PLURILINGUAL PEDAGOGY IN THE ARABIAN PENINSULA

This edited collection explores plurilingual education in the unique English medium instruction (EMI) context of the Arabian Peninsula.

The book argues that integrating a plurilingual pedagogy alongside current EMI in the region could enhance students' learning and contribute to a language policy that embraces linguistic diversity while fostering regional identity. It brings together the work of experts in Arabic and English language policy and planning, presenting empirical research relating to plurilingual pedagogical practices within the region. The book offers a range of recommendations for educators on how to integrate plurilingual pedagogies in classroom teaching. This becomes more important since many educators in the region are non-Arabic speakers and are teaching students with diverse linguistic backgrounds through English.

With a holistic and interdisciplinary approach to the linguistic landscape in the Arabian region, this book will be of great interest to researchers, scholars, and students in the fields of applied linguistics, language education, teacher education, and EMI.

Daniela Coelho is an assistant professor of Education at Abu Dhabi University, United Arab Emirates.

Telma Gharibian Steinhagen is an assistant professor of English Applied Linguistics at Zayed University, United Arab Emirates.

Routledge Research in Language Education

The *Routledge Research in Language Education* series provides a platform for established and emerging scholars to present their latest research and discuss key issues in Language Education. This series welcomes books on all areas of language teaching and learning, including but not limited to language education policy and politics, multilingualism, literacy, L1, L2 or foreign language acquisition, curriculum, classroom practice, pedagogy, teaching materials, and language teacher education and development. Books in the series are not limited to the discussion of the teaching and learning of English only.

Books in the series include:

Teacher Well-being in English Language Teaching
An Ecological Approach
Edited by Luis Javier Pentón Herrera, Gilda Martínez-Alba, and Ethan Trinh

Pluricentric Languages and Language Education
Pedagogical Implications and Innovative Approaches to Language Teaching
Edited by Marcus Callies and Stefanie Hehner

The Acquisition of English Grammar and Phonology by Cantonese ESL Learners
Challenges, Causes and Pedagogical Insights
Alice Yin Wa Chan

Using Digital Portfolios to Develop Students' Writing
A Practical Guide for Language Teachers
Ricky Lam and Benjamin Luke Moorhouse

Enhancing Beginner-Level Foreign Language Education for Adult Learners
Language Instruction, Intercultural Competence, Technology, and Assessment
Edited by Ekaterina Nemtchinova

For more information about the series, please visit www.routledge.com/Routledge-Research-in-Language-Education/book-series/RRLE

PLURILINGUAL PEDAGOGY IN THE ARABIAN PENINSULA

Transforming and Empowering Students and Teachers

Edited by Daniela Coelho and Telma Gharibian Steinhagen

Cover image: © Getty Images

First published 2023
by Routledge
4 Park Square, Milton Park, Abingdon, Oxon OX14 4RN

and by Routledge
605 Third Avenue, New York, NY 10158

Routledge is an imprint of the Taylor & Francis Group, an informa business

British Library Cataloguing-in-Publication Data
A catalogue record for this book is available from the British Library

ISBN: 978-1-032-32645-0 (hbk)
ISBN: 978-1-032-32646-7 (pbk)
ISBN: 978-1-003-31597-1 (ebk)

DOI: 10.4324/9781003315971

Typeset in Bembo
by KnowledgeWorks Global Ltd.

CONTENTS

EDITORS' BIOGRAPHIES

Daniela Coelho is an assistant professor of Education at Abu Dhabi University. She completed her graduate studies in the field of language pedagogy and curriculum development. Her research interests include plurilingual pedagogy, intercultural competence, teacher education, and curriculum development.

Telma Gharibian Steinhagen is an assistant professor at Zayed University in Abu Dhabi, UAE. Her research mainly focuses on multilingualism and the acquisition of English as an additional language. Her goal in research is to optimize language teaching practices, and she has engaged in a number of initiatives that help students foster critical thinking and reading.

CONTRIBUTORS

Amani Batakji Chazy is a senior education policy expert, working for the government of Dubai, the United Arab Emirates. She is a certified accreditation team member of the North England Association of Schools and Colleges (NEASC). Dr. Batakji Chazy has extensive experience in school evaluations and language policy regulation. In this role, she has significantly contributed to the development of quality assurance policies of the early childhood education and care in Dubai. Her doctoral research on Arabic language-in-education policies has been foundational in the context of the GCC and the UAE. Dr. Batakji Chazy is a regular peer reviewer of academic book chapters in the areas of language teacher education, policy, and training. She is a jury member of the prestigious Khalifa Award for Education, an annual event that seeks to advance regional educational talents and reward outstanding innovators in education.

Daniela Coelho is an assistant professor of Education at Abu Dhabi University. She completed her graduate studies in the field of language pedagogy and curriculum development. Her research interests include plurilingual pedagogy, intercultural competence, teacher education, and curriculum development.

Anna Dillon is a teacher educator in Abu Dhabi. She enjoys engaging in research about bilingual education, early childhood education, translanguaging, co-teaching, and third culture kids.

Aymen Elsheikh is an instructional assistant professor of English in the Division of Arts and Sciences at Texas A&M University at Qatar. He has over 15 years of teaching experience in different countries including Sudan, Oman, USA, UAE, and Qatar. His research interests include language teacher identity and knowledge, English as an international language, and language teaching associations, among others. He is the immediate past president of Africa ELTA (formerly known as Africa TESOL), and he has served as a member of the Editorial Advisory Board of the TESOL Journal.

Kay Gallagher is an Abu Dhabi-based teacher educator, educational leader and scholar in language-in-education, English education, and bilingual education. She has held roles as Acting Dean and Associate Dean in Education in the UAE, and she was a faculty member in English Education at the University of Hong Kong. Kay also has a strong school background, having been a school principal in her native Ireland. Her book, Education in the UAE: Innovation and Transformation, was co-authored with leading Emirates-based educational researchers.

Sarah Hopkyns has a PhD in Educational Research and Applied Linguistics from the University of Leicester, England. She is an assistant professor at Zayed University, United Arab Emirates. Her research interests include translingual practices, English-medium education, culture, identity, and linguistic landscapes. She is the author of "The Impact of Global English on Cultural Identities in the United Arab Emirates" (2020) and co-editor of "Linguistic Identities in the Arab Gulf States" (2022), both published by Routledge.

Melanie van den Hoven has a PhD in Intercultural Education from Durham University, England. She has lectured in the Language and Culture division at a teacher training institution in Abu Dhabi, UAE, to support the implementation of biliteracy in the New School Model. Currently, she leads a team of Korean-English interpreters in a nuclear power plant as a Cross Cultural Communications advisor. Melanie has published recent ethnographic research dealing with translanguaging and linguistic repertoires, interculturality and lingua franca communication, and linguistic landscapes in the Arabian Peninsula.

Sara Hillman is an assistant professor of English in the Division of Arts and Sciences at Texas A&M University at Qatar where she teaches courses in academic English, intercultural communication, and multicultural education, and coordinates the Foundations of English program. Her research focuses on language ideologies; language learner identities and emotions; EMI and transnational higher education in the Arabian Peninsula; and global Englishes. Her work has appeared in international journals such as TESOL Quarterly, System, Multilingua, and World Englishes. She is currently editing a special journal issue on the emotional impact of EMI in higher education.

Nadine Jaafarawi is a PhD holder in Applied Linguistics. Her teaching profile extends to more than 20 years. She was an English coordinator, curriculum developer, and university lecturer in Lebanon for more than 15 years. She joined

Zayed University in Spring 2018 and is currently an assistant professor there. She is a "fellow" in the Higher Education Academy (Advance HE) and trainer in *Child Protection Training Certification Program* with Georgetown University and Abu Dhabi Childhood Authority.

Dudley Reynolds is the senior associate dean for Education and teaching professor of English at Carnegie Mellon University Qatar. He served as the president of TESOL International Association in 2016–2017 and has been a teacher and researcher of multilingual language learners for over 30 years working primarily with learners of English. His research addresses language education policy, developmental patterns in additional language learning, curricular and pedagogical approaches to literacy development, teacher education, and learning.

Telma Gharibian Steinhagen is an assistant professor at Zayed University in Abu Dhabi, UAE. Her research mainly focuses on multilingualism and the acquisition of English as an additional language. Her research goal is to optimize language teaching practices, and, as such, she is engaged in a number of initiatives that help students foster critical thinking and reading skills.

Hanada Taha Thomure (PhD) is a professor of Arabic Language Teaching and Learning. Her main research interest revolves around the modernization of the teaching of Arabic language and literacy, standards- and literature-based instruction, and national literacy strategies. She is the endowed chair of Arabic language at Zayed University and is the director of the Zayed University Arabic Language Center for Research and Development, UAE.

ACKNOWLEDGMENTS

We would like to thank Dr. Christina Gitsaki for sharing with us an excellent reviewer report form which we adapted to our needs.

A special thanks to Dr. Ileana Baird for her detailed proofreading of our proposal.

Many thanks to our many external chapter reviewers for their thorough reviews:

- Dr. Christine Hélot
- Dr. David Plafreyman
- Dr. Glenda El Gamal
- Dr. Mark Wyatt
- Dr. Mónica Lourenço
- Dr. Sunny Lau
- Dr. Yecid Ortega

INTRODUCTION

Daniela Coelho and Telma Gharibian Steinhagen

Introduction

In his presentation at the UNESCO *Forum on Higher Education, Research and Knowledge*, Darim Albassam (2007), Chief Adviser at the United Nations Development Program, addressed the implications of globalization on education within the Regional Seminar *The Impact of Globalization on Higher Education and Research in the Arab States*. He highlighted specifically the need for readiness on the part of the states to embrace the impacts of globalization in pluralistic communities:

> Only those countries and regions, which take pre-emptive measures but are endowed with vision, strategic thinking, and determination to understand the globalization process and, nevertheless, its oncoming threats and opportunities, will be able to secure a strong foothold and productive co-existence in the global pluralistic international community.
>
> *(Albassam, 2007, p. 4)*

Globalization, technologicalization, interconnectedness, and migration have transformed societies in general in many aspects, namely their educational systems. Today, teachers encounter classrooms that do not resemble much of those just some decades ago, yet "a number of [educational] assumptions continue to survive, rendering many aspects of today's schooling systems irrelevant to the world we actually live in." (Albassam, 2007, p. 10). Some of the transformations seen in schools and universities nowadays include increased cultural diversity and enhanced multilingualism. This is particularly true for the Gulf Cooperation Council (GCC) countries, which include the United Arab Emirates, Saudi Arabia, Qatar, Oman, Kuwait, and Bahrain. According to GoGulf statistics

DOI: 10.4324/9781003315971-1

(2016), expats in the GCC area account for 48.1% of the whole population, most coming to the region as a specialized workforce. This large community of "non-locals" living in each of these countries enriches their multicultural and multilingual landscape but also brings about dilemmas, namely at the language policy level. The need to cater to these countries' superdiverse communities, as well as a realization that economic prosperity and profit maximization usually come associated with the use of the English language, triggered the neoliberal emergence of English as a *lingua franca* and inevitably prompted many Arabian Peninsula countries to increase the presence of English in educational institutions (Baker, 2017). Thus, higher education institutions have come up with a pragmatic solution to offer the great majority of programs in the English language, and public schools have also seen an increase in the number of subjects taught in English. Although there have been voices from local scholars showing concern in regard to the role of Arabic and to the Arabic language policy trends, resulting in calls for more Arabic as the language of instruction, English seems to have come to stay as the academic lingua franca (Corrigan, 2018). One would consider that the circumstances make this region a perfect place to implement the English as a medium of instruction (EMI) model where the content and language can be taught at the same time. Ironically, the EMI model in this region is not fully pedagogically or linguistically developed and conceptualized, and it seems to be applied under the assumption that the Arabian Peninsula students are "native" speakers of English. This Englishization of schools and universities does not appear without its challenges and even disappointments (Corrigan, 2018), mainly related to unreadiness and lack of language proficiency on the part of students to fully embrace an EMI model (Baker, 2017). This has naturally prompted concerns and calls for research on pedagogical approaches which may better serve the needs of these multilingual, multicultural, and "englishized" students (Baker, 2017 citing Lambelet & Berthele, 2015) and even the needs of the teachers themselves (Corrigan, 2018). Integrating a plurilingual pedagogy stance in current schools and universities in the region could enhance student learning and contribute to a language policy that embraces linguistic diversity while fostering regional identity. Contrary to monolingual approaches, this pedagogy builds on students' varied linguistic repertoires to foster Cognitive Academic Language Proficiency (CALP) and identity affirmation as suggested by Cummins (1979), taking advantage of the symbiosis that arises from welcoming several languages in the classrooms.

Following the *multilingual turn* (May, 2014), the understanding of how teaching and learning happens in language-in-education contexts seems to have shifted, with many teachers gradually embracing the plurilingual paradigm. Small-scale applications of plurilingual pedagogy appear to be flourishing in isolated, individual initiatives by teachers in the region as well. Therefore, this edited volume explores plurilingual education from the theoretical and practical points of view, considering the unique educational context of the Arabian Peninsula. The volume presents three sections which aim to provide a) an overview of the current linguistic landscapes in the region, b) an outline of plurilingual pedagogical practices within the region based on empirical research followed by c) a range of recommendations for integrating plurilingual pedagogies.

Clarification of terms in the scope of this volume

Garton and Kubota (2015) have once highlighted that, in the field of applied linguistics, "there is a need for conceptual clarity, with a multitude of terms currently being used without a clear distinction or definition" (p. 418). As Lau and Van Viegen (2020) stated, "language often fails us and the naming of the terms itself can become a site of 'translingual reflexivity'; terms themselves crossing, mixing, merging and diverging, in contestation and negotiation" (p. 6). We too believe a myriad of terms is currently being used in an attempt to describe sociolinguistic or pedagogical practices that involve the fluid use of several languages in daily life or in classroom settings, rejecting the compartmentalization of languages known by an individual. Some examples are plurilingualism, multilingualism, plurilingual pedagogy, and translanguaging. With this in mind, a brief clarification of the differences between these terms was deemed necessary within the purpose of this volume. Other terms such as code-meshing, code-switching, or polylanguaging may occasionally appear in a few chapters, but they are used mainly in chapter introductions to locate the reader in the variety of terms available associated with plurilingualism and not as the preferred or research adopted terms; therefore, the editors did not see a need to dwell on definitions of these latter terms.

As far as multilingualism is concerned, Moore, Lau, and Van Viegen (2020) explained that it is regarded as the sum of more than two languages known by an individual as in the "amount of monolinguals" within a person. If an individual speaks English, Arabic, and French, this person is considered monolingual in three languages, making them a multilingual. However, the term multilingual implies that there is a clear "separateness of language abilities" (Moore, Lau & Van Viegen, 2020, p. 31) in the languages known, while the term plurilingualism renounces that idea, emphasizing the belief that languages act symbiotically instead. Plurilingualism is hence seen as a flexible and varying language competence that draws on all the (uneven) knowledge of several languages of an individual to serve communication episodes (Herdina & Jessner, 2002).

Plurilingual pedagogy (also referred to as *plurilingual education* or *pluralistic approach*) is a term predominately used in the European context with an undoubted didactic stance which concerns approaches that "involve the use of more than one/several varieties of languages or cultures simultaneously during the teaching process." (Candelier et al., 2013, n.p). Plurilingual approaches promote an "optimisation of relations between languages" (Candelier & Schröder-Sura, 2015) and encourage the integration and active use of several languages in the learning process of any subject in general education. As for translanguaging, on the other hand, it is usually applied in the anglophone and North American world and is more focused on bilingual education (Candelier & Schröder-Sura, 2015). Translanguaging was originally applied and supported by Williams in Wales in the 90s in the context of Welsh revitalization programs in which the teacher would teach in Welsh but allow for answers from the students in English (Wei, 2018). Williams believed that such approaches helped "maximize the learner's, and the teacher's, linguistic resources in the process of problem-solving and knowledge construction" (Wei, 2018, p. 15). Canagarajah (2011) defined translanguaging as "the ability of multilingual speakers to shuttle between languages, treating the diverse languages that form their repertoire as an integrated system" (p. 401). With this in mind, it is clear that the underlying notion and beliefs of both plurilingual pedagogy and translanguaging are similar and transversal to both terms, the only difference being the geographical contexts they are more often used in; therefore, both terms could and will be used interchangeably in this volume.

Overview of sections and chapters in this volume

This collection has been organized into three parts. The first part, entitled *Language planning, policy, and practices in the context of English as a Medium of Instruction (EMI) in the Arabian Peninsula: Challenges and success stories*, provides an account of the language policy trends in the region and draws connections between current language planning processes, future language planning needs, and teacher education. Chapter 1 in this section, **Batakji Chazy**'s *Steering the Arabic Language Policy and Planning Agenda: The way forward for Arabic as a language of the future*, explores the perceptions of the Arabic language by its speakers and accounts for the language policy and planning efforts made so far in order to revive the presence of Arabic across multiple contexts in the region, namely the education sector where English prevails. Next, Chapter 2 (*Current Discussions on Plurilingual Pedagogy: Language Learning Implications in the Arabian Peninsula*) examines the potentialities of plurilingual pedagogies within the Arabian Peninsula's educational institutions given the remarkable presence of English as the language of instruction and the precarious use of Arabic. **Jaafarawi** starts with an overview of the emergence of plurilingualism-related pedagogies worldwide, moving on to defining these pedagogies in detail, and concludes with a personal account of her own experience in shifting from a monolingual stance to a plurilingual one and with a note on how these approaches may be particularly fruitful in teaching and learning contexts in the region, implying that these pedagogies are transformative in nature. **Thomure**'s Chapter 3, *Arabic language teacher training in the Arabian Peninsula: Great teachers don't grow on trees*, delves into the problem of the adoption of English as the language of instruction in the Arabian countries in general. Thomure focuses on the generalized poor performance of some students in the Arabic language and, based on a success case in Saudi Arabia, she opens a discussion on how teacher training can be the key to a shift in the pedagogies adopted to teach Arabic which can lead to improved student performance. This part concludes with a chapter by **Gallagher** and **Dillon** entitled *Teacher education and EMI in the UAE and Arabian Peninsula – Past, present, and future perspectives.* It explores the challenges faced by local student teachers while being trained to become bilingual teachers, to teach in Arabic and English, without formal training on plurilingual language education approaches. It also addresses the potentialities of translanguaging in the teacher training of these future teachers.

Part 2, *Empirical research on plurilingual education in the Arabian Peninsula context*, presents three empirical studies developed in the UAE and Qatar. Chapter 5, by **van den Hoven** and **Hopkyns**, is entitled *From binaries to plurality: Emirati college students' perspectives on the plurilingual identities of English users and expatriate teachers*. It gathers responses from Emirati students on English users' and their own teachers' linguistic profiles and offers plurilingual-oriented strategies that could enhance local prospective teachers' cross-cultural and linguistic awareness. This chapter is followed by **Coelho**'s *Plurilingual pedagogy in Higher Education in the UAE: Student voices in an academic writing course*, which provides the results of a study carried out with undergraduate UAE students who engaged in plurilingual activities in their academic writing in English course throughout three terms. The students' opinions point to a positive acceptance of the approach as well as enhanced learning. In Chapter 7, *Expanding communicative repertories through plurilingual pedagogies in international branch campus classrooms in Qatar*, **Hillman**, **Reynolds,** and **Elsheikh** give personal accounts of their own initiatives to challenge the monolingual biases by enhancing the presence of plurilingual pedagogy in their courses, aiming to improve their students' English proficiency and develop their full communicative repertoires.

The last part, *Implications and applications of plurilingual pedagogy in teaching and learning*, has two chapters which offer suggestions of ways to apply plurilingual pedagogy in the Arabian Peninsula based on approaches utilized by the authors themselves. It intends to meet the need for more practical and authentic texts that present feasible strategies that have been and could be used with students. The first chapter of this part, *Rethinking Learning and Teaching Using Plurilingual Pedagogy in the UAE: Challenges and Success Stories*, takes us on a journey of its author, **Gharibian Steinhagen**, through her own growth as a plurilingual-oriented, non-Arabic-speaking teacher in the UAE, offering examples of her own classroom practices. The last chapter by **Coelho** and **Gharibian Steinhagen** appears in an unconventional format, resembling a manual, with the intention to provide teachers and future teachers a go-to guide which helps them understand their plurilingual selves as well as their students' and their own readiness to embrace plurilingual pedagogy. *From theory to practice: Ways to implement plurilingual pedagogy in education institutions in the Arabian Peninsula* concludes with a list of strategies and real examples of plurilingual pedagogy uses in the region's classrooms.

References

Albassam, D. (2007). *Globalization and Education*. Presented at the Regional Seminar "The Impact of Globalization on Higher Education and Research in the Arab States". UNESCO Forum of Higher Education, Research and Knowledge. UNESCO Digital Library.

Baker, F. S. (2017). National pride and the new school model: English language education in Abu Dhabi, UAE. In R. Kirkpatrick (Ed.), *English Language education policy in the middle East and North Africa. Language policy, 13* (pp. 279–300). Springer.

Canagarajah, S. (2011). Codemeshing in academic writing: Identifying teachable strategies of translanguaging. *Modern Language Journal, 95*, 401–417.

Candelier, M., de Pietro, J.-F., Facciol, R., Lorincz, I., Pascual, X., & Schröder-Sura, A. (2013). *CARAP– FREPA: A framework of reference for pluralistic approaches to languages and cultures.* Council of Europe. http://carap.ecml.at/

Candelier, M., & Schröder-Sura, A. (2015). Les approches plurielles et le CARAP: origines, évolutions, perspectives. *Babylonia, The Journal of Language Teaching and Learning, 2*(15), 12–19.

Corrigan, P. (2018). Building EMI pedagogy to support EMI policy. In H. M. Fardoun et al. (Eds), *The future of higher education in the middle East and Asia* (pp. 1–10). Springer.

Cummins, J. (1979). Cognitive/academic language proficiency, linguistic interdependence, the optimum age question and some other matters. *Working Papers on Bilingualism, 19*, 121–129.

Garton, S., & Kubota, R. (2015). Joint colloquium on plurilingualism and language education: Opportunities and challenges (AAAL/TESOL). *Language Teaching, 48*, 417–421.

GoGulf (2016*). Expats in Middle East – Statistics and Trends.* Retrieved from https://www.go-gulf.ae/expats-middle-east/ (11 April 2022)

Herdina, P., & Jessner, U. (2002). *A dynamic model of multilingualism: Perspectives of change in psycholinguistics* (1st ed.). Multilingual Matters.

Lau, S. M. C., & Van Viegen, S. (2020). Plurilingual pedagogies: An introduction. In S. Lau, & S. Van Viegen (Eds.), *Plurilingual pedagogies: Critical and creative endeavors for equitable language (in) education* (pp. 3–22). Springer.

May, S. (2014). Introducing the "Multilingual turn". In S. May (Ed.), *The multilingual turn: Implications for SLA, TESOL and bilingual education* (pp. 1–6). Routledge.

Moore, D., Lau, S. M. C., & Van Viegen, S. (2020). Mise en Echo des perspectives on plurilingual competence and pluralistic pedagogies: A conversation with Daniele Moore. In S. Lau, & S. Van Viegen (Eds.), *Plurilingual pedagogies: Critical and creative endeavors for equitable language (in) education* (pp. 23–45). Springer.

Wei, L. (2018). Translanguaging as a practical theory of language. *Applied Linguistics, 39*(1), 9–30.

Wisbey, M. (2014). *MTB-MLE: Mother Tongue-based multilingual education; Lessons learned from a decade of research and practice.* Asia-Pacific Multilingual Education Working Group: UNESCO Digital Library.

PART 1

Language planning, policy, and practices in the context of English as a medium of instruction (EMI) in the Arabian Peninsula: challenges and success stories

1

STEERING THE ARABIC LANGUAGE POLICY AND PLANNING AGENDA

The way forward for Arabic as a language of the future

Amani Batakji Chazy

Introduction

This chapter sets out a critical discursive lens for identifying directions for advancing the Arabic language-in-education policy agenda in the Arab region, particularly in countries of the Arabian Peninsula. For this purpose, I adopted the *What's the problem represented to be* framework, known as the WPR framework, by Bacchi (2009), to analyze the most recent Arabic language policy texts.

The chapter argues that an Arabic language policy and planning (LPP) process in the Arab region is overdue, as the elements and the ecosystem for a language policy are primed. In so doing, I discuss how most recent policy initiatives and developments in a few Arab countries have contributed largely to shifting the perceptions about the Arabic language through a renewed discourse. Secondly, I discursively analyze the elements of the most recent Arabic language policy developments, mainly appearing in a seminal Arabic language status report, that I will refer to as the *"status report"* (MCY, 2021) and the Arabic Language Declaration of the UAE (Dubai Media Office, 2021) that I will refer to as the "*declaration,*" to highlight this renewed policy discourse and analyze how these developments can lead to further improvements in language-in-education policies and practices.

My selection of these two most recent documents for analysis is intentional. The *status report* is a massive effort by institutions, researchers, and government entities, to provide a full landscape analysis of the Arabic language across the Arab region and beyond. It is a substantial policy process constructed by a government entity (Ball, 2021) to assess the situation with the Arabic language. The *status report* is research based and contextualized with case studies from all Arab countries. It also sets out a model for future opportunities for advancing the Arabic language in key aspects of the language, such as constitutional legislative

DOI: 10.4324/9781003315971-3

texts, Arabic digital content, and the teaching and learning status of the Arabic language across the region.

The second policy source that I use in this analysis is the UAE Declaration for the Arabic language, which was launched by the government of the UAE in parallel with the proceedings of the Arabic Language Summit 2021, in Dubai, marking the annual celebration of the international day of the Arabic language. The *declaration* is a concise document that emerged in response to the *status report* as a guidance and direction, and a tool to implement the recommendations of the *report* to advance the Arabic language (Dubai Media Office, 2021).

The What's the problem represented to be (WPR) framework

I selected the WPR framework for two key reasons. The theoretical premises of the framework of Carol Bacchi (2009) enable a deeper understanding of how a language-in-education policy can move forward and serve the purpose of interpreting policy discourse, in this case, the changing discourses around the Arabic language. I am of the view that language policies filter broadly through social systems, particularly the educational system, and impact first language speakers, educators, and general users. Any policy text, practices, and discourses are powerful and impactful and contribute to a range of linguistic practices among users of the language (Canagarajah, 2005; Spolsky, 2017; Tollefson & Tsui, 2017). However, understanding how policies are interpreted, mediated, and implemented will always be a complex endeavour (Ball, 1993). Analyzing discourse is a significant ingredient of policy analysis because discourse extends beyond the "text" and the "talk" to impact practices and experiences (Ball, 1993; Fairclough, 2013; Wodak & Meyer, 2009).

The second reason for my choice of the WPR as a policy analysis framework is that it utilizes a conceptual analysis questioning tool, comprised of six questions, that provides a simple and meaningful approach to policy analysis (Bacchi, 2009; Bacchi & Goodwin, 2016). These questions interrogate the "taken-for-granted" policy premises and establish the understanding of the context of the policy, its implications, and how it problematizes the key issue of the Arabic language (Bacchi, 2009). Often, this methodological process uncovers ways of governing and potentially opens opportunities for identifying solutions that may be inherent in the policy text itself (Bacchi, op. cit).

Current initiatives to support the Arabic language in the Arabian Peninsula

The endorsement of the General Assembly of the United Nations Educational, Scientific and Cultural Organization (UNESCO), on December 18th, 1973, of Arabic as one of its official languages is a recognition of the significance of disseminating knowledge from the Arab world countries and speakers globally. The United Nations Organization (UN) has been leading initiatives, since 1966, to position Arabic on equal footing with other world languages; the most significant is the

Sultan Bin Abdelaziz Al Saud Foundation program in 2017 to support the Arabic language at the UNESCO (UNESCO, 2017). One of these efforts is a program started in 2005 to expand the use of Arabic at the institutional level at the UN and develop its digital content since the beginning of the decade (Dewachi & Aita, 2012).

Few Arab countries have been leading efforts and initiatives to improve the use of the Arabic language through language-in-education policies, or broader language policies. Some of the efforts were intended to focus on the social and cultural aspects of the language and produce research work around cultural topics. The Kingdom of Saudi Arabia (KSA) started the King Abdullah Initiative for Arabic content, planned and executed in collaboration with the City of King Abdullah for Science and Technology (KAICA, 2019). The efforts included decisions such as enhancing the Arabic Wikipedia content and the translation of 2100 books, with the purpose of contributing to the Arab knowledge economy (KAICA, op cit). Most recently, the KSA's diligent efforts lead to registering the Arabic calligraphy as the first intangible cultural heritage of UNESCO (UNESCO, 2021). Another example of Arab's efforts to impact resources for the teaching and learning of Arabic is the Arab Thought Foundation (ATF), an independent regional non-governmental organization with the mission to support the Arab body of knowledge and preserve the Arab identity through cultural, educational, and language policy research projects. The ATF has been funding growing Arabic language education projects such as *Arabi 21*, which included the levelling of Arabic children's readers to consolidate the habit of reading (Arab Thought Foundation, 2022).

Last, and most importantly, the UAE established an integrated strategy for transforming the country into a centre of excellence for the Arabic language, through the Arabic language charter (Emirates 24/7, 2012). A series of initiatives spearheaded by the UAE were rolled out in the last 10 years to advance the Arabic language, under the umbrella of the Arabic Language Charter (Batakji Chazy, 2020). From these initiatives, the latest achievement saw the light through the launch of the first 17 volumes of the historical Arabic language dictionary, by HRH Sh. Sultan Al Qassimi, Ruler of Sharjah (Al Khaleej Times, 2022).

I would like to acknowledge that this list of initiatives is not exclusive. There is a wider list of government, regional, and global efforts, including literary competitions, awards, literary research efforts, digital content, publications, and curricular initiatives that are tracked in other prominent sources and publications (Arab Thought Foundation, 2012; MCY, 2021), but are beyond the scope of this chapter. Many of the efforts that were meant to revive the Arabic language have contributed to raising the profile of the Arabic language at social, cultural, and educational levels, and mostly through the media. There is little evidence to suggest the impact of such policy efforts and initiatives on the learners themselves (see Batakji Chazy, 2020).

The Debate

The prominence of the Arabic language has fluctuated over time as a result of post-colonial political and historical developments, paralleling socioeconomic and demographic changes (Boyle, 2012; Canagarajah, 2005; Fehri, 2013b). Despite the most recent efforts, the Arabic language outcomes for learners and native speakers are still alarming (PIRLS, 2012, 2016). The literature projects a perceived decline in the usage of the Arabic language in the Arab world, primarily by its native speakers (Abanmi, 2017; Al Issa & Al Dahan, 2011; Arab Thought Foundation, 2012; Boyle, 2012; Fehri, 2013b; Taha-Thomure, 2008).

The discourse that favors English as the language of progress and growth is commonly seen through the choices of governments of the Arabian Peninsula to infuse English as a language of instruction at all phases of education to ensure access of students to international universities and support the economic growth. As suggested by Karamani, "English was widely becoming identified as a powerful tool in facilitating the region's course to modernization" (Karamani, 2005, p. 92). Barnawi (2018) echoes the narrative that English reached the status of the *lingua franca* in Arab countries, motivated by these countries' will to advance their economies and compete globally. Similarly, Al Fahham (2017) argues that there are factors that prevent Arab countries from investing in the Arabic language, which are the inability to make Arabic fully the language of commerce, culture, health, and other economic areas in individual countries (Al Fahham, 2017).

The tensions resulting from the enforcement of the English language during colonization have had implications on the peoples of colonized countries (Canagarajah, 2005). Colonized countries were still recovering from the state of colonization through affirming their nationalism and identities, while at the same time they were trying to come to grips with globalization and the pressing need to embrace English for the betterment of their societies (Canagarajah, Op cit.). This process is identified as a feature of linguistic imperialism where colonial dominance in developing countries has contributed to marginalizing national languages with the purpose of prioritizing the colonial language (Phillipson, 2009).

In parallel, the narrative that Arabic is challenged to be the language of science, advancements, and the future aspirations seems to undermine most policies and efforts that offer to strengthen the position of the Arabic language. This is not the only narrative that impacts learners' attitudes toward their first language, as seen in the Arabic *status report* (MCY, 2021). I am of the view that power, ideology, and political decisions are perceived as factors that sustain a language, and reviving the Arabic language must be political through strategic planning (Fehri, 2013a; Troudi & Al Hafidh, 2017). Political will is what drives language-in-education policies, as will be demonstrated in this chapter's analysis of the *status report*.

The WPR policy analysis

The questioning tool of the WPR policy analysis framework is a set of six questions that interrogate the policy text and help to unpack the assumptions, the premises, problematizations, and implications of the Arabic language *status report* and *declaration*. According to Bacchi and Goodwin (2016), policy documents and discourses focus on what needs to be changed, and in doing so, they contain

TABLE 1.1 This table is an adaptation from Bacchi and Goodwin (2016, p. 20) which includes all the six conceptual questions of the WPR model "What's the problem represented to be" with slight modifications to align with the context of analysis in this chapter

Question 1:	What's the problem represented to be in the *report* and the *declaration*?
Question 2:	What deep-seated prepositions and assumptions underlie this representation of the Arabic language?
Question 3:	How has this representation of the Arabic language come about?
Question 4:	What is left unproblematic in this representation? Where are the silences? Can issues of the Arabic language be conceptualized differently?
Question 5:	What effects (discursive, subjectification, and lived) are produced by this representation of the Arabic language?
Question 6:	How and where has this representation of the Arabic language been produced, disseminated, and defended? How has it been and/or how can it be disrupted and replaced?

implicit representations of the problems or "problematizations" for whom the policy was created the first place (Bacchi & Goodwin, 2016). The six conceptual questions are listed in Table 1.1 above, with adaptation for the context of the analysis in this chapter. I have focused on some questions more than others. For example, I left out WPR Question 3 because the analysis of Question 2 serves the purpose of uncovering deep-seated assumptions in the text, and as Bacchi (2009) suggests, it is useful to highlight certain questions more than others for certain policy contexts and texts.

Methodologically, I examined selected sections of the executive summary of the Arabic *status report* and the *declaration* that I refer to as "(SR, 2020)" and "(D, 2021)" in citations followed by page/article numbers, respectively. It is important to note that the *status report* was originally published in Arabic, while translations to English of the executive summary are available through the official website of the Ministry of Culture and Youth of the UAE (MCY, 2021).

WPR Question 1: What's the problem represented to be in the status report *and the declaration?*

There are several representations of the Arabic language that I could identify in the *status report* that are most vividly articulated in its executive summary entitled "current approaches to develop Arabic language curricula." Arabic language teaching and learning are represented in the *status report* in positive overtones, whereby the authors summarized recent emerging approaches in curriculum modification and design, acknowledging a renewed focus on the role of teacher preparation and capacity building. The positive tones are mostly reflected in the increased attention of Arabic language educators on the learners of Arabic (SR, 2020, p. 427). At the same time, the *status report* represents the Arabic language curricula as deficient and implies an outdated curricular philosophy (SR, 2020, p. 430). The text also touches upon "unbalanced approaches to pedagogies" and "assessments that are not to the level of updated pedagogies" and therefore does not do justice to learners (SR, 2020, p. 430). The *report* uses the terms "up-to-date approaches that are linked to real life ..." (SR, 2020, p. 341), implying that the current approaches are not in line with the recent best practices. Curriculum approaches are described as being variable across the country case studies and are not based on a clear set of standards (SR, 2020, p. 340). In summary, the representations of Arabic, in regard to pedagogies, are identified as the curriculum, the teacher preparation, and the focus on the learners and their context.

These representations of the Arabic language overlap in both the *report* and the *declaration*. One single Article 2 in the *declaration* addresses Arabic curricula, representing Arabic language pedagogies as requiring updates, "... develop new methodologies of teaching and learning the language in schools ..." (D, 2). The *declaration* is meant to be a response to the issues raised in the *report,* providing direction on future next steps, and therefore it addresses the key priorities of the *status report.*

The *declaration* makes an additionally intriguing representation of the issues around Arabic when it asserts that learning Arabic needs to be treated as "... a building block for our society and our economy" (D, 2022, Article 2), establishing a new link that has not been commonly raised in previous Arabic language policy discourse, the link to the economy, growth, and advancement. This direct connection between language learning and economic growth and societal development is powerful and futuristic in its tone, and what makes it so is that it is highlighted in the only agenda item about Arabic teaching in a high-level policy document as the *declaration.* It is important to expand on this link in future policy research on Arabic language policy, as this may be a critical mobilizer of prospective policy efforts.

This said, the concept of investing in the Arabic language and linking it to societal growth may be aspirational, to say the least, when minimum requirements of language acquisition of first language learners are a source of alert. It is a clear reminder of the World Bank's most recent publication on learning poverty in the Arab world (Gregory et al., 2021). The researchers in this report present the Arabic first language learner gaps as an indicator of learning poverty, a stark alert for Arab countries. The report consolidates the link between the outcomes of learning Arabic as a first language to the overall learning competencies of students and their abilities to access the entire curriculum (Gregory et al., 2021). The research presented needs to be read and reflected upon critically when designing any future policy initiatives in the Arab world and the Arabian Peninsula in particular.

WPR Question 2: What presuppositions and assumptions underlie this representation of the Arabic language?

The purpose of this question is to look for assumptions in the text itself, rather than in the minds of the social actors (Bacchi & Goodwin, 2016). It refers to the basic knowledge that must be in place for these representations of Arabic to make sense. I found that the key problematization of teachers' competencies is that teacher preparation provisions require attention, and as a result, pedagogies of Arabic are flagged in the *status report*. The *report* discusses, with quite negative overtones, the underperforming teachers of Arabic who lack appropriate preservice and/or in-service preparation and who cannot meet the goals of language curricula. They are even portrayed in the *status report* as submissive to conventional approaches, resistant to change, and reluctant to use the standard variety of Arabic in lessons (SR, 2020, p. 340).

The *status report*, in its research sections, does not specify the provisions for teacher preparation programs that are currently operational in the Arab world, nor addresses their quality. With their negative implications, these claims about teacher preparation gaps that impact the quality of Arabic language curriculum and pedagogies in the summary of the *status report* are worth further reflection at policy level and need to be approached as policy problematizations. Therefore, there is a clear gap in teacher preparation, which was not problematized by the *status report* sufficiently. I believe, with the same token, this assumption links to the representations about learners and how future policy in curriculum design needs to engage the learners and perceive them as drivers of the learning process.

Moving on to the *declaration*, the text clearly follows the mentioned assumptions in the *status report*. It complements it clearly when it asserts the need to "... develop programs for Arabic language teachers to enhance their skills to teach the language in a scientific way that facilitates its learning and makes it relatable and relevant to new generations" (D, 2020, Article 2).

The text of the *status report* argues that the Arabic language curricula lack a unified vision and/or philosophy, which is a crucial requirement across Arab countries. A unified vision sets the scene for non-negotiable research-based Arabic language pedagogies. A key criticism that the *status report* presents is that the curricula of Arabic are very diverse, not yet benchmarked, and lack a unified Arab national direction (SR, 2020, p. 340).

I would further interrogate this piece of information and suggest that it is not well linked in the *status report* text itself. The curricula of Arab countries have been discussed individually, and the obvious conclusion is that all curricula are very diverse and require a unified philosophy. However, the *status report* does not sufficiently explain the rationale for having a unified curricular vision or philosophy. It does not elaborate on the value of a unified curriculum vision and how that would support learners at every level. Future policy efforts may want to consider lessons learned and benchmarking analyses from other languages and curricular development experiences to pinpoint useful research-into-practice applications of a unified curriculum philosophy to support educators and practitioners of the Arabic language.

WPR Question 4: What is left unproblematic in this representation? Where are the silences? Can the "problem" be conceptualized differently?

In the *status report*, the three problematizations of Arabic seem to include some "silenced" discourses. Although the *status report* problematizes teacher competence and planning and speaks about the need to update pedagogical practices, the *status report* becomes silent about a very significant area which is how teacher preparation programs are currently performing. The text hardly addresses how the provisions of teacher preparation across Arab countries have or have not achieved. This is the link required to understand the recommendations brought forward at the conclusion of the *status report*. The text eventually raises four critical issues about the professionalization of the teaching profession through: (1) licensing schemes, (2) creating the research knowledge base of academic and refereed journal content that is accessible to all practicing teachers, (3) designing immersive teacher training programs, and (4) evaluating and analyzing curricula (ST, 2020, p. 437). In future directions in teacher preparation, policy efforts need to highlight the rationale and the assumptions for a new approach to teacher preparation and training and establish clear links to how these efforts can complement and support teacher education programs. For example, the work by Taha (2017) needs to be extended with additional investigation around this area to inform policy practices (Taha, 2017a, 2017b).

The *status report* again seemed to "silence" the linguistic ecosystem of Arab first language speakers and learners. In the section about teaching and learning, the *status report* addresses the diverse speakership of the Arabic language and approaches diglossia in a new manner. It proposes a model whereby the Arabic language needs to be seen in the context of its diverse dialects and that it should not be approached from monolingual parameters that deny the diverse situations and scenarios where Arabic is used (SR, 2020, p. 431). This said, the text, however, did not raise the issue of the plurilingual learner (Erling & Moore, 2021), and how the Arabic first language speakers' repertoire of knowledge and use of other languages side by side with the Arabic language are impacting how Arabic is being used and learned.

Additionally, there is one more silenced discourse. The *status report* did not account for the contention that Arabic may not be the "first language" of many Arab learners. This is again a contextual debate. Current Arabic learners and speakers are theoretically first language speakers, but practically their first contact with Arabic may only begin through formal schooling, not from the family environment. Therefore, both issues of the plurilingual context of the Arabic first language learners as well as the realistic identification of their first language are factors to be accounted for in any future policy attempt.

WPR Question 5: What effects (discursive, subjectification, and lived) are produced by this representation of the "problem"?

The *status report* identifies the following problematizations: (1) the Arabic language curriculum and assessment approaches, (2) teacher preparation, and (3) learner agency. The discursive effects of these problematizations are clearly addressed in the *declaration,* where it focuses in its sole Article 2 on responses to these three core issues. Discursive effects of a policy can also refer to any "silenced" or left out issues that needed to be highlighted. I already mentioned the diverse contexts and linguistic profiles of Arab speakers, how their linguistic repertoires and first language profiles affect the way they learn the Arabic language, and how these factors are not raised in the *status report*. Additionally, the issue of teacher preparation rationale and contextualization is not well emphasized. Future policy agenda items may need to address these significant factors.

WPR Question 6: How and where has this representation of the "problem" been produced, disseminated, and defended? How has it been and/or how can it be disrupted and replaced?

The *status report* encourages stakeholders to rethink the vision for the Arabic language, taking a realistic pragmatic stance toward the identified problematizations. It proposes an inclusive conceptual model to address all the problematizations of Arabic and highlights opportunities. By taking this stance, it disrupts the "traditionally" anticipated policy responses to the issues at hand. For example, the *status report* does not stop at the point of raising recommendations for curriculum and pedagogies, learner agency, and teacher preparation. The text provides a list of recommendations, and it further proposes a new vision for Arabic through a conceptual and inclusive model that rethinks the historic diglossia debate (SR, 2021, 431). The proposed model suggests that the individual dialects can continue to operate as crucial ingredients complementing a "whole" Arabic language repertoire. For example, any dialect can serve as a stepping stone through a bridging process to learning the "Fus'ha" or Modern Standard Arabic (MSA).

I believe that, in this proposal, the problematization of Arabic as being in a challenging and critical phase of its development has been disrupted and replaced. To say the least, it is a discourse that is futuristic in its outlook, reflecting an anti-antiquity perception of "Arabic" that celebrates diversity within the language and embraces its challenges.

Turning to the *declaration,* the single agenda article on teaching and learning, as seen under WPR Question 1, establishes a powerful link between Arabic language pedagogies and advancing the society. This discourse is new in its presence in a high-level policy document as the *declaration,* symbolic in its discursive effects, and firm in the authority it portrays. It does disrupt traditional policy proposals that could have emerged in similar debates about language pedagogies. The critical consideration is how this statement will be further disseminated and consolidated in future policy texts that will mediate the *declaration* and the users, the educators, and the learners. For example, Arabic speakers and learners would be interested to know realistically how "treat[ing] [Arabic] as a building block for our society and economy" (D, 2022, Article 2) will translate into operational and pragmatic policies, while research still reports significant Arabic language learning gaps.

WPR analysis summary

A closer reading of the debate through the WPR framework allowed me to interrogate the different problematizations of Arabic in the two texts, analyze their deep-seated assumptions and highlight their silences. It also helped me identify how the discourse could be disrupted and replaced.

The discourse analysis of the two recent policy texts reflects an emerging emphasis on the potential role of the Arabic language. The analysis highlights how improving the Arabic language can contribute to advancement and growth at a societal level. It also portrays a renewed emphasis on key players, the learners, and the teachers and proposes a new vision to overcome long-held debates about the Arabic language and turns them into opportunities.

The caveats appear in some silenced discourses that are not sufficiently addressed, mainly the issue of teacher preparation programs and how the current provisions can progress toward the vision of teachers of Arabic operating in a fully professionalized space, from pursuing research to upskilling themselves, to being empowered to use the updated curricula rigorously and professionally and achieve real outcomes with learners. Also, the analyzed texts do not approach the linguistic profiles of Arab first language speakers and their plurilingual realities that inform how they learn languages and how they use them. The analysis reflects that future policy needs to convey greater clarity around the unified vision for an updated Arabic language curriculum.

The question remains about how these policy discourses can move the policy forward to the next space, the space of the Arabic language policy and planning (LPP), and how any form of LPP can impact the perceptions of the Arabic language by its first language speakers, amid a plurilingual landscape in the Arabian Peninsula. I believe that the Arabic LPP agenda is moving toward a new space, in a fertile environment of policy readiness and political convenience.

Discussion: Arabic language policy and planning (LPP): possible directions

After having focused exclusively on the educational and pedagogical sections of the *status report,* I wish to draw attention to its intriguing section on "Arabic in laws, legislations and regulating authorities" (SR, 2020, p. 433). The premises of this section have a direct link to all potential language-in-education policy efforts. The *status report* builds on a three-pillar premise: a) a binding language policy, b) effective regulating authorities that will make it happen, and c) political will (SR, 2020, p. 433). I believe that these pillars are crucial and discursively powerful, as they signify a moment of policy readiness. We have not encountered high-level reports that articulate accountabilities and responsibilities explicitly in this manner. This means that there is political convenience for saying what has been said (Ball, 1993). This view aligns with my understanding that words are powerful because they signify processes and produce discursive effects when they come from a formal authority as the *status report.*

The Arabic language policy is in need for moving to a new space, to the space of action and implementation. Liddicoat (2013) and Fehri (2013) discuss key processes in language planning. The first is *status planning*, which involves the choices made about language varieties for specific purposes in a community, including decisions about language use in education or the language of instruction. The second level of processes is *corpus planning* that refers to decisions about how a language is to be codified and designed at the levels of lexicon while developing the needed resources for this process. Thirdly, *image planning* refers to the ways in which language varieties are given importance or value in a community (Liddicoat, 2013). Fourth and the last, the notion of language planning involves *language-in-education or acquisition planning* whereby the teaching and learning issues are addressed.

Fehri (2013) argues that many of the Arabic language policies and initiatives at the regional level contribute to *corpus planning* as identified by Liddicoat (2013). Fehri (2013) suggests that there is little evidence of *status planning* for the Arabic language, which in his opinion hinders the strategic view of Arabic as a language to be protected, sustained, disseminated, and maintained. Almost nine years after Fehri's seminal publication, the Arabic *status report* and the UAE Declaration of the Arabic language both embody a vision for *status planning* of the Arabic language that has implications beyond protecting the Arabic language. It moves ahead to propose a more inclusive and forward-looking model of how to perceive the Arabic language and its renewed vision as a medium of accommodating all the dialects and proposing how they can be used to allow an inclusive speakership of Arabic. This model is practically a tool for growth, and an emerging fertile linguistic policy and planning area for the future.

Additionally, *image planning* as suggested by Liddicoat (2013) is a key component of the themes of the *status report*. The *report* discusses how Arabic is perceived by university students and dedicates sections to frame Arabic as a language of the future, rather than a language of antiquity. The efforts to change the mindset and attitudes around the Arabic language fall under *image planning* as defined by Liddicoat (2013). I believe that sound language-in-education policy reforms can fill much of the gaps in this significant policy area. The *status report* uncovers that the Arab youth found the pedagogies as a main cause for changing their attitudes toward it (SR, 2020, p. 430).

Finally, a consideration of the concept of "plurilingualism" and what it means to the Arab first language speakers and learners is worth reflecting and expanding on. Plurilingualism, according to the Council of Europe, refers to the individual's ability to learn and use more than one language symbiotically (Erling & Moore, 2021; Vallejo & Dooly, 2020). Vallego and Dooly (2020) discuss how plurilingual speakers develop communicative skills and implement hybrid and complex linguistic practices. Arab learners are plurilingual and tend to utilize their repertoires in other languages and dialects of Arabic in the Arabic learning situations. I am an advocate of the paradigm shift from monolingualism parameters to the perspective that speakers can develop hybrid and fluent communicative practices that can work for multiple languages or dialects within a language (Erling & Moore, 2021; Vallejo & Dooly, 2020). However, this may not be fully applicable to the case of the Arabic language. The literature acknowledges that this research area is still emerging but offers the possibility for further research and reflection on how learners process Arabic as their first language amid a plurilingual landscape.

It is important to reflect on designing curricula and pedagogies that build bridges between the learners' realities, namely their dialects, contexts, and needs, and scaffold their language learning to achieve the targets, be this in the choice of literary content, vocabulary, or contextually adapted and relevant pedagogies (see Harb & Taha Thomure, 2020). An enhanced curriculum design can lay the ground for learners and move them smoothly from their current competencies, their dialects, or lack thereof, to the MSA (Batakji Chazy & Taha Thomure, 2022). The renewed focus on the Arabic language learner in the *status report* can be the point of entry for empowering the learner, achieving linguistic justice, and acknowledging the linguistic wealth and diversity that they bring to the learning space, an argument in favour of Arabic as a language to be utilized, lived, and enjoyed as a language of the future.

Conclusion

This chapter sets out to argue for an emerging language-in-education policy agenda for the Arabic language through discourse analysis. The analysis focused on the latest policy developments in this area, namely the report on the status of the Arabic language (MCY, 2021) and the latest UAE Declaration of the Arabic language (Dubai Media Office, 2021), using the *WPR framework* approach to policy analysis (Bacchi, 2009). The analysis revealed that these two policy texts and processes embody an emerging and growing discourse that draws the lines of a way forward for Arabic LPP. The *status report* analysis uncovered the key areas of focus of the policy makers: the need to update the Arabic language curriculum, focus on the learner, and rethink teacher preparation. The analysis shed light on gaps and rather silenced discourses, namely the assumptions about teacher preparation and the plurilingual environment of the learner of Arabic as a first language. The *declaration* text came in as a powerful response to the *status report*, emphasizing the link between Arabic language and economic growth of societies.

Most importantly, the analysis revealed that the proposed vision for the Arabic language, through the acknowledgement of the need for a binding language policy, effective regulatory authorities that can act to oversee it, and political will to back it up are key pillars for the way forward to Arabic LPP. The proposed model for rethinking the vision for Arabic and adopting an inclusive approach to language has the potential to filter through subsequent and future language-in-education policy agenda items. There is a powerful argument to support Arabic as a language of the future when language-in-education policies are well designed. This is where the immense criticality and challenges lie. Future policy work is now primed for more efforts to unpack the two analyzed documents, particularly the *declaration*.

I envisage future policy plans to be spearheaded by middle-leadership policy makers who will focus on the learners as agents. An enhanced curriculum needs to be designed based on the Arab learners' current achievements, vulnerabilities, and plurilingual realities in mind. Expert educators and policy makers are aware of these vulnerabilities, but there is no evidence that they have filtered them yet into the language planning space.

Similarly, any future work needs to break down the journey of teachers as professionals and how they can grow to the level of researchers, decision-makers, and strong advocates of the Arabic language. As key players, teachers need to be well prepared, coached, supported, and professionalized in their status, and so policy planning work will move in the direction of licensing and professionalization and re-inventing teacher higher education. Currently, a few promising licensing plans are underway in few Arab countries. However, there is little evidence on how the teaching workforce will be sufficiently prepared in their preservice journey.

Finally, the curricula and pedagogies that live up to the promise of a pragmatic, futuristic, and aspirational Arabic learner will require a vision and a clear philosophy across the countries of the Arabian Peninsula. Contentions around diglossia, contextualization, and relevance need to be part of the next curriculum, pedagogy, and assessment reforms.

The way forward will be through accommodating all the factors that an LPP process will require. The *status report* and the *declaration* both advanced the Arabic LPP discussion and honed the focus on the most important ingredients of an Arabic language-in-education policy: the learner, the teacher, and the curricular updates, and at the same time, linked this plan to the advancement and future aspirations.

References

Abanmi, I. B. M. (2017). Mustaqbal al lughatil Arabiyaa fi thilli tadafo'o al lughat (The future of the Arabica language in light of language competition). In I. Y. Al Balawi (Ed.), *Ala Lughal Ala Arabiyaa hadiran wa mustaqbalan (The Arabic language: Present and future)* (pp. 163–177). Delegation du Royaume d'Arabie Saoudite auprès de l'UNESCO.

Al Fahham, A. A. (2017). Tahadiyat al istithmar fi lughatil Arabiyaa (Challenges of investing in the Arabica language). In I. Al Balawi (Ed.), *Ala Lughal Ala Arabiyaa hadiran wa mustaqbalan (The Arabica language: Present and future)*. Delegation du Royaume d'Arabie Saoudite auprès de l'UNESCO.

Al Issa, A., & Al Dahan, L. S. (2011). Global English and endangered Arabic in the United Arab Emirates. https://doi.org/https://www.researchgate.net/publication/313766869

Al Khaleej Times. (2022). Sharjah Ruler launches first 17 volumes of "Historical Dictionary of the Arabic Language." Retrieved from https://www.khaleejtimes.com/books/sharjah-ruler-launches-first-17-volumes-of-historical-dictionary-of-the-arabic-language

Arab Thought Foundation (2012). *Li nanhada bi lughatina: mashrou'h li istishraf mustaqbal al lughati el arabiya (reviving our language: A project for envisaging the future of the Arabica language).* Beirut.

Arab Thought Foundation. (2022). Arabi 21. Retrieved from https://arabthought.org/ar/arabi21/index

Bacchi, C. (2009). *Analyzing policy: What's the problem represented to be.* Pearson.

Bacchi, C., & Goodwin, S. (2016). *Poststructural policy analysis* (ebook). Palgrave Macmillan US. https://doi.org/10.1057/978-1-137-52546-8

Ball, S. J. (1993). What is policy? Texts, trajectories and toolboxes. *Discourse: Studies in the Cultural Politics of Education, 13*(2), 10–17. https://doi.org/10.1080/0159630930130203

Ball, S. J. (2021). *The education debate (fourth).* Policy Press.

Barnawi, O. Z. (2018). *Neoliberalism and English language education policies in the Arabiana Gulfg.* Routledge.

Batakji-Chazy, A. (2020). *The fall and rise of the Arabica language: A discursive analysis of Arabica language initiatives of the United Arab Emirates.* University of Bath. Retrieved from https://researchportal.bath.ac.uk/en/studentTheses/the-fall-and-rise-of-the-arabic-language-a-discursive-analysis-of

Batakji Chazy, A., & Taha Thomure, H. (2022). Arabic Language-in-Education Policy Opportunities: Pathways to policy change. Unpublished Manuscript.

Boyle, R. (2012). Language contact in the United Arab Emirates. *World Englishes, 31*(3), 312–330.

Canagarajah, S. A. (2005). Dilemmas in planning English/vernacular relations in post-colonial communities. *Journal of Sociolinguistics, 9*(3), 418–447.

Dewachi, A., & Aita, S. A. (2012). *Status of the Arabic digital content industry in the Arab region.* Retrieved from https://digitallibrary.un.org/record/1292297?ln=en

Dubai Media Office. (2021). UAE Declaration of the Arabic Language. Retrieved from https://mediaoffice.ae/en/news/2021/December/19-12/Mohammed-bin-Rashid-2

Emirates 24/7. (2012). Mohammed unveils Arabic Language Charter. Retrieved from https://www.emirates247.com/news/government/mohammed-unveils-arabic-language-charter-2012-04-23-1.455274

Erling, E. J., & Moore, E. (2021). INTRODUCTION–Socially just plurilingual education in Europee: Shifting subjectivities and practices through research and action. *International Journal of Multilingualism, 18*(4), 523–533. https://doi.org/10.1080/14790718.2021.1913171

Fairclough, N. (2013). *Critical discourse analysis.* Routledge.

Fehri, A. K. F. (2013). *Al siyasa al lughawiya fil bilad el Arabiyaa (Language policies in Arab countries).* Dar al Kitab al Jadeed al Muttahida.

Gregory, L., Thomure, H. T., Kazem, A., Boni, A., Elsayed, M. A. A., & Taibah, N. (2021). *Advancing Arabic Language Teaching and Learning a Path to Reducing Learning Poverty in the Middle East and North Africa.* Retrieved from https://www.worldbank.org/en/events/2021/06/29/advancing-arabic-language-teaching-and-learning-in-mena#:~:text=The World Bank's Advancing Arabic,learning of Arabic more effective

Harb, M., & Taha Thomure, H. (2020). Connecting literacy to curriculum ideologies. *Curriculum Perspectives, 40*, 27–33. https://doi.org/10.1007/s41297-020-00099-0

KAICA. (2019). King Abdullah bin Abdulaziz Int'l Center for the Arabic Language. Retrieved from https://kaica.org.sa/site/news/34

Karamani, S. (2005). Petro-linguistics: The emerging nexus between oil, English and Islami. *Journal of Language, Identity, and Education, 4*(2), 87–102. https://doi.org/10.1207/s15327701jlie0402_2

Liddicoat, A. J. (2013). *Language in education policies: The discursive construction of intercultural relations*. Multilingual Matters.

MCY. (2021). *Taqreer Halat Al Lugha Al Arabiya wa Mustaqbalaha (Report on the Arabic Language Status and Future Prospects) of the Ministry of Culture and Youth of the United Arab Emirates*. Retrieved from https://www.mckd.gov.ae/ar/wp-content/uploads/sites/3/2020/12/Arabic-Status-Report.pdf

Phillipson, R. (2009). *Linguistic imperialism continued*. Routledge.

PIRLS. (2012). *PIRLS 2011 international results in reading. TIMSS & PIRLS International Study Center*. https://doi.org/10.1097/01.tp.0000399132.51747.71

PIRLS. (2016). PIRLS 2016 international results in reading. Retrieved August 21, 2019, from http://timssandpirls.bc.edu/pirls2016/international-results/pirls/student-achievement/

Spolsky, B. (2017). Language policy in education: Practices, ideology, and management. In T. L. McCarty & S. Mary (Eds.), *Language policy and political issues in education, encyclopedia of language and education*. https://doi.org/10.1007/978-3-319-02344-1_1

Taha-Thomure, H. (2008). The status of Arabica language teaching today. *Education, Business and Society: Contemporary Middle Eastern Issues, 1*(3), 186–192. https://doi.org/10.1108/17537980810909805

Taha, H. (2017a). Arabic language teacher education. In A. Gebril (Ed.), *Applied linguistics in the middle East and North Africa* (pp. 267–287). John Benjamins. https://doi.org/10.1075/aals.15.12ta

Taha, H. (2017b). Investing in cutting edge arabic language education. In I. AlBalawi (Ed.), *L'Arabea langue de culture universalle: Ouvrage publie a l'occasion de la celebration de la journee mondiale de la langue Arabea* (pp. 67–76). UNESCO Plan Arabia.

Tollefson, J. W., & Tsui, A. B. (2017). Language policy and the construction of national cultural identity. In J. W. Tollefson & A. B. Tsui (Eds.), *Language policy, culture, and identity in Asian contexts*. Routledge. Retrieved from https://books.google.ae/books?id=gB03DwAAQBAJ&printsec=frontcover&hl=ar&source=gbs_ge_summary_r&cad=0#v=onepage&q&f=false

Troudi, S., & Al Hafidh, G. (2017). The dilemma of English and its roles in the United Arab Emirates. In A. Mahboob & T. Elyas (Eds.), *Challenges to education in the GCC during the 21st century* (pp. 93–117). Gulf Research Centre Cambridge.

UNESCO. (2017). History of the Arabic language at UNESCO. Retrieved from http://www.unesco.org/new/en/unesco/resources/history-of-the-arabic-language-at-unesco/

UNESCO. (2021). Arabic calligraphy: Knowledge, skills and practices. Retrieved from https://ich.unesco.org/en/RL/arabic-calligraphy-knowledge-skills-and-practices-01718

Vallejo, C., & Dooly, M. (2020). Plurilingualism and translanguaging: Emergent approaches and shared concerns. Introduction to the special issue. *International Journal of Bilingual Education and Bilingualism, 23*(1), 1–16. https://doi.org/10.1080/13670050.2019.1600469

Wodak, R., & Meyer, M. (2009). Critical discourse analysis: History, agenda, theory, and methodology. In R. Wodak & M. Meyer (Eds.), *Methods for critical discourse analysis* (2nd Revise, pp. 1–33). Sage. https://doi.org/10.1016/S0376-7361(09)70018-4

2

CURRENT DISCUSSIONS ON PLURILINGUAL PEDAGOGY

Language learning implications in the Arabian Peninsula

Nadine Jaafarawi

Introduction

Teaching English as a second or foreign language has traditionally been associated with teaching practices that encourage the isolation of English from other languages in the student's repertoire and in the school curriculum (Cenoz & Gorter 2013; De Houwer & Wilton, 2011; Gorter, 2013). As a result, teachers of language are often expected only to use English and avoid any reference to elements of the first/home language (L1) or other languages. This is a product of behaviorism and its influence on the acceptance of how the second language (L2) should be taught and learned (Nor & Ab Rashid, 2018). These ideas are deeply rooted both in society at large and in second/foreign language teaching. It has been reinforced in Europe by the one nation-one language ideology since the 18th century, and it is still prevailing in many parts of the world (Lüdi & Py, 2009).

However, recent research on plurilingualism and language education proposes a softening of borders between languages and the use of plurilingual repertoires of students and teachers for learning (Duarte & Van der Ploeg, 2019). The notion of softening boundaries between languages is not new. Decades ago, Grosjean (1985) and Cook (1992) discussed the specific characteristics of bilingual speakers. Grosjean (1985) considered bilinguals to be fully competent learners with unique linguistic profiles that cannot be divided into separate parts. Cook (1992) proposed the term multicompetence as a complex type of competence, which is qualitatively different from the competence of monolingual speakers of a language. Consequently, a bilingual or plurilingual person's communicative competence is not comparable to that of a monolingual speaker. That is why he considered that L2 learners are fundamentally different from native speakers. Cook (1999) further discussed the fallacy of comparing L2 learners to native

DOI: 10.4324/9781003315971-4

speakers, because these new language learners bring with them part of their L1, and therefore judging them against native L1 speakers is inappropriate.

Today, the boundaries between languages are becoming softer considering the evolving nature of the teaching approaches utilized by instructors in higher education and other levels of education. Things are now changing as recent research is starting to acknowledge the plurilingual resources of students and instructors and has called for a restructuring of higher education beyond English medium orientation in countries in which English is not the official language (Coleman, 2013). This has important implications for a number of countries in the Arabian Peninsula, especially in those countries where both teachers and students are facing enormous challenges as a result of the educational reforms that were undertaken to increase the adoption of English as a medium of instruction (EMI) in higher education institutions (HEIs) (Solloway, 2016).

Keeping this in mind, the main aim of this chapter is to explore implications of the plurilingual pedagogy to improve language education in countries within the Arabian Peninsula. To achieve this aim, this chapter first briefly describes the need for a paradigm shift toward plurilingualism within the Arabian Peninsula, providing then a brief overview of the concepts of plurilingualism and translanguaging along with the potentialities and practical applications of these pedagogies in learning languages. It will be in this section that the relevance of these two pedagogies in transforming the education and learning of language in the countries of the Arabian Peninsula will be discussed. The final section will conclude with potential recommendations for educators in the region on how to bring about an actual shift in language education based on plurilingualism and plurilingual pedagogies.

The need to shift toward plurilingualism/translanguaging in language education

The shift toward plurilingualism in language education first took place in Europe when the Council of Europe (2001) supported the position that all European citizens should learn two additional languages besides their first/home language. Several researchers started (Bell, 2003; Bialystok, 2001; Bickes, 2004; García, 2009; Kumaravadivelu, 2001; Lantolf, 2011) examining the benefits of plurilingualism from a variety of perspectives namely the psychocognitive (Bialystok, 2001; Bickes, 2004; Perani et al., 2003), sociocultural (Lantolf, 2011), and pedagogical (Bell, 2003; García, 2009; Kumaravadivelu, 2001) perspectives. According to this stream of research, acquiring a new language modifies the individuals' global language competence and shapes their linguistic repertoires, and in the process of learning languages, errors should no longer be seen as pure by-products of interference but should be seen as a way of progressing in language learning.

Consequently, plurilingualism and translanguaging are terms that are currently being used in an attempt to "didacticize" or transform them into classroom teaching methodology. In this chapter, the terms are synonymous, and both reject the compartmentalization of languages favoring the optimization of relations between languages. Unfortunately, I found that there is still fear associated with the use of "home" languages among the monolingual demographic of the teaching profession. As a teacher, I myself was biased by the monolingual stance, and as a teacher of English, I was told to exclusively use English inside and outside class. In fact, we were conditioned in our schooling and in our training as teachers not to use another language besides English believing that if we did, it would lead to losing control of aspects of the learning process, especially in language learning. However, it is time to change our perceptions on adopting the monolingual ideology and start developing a good understanding of the social, cultural, emotional, and linguistic benefits of using the students' home language in the learning process. In fact, there are increasingly positive stories demonstrating the innovative use of multiple languages in teaching to make the most of a classroom's linguistic diversity which will be mentioned in the next sections.

Plurilingualism: Definition

Plurilingualism was first introduced to the European education system in 1996. It was a consequence of waves of migration in Europe. These waves resulted in a plurality of languages and cultures, which were seen either as a problem or as an asset. Being in the front line, language became the catalyst of change as languages and cultures of migrants interacted with the languages and cultures of host societies. That is why, according to the Council of Europe (2001), it is imperative that students learn to be plurilinguists from a young age so that they can be not only more competitive in an increasingly globalized world, but also able to integrate within societies when necessary. Consequently, Plurilingual education was developed in the European Union due to the growth of these multilingual and multicultural communities.

Several researchers reviewed the term and have made attempts to define it. In most studies conducted in this field, researchers made sure to clarify the difference between *pluri*lingualism and *multi*lingualism to make it clear for the reader before they proceed, as is the case in the introduction to this volume.

Plurilingualism has been defined in the Common European Framework of Reference for Languages (Council of Europe, 2001, p. 168) in the following way:

> [Plurilingualism is] the ability to use languages for the purposes of communication and to take part in intercultural interaction, where a person, viewed as a social agent, has proficiency of varying degrees, in several languages, and experience of several cultures. This is not seen as the superposition or juxtaposition of distinct competences, but rather as the existence of a complex or even composite competence on which the user may draw.
>
> *(Council of Europe, 2001, p. 168)*

Looking through a plurilingual lens, Marshall and Moore (2016) stressed the notion that individual's languages and cultures are inseparable. The authors suggest that plurilingualism should be viewed as the interrelation of an individual's languages and cultures in a complex way. This interrelation, the authors argue, largely depends on individuals' biographies, lived experiences, social trajectories, and life paths and is subject to change with time and circumstances. Hence, it can be argued that plurilingualism challenges the concept of bilingualism which conceptualized the learning and use of more than one language as a full and balanced competence rather than as an ideological construction that develops over time.

Additionally, in their attempt to explore plurilingual pedagogy, Dooly and Vallejo (2019, p. 81) defined plurilingualism as "social reality," and also a "reality of the classroom" that needs to be transformed into classroom teaching methodology.

Based on the definitions of plurilingualism provided above, plurilingualism can be understood as a concept that refers to the learning and use of more than one or two languages to facilitate communication and understanding that is based not on the discreetness and full competence required to master multilingualism, but as a constantly emerging and evolving language competence. Consequently, plurilingual pedagogy refers to bringing into the classroom strategies employed by both teachers and students that will allow the learners to overcome the barriers that might arise when encountering other languages and/ or other cultures. Keeping this in mind, we will now discuss the transformative aspects of plurilingualism.

The transformative aspect of plurilingual pedagogies

Though in higher education the pedagogical practices remain largely monolingual, it has been argued by prominent scholars within the field of plurilingualism that plurilingualism should be the focus of language education and learning and the goal of all educators (Dooly & Vallejo, 2019). It has changed traditional foreign language education where the goal is to have partial competence in multiple languages, rather than full competence in two or three. In the European context, García and Otheguy (2020) stressed the point that "not only has the concept of plurilingualism influenced the teaching of additional languages for all European citizens, but it has also influenced instruction of the national language for the increasing number of black and brown refugees that enter the European Union" (p. 22). That is why it is essential not to neglect the unique opportunity to turn students' spontaneous plurilingual practices into pedagogical strategies (Galante et al., 2019). Studies in higher education have shown that recognizing and valuing students' plurilingual competence is essential for better learning. To prove this point further, in their study, Marshall and Moore (2016) showed that international students in Vancouver, Canada, had agency over their plurilingualism in both social and educational contexts and were able to utilize their linguistic repertoire as a resource to communicate, even if only English was used as the medium of instruction. Consequently, and since students showed that they use languages other than English in their academic studies, the main concern should be how to support and supply educators with suitable materials to be able to implement pedagogy that can harness students' plurilingual practices. Galante et al. (2019) conducted a researcher-instructor collaboration that aimed at implementing plurilingual practices, such as translanguaging, plurilingual identity, and intercomprehension over four months in an English for Academic Purposes (EAP) program at a university in Toronto, Canada. They proposed a framework for the integration of plurilingual tasks where they carefully initiated the process of shifting pedagogy from English-only to more linguistically and culturally inclusive practices. They discovered that instructors could make use of existing materials and adapt them by introducing one or more plurilingual strategies such as intercomprehension and translanguaging (Galante et al., 2019). Through this, the balance of plurilingual versus nonplurilingual tasks can be established, and this will help the shift in the classroom pedagogy in higher education to be more systematic for students and instructors.

Translanguaging: Background

Among the plurilingual pedagogies, translanguaging theory builds on scholarly work that has demonstrated how colonial and modernist-era language ideologies created and maintained linguistic, cultural, and racial hierarchies in society. Originally, in Wales, Cen Williams created the term translanguaging (in Welsh) (Vogel & García, 2017) to refer to pedagogical practices in which English and Welsh were used for different activities and purposes (i.e., reading in one language and writing in another). Colin Baker (2001) then translated the term into English as translanguaging (cited in Vogel & García, 2017).

There have been numerous debates among scholars on the term's definition. However, García (2009) noted that the term is not just something bilinguals do when they feel they are lacking words or phrases needed to express themselves in a monolingual environment. In fact, translanguaging is a pedagogical practice, which leverages the fluid languaging of learners in ways that deepen their engagement and comprehension of complex content and texts (Vogel & García, 2017) where the *trans* prefix communicates the ways that multilingual people's language practices in fact "go beyond" the use of state-endorsed named language systems (García & Li Wei, 2015, p. 42; Wei, 2011). For García (2013), translanguaging is not a mere strategy and is more than code switching, which considers that the two languages are separate systems (or codes) and are "switched" for communicative purposes (Velasco & García, 2014). "Translanguaging is the process of making meaning, shaping experiences, gaining understanding and knowledge through the use of two languages" (Baker, 2011, p. 288). To go deeper, translanguaging is a process whereby multilingual speakers utilize features taken from different languages that have been previously separated by sociopolitical forces but are now experienced in speakers' interactions as an integrated communication repertoire (Paulsrud et al., 2017), thus creating more learning opportunities for multilinguals (Rasman, 2018). For Wei (2011), translanguaging and the idea of translanguaging space derive from the psycholinguistic notion of languaging, which moves from language as a noun to language as a verb, thus stressing an ongoing psycholinguistic process.

For García and Otheguy (2020), translanguaging is a theoretical lens that provides an opportunity to view bilingualism and multilingualism from a different perspective. According to the authors, the theory of translanguaging posits that contrary to the common belief of having more than two autonomous language systems, it is better that all users of language select and deploy specific features from a unitary linguistic repertoire. This way it becomes easier for users to not just understand the meaning but also negotiate specific communicative contexts. The authors add that translanguaging can also be used as an approach to language pedagogy as it can help to leverage students' diverse and dynamic language practices in teaching and learning.

Finally, still according to García (2009), translanguaging empowers both the learner and the teacher, transforms the power relations, and focuses the process of teaching and learning on making meaning, enhancing experience, and developing identity. More importantly, it is a process of knowledge construction that goes beyond language(s). It takes us beyond the linguistics of systems and speakers to a linguistics of participation: "It is an action to transform classroom discourses, including both the discourses by the participants of the classroom activities and the discourses about the classroom" (Wei & Lin, 2019).

Despite their different origins, both terms, plurilingual pedagogy and translanguaging, represent instances and practices where languages interact symbiotically as part of the one single linguistic repertoire of an individual, be it in day-to-day situations or in teaching and learning contexts. Therefore, as explained in the introduction of this volume, they can be used interchangeably at times.

The case in Arabian Peninsula

In the Arabian Peninsula, this gradual introduction of plurilingual strategies appears much needed in the education systems. This is mainly because in many of these countries, both students and teachers find it difficult to learn and teach (through) English but are compelled to do so by the policy of the institutions that states that English is "the" language of science and technology (Al-Mahrooqi, 2012; Solloway, 2016).

In many of the countries of the Arabian Peninsula, many educational institutions use content and language integrated learning (CLIL) in English as they consider it vital for students who must function in an increasingly globalized marketplace. Over the years, initiatives to increase the adoption of EMI in schools as well as higher education have been observed which resulted in many content subjects being taught via English. This shift can be largely seen from the fact that since the 1990s, a number of educational language policies making English as the primary medium of instruction in higher education have been implemented in these countries (Hopkyns et al., 2018). These policies have been implemented to ensure that the peoples of these countries are on par with the international academic community and also to achieve country-specific goals (Alhassan, 2021; Al-Mahrooqi, 2012). This was largely a result of the government policies who realized that English was not just a dominant language of science, research, and technology but was also widely present in the international academic community. However, little thought was given to what this might mean for the status of Arabic.

To go further, in the United Arab Emirates (UAE), the move to adopt EMI in HEIs was mainly influenced by the government's move to transform the country from an oil-based economy to a knowledge-based economy (Siemund et al., 2020). However, we cannot deny the fact that due to the rise of the translingual society in UAE where a large number of the population, especially young people, speak different varieties of English and Arabic (O'Neill, 2017; Siemund et al., 2020), many initiatives have been spearheaded by the UAE in an effort to develop the teaching and learning of Arabic in the country (Taha-Thomure, 2019).

In the State of Qatar, the ruling family, in the year 2003 as a part of the Education for a New Era (EFNE) reform policy, decreed the establishment of a bilingual education system as a means of transition to EMI. The move toward EMI was often cited as a way to realize the Qatar National Vision 2030 (Ahmadi, 2017). However, the decree was abandoned in the year 2012 by the Qatari authorities as a remedy to correct the various pitfalls that occurred in the education system as a result of the implementation of the EFNE (Mustafawi et al., 2022).

In addition, the growing use of EMI in almost all these countries has been found to have created numerous challenges for both teachers and students, indicating a failure of these policies to enhance language education among the populace of these countries. The reasons for these policy failures are numerous and have been documented by various studies (Ahmadi, 2017; Alhassan, 2021; Ellili-Cherif, 2014; Mustafawi et al., 2022; Solloway, 2016) examining the use of EMI in HEIs in many of these countries from both students' and teachers' perspectives. The primary conclusions that can be drawn from these studies are the fact that the adoption of EMI in HEIs has brought stress to the parents as well as students (Ahmadi, 2017), has negatively affected academic performance of students in English as well as other subjects (Mustafawi et al., 2022; Solloway, 2016), and has been regarded as a threat to Arabic (which is the official language in many of these countries), their religious identity, and cultural integrity (Ahmadi, 2017; Ellili-Cherif, 2014; Solloway, 2016). Nevertheless, it is worth noting that many of these studies recommend that in order to improve language education, it is not only important to improve the pedagogical training of teachers but also to alter the EMI content in a way that meets the learning styles and preferences of the students (Alhassan, 2021). This is where the concepts of plurilingualism and translanguaging can greatly help in reducing the conflict between English and

Arabic that has been found in many of the countries in the Arabian Peninsula (Ahmadi, 2017; Ellili-Cherif, 2014; Solloway, 2016).

The task of translating plurilingualism into teaching pedagogy for language education can be a relatively smoother process in the Arabian Peninsula since the social interaction and communication in many of these countries take place in multiple languages or language varieties specific to the country. For example, in Qatar, daily interactions often take place in languages that include Qatari Arabic, Standard Arabic, Gulf Pidgin Arabic, English, and others (Mustafawi et al., 2022), whereas in the UAE, an increasingly diverse country social interaction, especially among young people, mostly takes place in "Arabizi" or "Arabish," a mixture of English and Emirati Arabic (Hopkyns et al., 2018; O'Neill, 2016).

A plurilingual pedagogical practice is particularly needed in countries in the Arabian Peninsula where both teachers and students have been found to lack English proficiency, and students are more likely to prefer receiving instructions in Arabic rather than English (Alrabah et al., 2016). Additionally, creating pedagogical practices comprising two (L1 and L2) or more languages can not only help teachers to respond to the students' preferred ways of learning but will also help them to create a relaxed classroom experience. This can greatly help the students to learn L2 more effectively as compared to just using L2 as the sole language of instruction. However, it is recommended that the implementation of such plurilingual-inspired activities/tasks be gradually introduced in the language program and that collaboration between instructors and administrators be set up. In fact, Ellis (2013) investigated English as a second language (ESL) teachers' views about language teaching and learning and found that plurilingual teachers are aware of their own plurilingual strategies but still need support to transform this knowledge into pedagogical practice. Other teachers in Kuwait showed negative attitudes toward the use of these strategies when teaching English (Alrabah et al., 2016).

My personal experience in an Arabic-speaking country

Based on the above and on how teachers show negative attitudes toward implementing plurilingual pedagogies and others even fear, the term plurilingualism to begin with, let alone to use it in class, drives me to mention a study that I did years ago in this area. Back when I was a preschool homeroom teacher and coordinator of English in a school in Lebanon and being a native speaker of Arabic, my main concern was to find ways to develop my students' L2 acquisition and comprehension of the content with the use of their native "home" language which was Arabic. For this purpose, I decided to conduct an experimental study on this through a read-aloud lesson which was part of my PhD dissertation. The target samples (275 students) were divided into two groups, one experimental and the other controlled. In the experimental group (137 students), I used the students' mother tongue (Arabic/L1) and their second foreign language (English/L2) in reading the story. While in the control group (138 students), I delivered the same lesson using English only. Students (in both groups) were asked to draw the story followed by open-ended questions to reflect on their drawings. The students' drawings were taken to a child psychologist to interpret them according to a specific rubric that targets the concepts of language acquisition, comprehension, and empathy. The drawings of students, in this study, were analyzed by looking at four main things: image themes, image features, image location, and pencil pressure.

Results showed that the integration of L1 and L2 yielded favorable results to comprehension and cultural awareness, where the students, through their drawings, could relate and feel empathy toward the character in the story under study. All values and associations were in place in the student's mind. The drawings were expressive of comprehension and cultural awareness acquisition. This indicated that introducing the mother tongue can be positive, especially since it makes the student culturally familiar to the study material. By integrating their home language, the students developed a better feel for the culture studied, as well as a better understanding of themselves. So, teachers do not need to feel as if they are "betraying" their mission and profession by introducing the mother tongue into their classes. As English teachers are not advised to use the mother tongue (Arabic) in their teaching, they feel very guilty about introducing this language, regardless of how effective it may be in terms of language acquisition.

So, in the above study, I was trying to use the students' "home" language to build a better classroom environment that fosters a *Culture Vulture Child* (Jaafarawi, 2018). Though it was conducted years ago, it proved the effectiveness of the use of the mother tongue in language learning. Consequently, the above study could help teachers realize the real benefit of plurilingualism and translanguaging so they can defy the ideology of isolating English from other languages in the curriculum. This corroborates what García and Wei (2015) noted in their work that "Translanguaging in schools not only creates the possibility that bilingual students could use their full linguistic and semiotic repertoire to make meaning but also that teachers would 'take it up' as a legitimate pedagogical practice. Rather than just being a scaffolding practice to access content or language, translanguaging is transformative for the child, for the teacher, and for education itself, and particularly for bilingual education" (García & Wei., 2015, p. 227). Translanguaging allowed me, as a teacher, to cognitively engage every child in the class, which in turn made me sure that each individual child is able to receive the linguistic input appropriately, is able to produce linguistic output adequately, and is cognitively involved. Consequently, there should be no fear of using these approaches in language learning.

Translanguaging and plurilingualism as pedagogies or practices

Questions are raised regarding what the best practices for translanguaging within the classrooms are. There is evidence within the literature that the best translanguaging practice within classrooms is the one that is student directed or that facilitates learner–learner interactions. For example, in their work, Lewis et al. (2012) refer to this practice as the one that involves only students and little teacher support. One of the major benefits of this practice as observed by García (2009) is that student-directed translanguaging practice greatly allows students to construct meaning on their own and even demonstrate knowledge of other languages. This largely facilitates language acquisition among students without having to wait for their teachers to assume their role. However, García (2009) urges that such translanguaging practice must be implemented with some caution, especially in countries or settings where there exists unequal power between two languages.

For example, in UAE, the increasing spread of English, along with the value assigned to it, has elevated the status of English and marginalized the status of Arabic. This has forced some parents, who want Arabic-only instruction for their children, to "seek out private fee-paying Arabic-medium schools" (Baker, 2017, p. 286). For this purpose, I believe the introduction of L1 in education is necessary to facilitate multilingual competencies starting in schools. To explain my point of view, throughout my teaching career, I was hired to teach Arabic to native speakers of English in an American standard-based curriculum school in UAE. I had to mix the two languages to be able to communicate and teach the difficult concepts to the students. Hearing their "home" language used by the teacher helped students not only to accept but also to enjoy learning Arabic. I developed materials that helped me in teaching Arabic such as reading dual-language story books, dual-language flash cards, recordings of other students talking or singing in Arabic, and real-life scenarios (dialoging). The students started to exhibit improved executive function and cognitive flexibility and creativity.

Consequently, I started reading and researching more about plurilingualism and translanguaging practices in higher education context too. In teaching English composition courses, I asked my students to look up meanings of certain key terms in Arabic to help bring students closer to the material and to help them comprehend the content better. Being a native speaker of Arabic gave me the advantage of discussing the content freely using L1 and L2 and understand any word used by students in class in any of the two languages. This was also emphasized in an intervention that was carried out in UAE higher education classrooms by two university professors (Steinhagen & Said, 2021). Students were offered academic papers in English and Arabic and were provided the space to learn information through their languages. Using combined principles of translanguaging practice, the project yielded positive results. Students found the intervention empowering as it renewed their sense of respect for Arabic (Steinhagen & Said, 2021).

Throughout my teaching journey in higher education, I saw students use translanguaging in note-taking as they stated that it helps them "understand" and it "feels more comfortable and natural" to them. In other cases, students use their L1 (Arabic) in summarizing a text in L2 (English), and if not summarizing the whole text, they choose to look up unfamiliar terms in Arabic. Those approaches can be supported by the teacher by intentionally guiding students to use all of their linguistic abilities to mediate understanding. By helping students take part in their learning process, we are helping them to validate who they are and what they bring to the classroom. Consequently, teachers can provide translanguaging spaces where students are encouraged to communicate naturally through any language or mix of languages they choose. This fosters a sense of belonging as bilingual individuals through using their full linguistic repertoires to support learning.

Hence, the use of translanguaging in different education settings that range from preschool learning to young adults, as seen in the examples of my own experience, speaks for the potential of plurilingualism and translanguaging as a pedagogical tool. This should give insights to teachers and curriculum developers on the need to develop and implement translanguaging pedagogical practices in the education system of the countries within the Arabian Peninsula.

Conclusions and recommendations

Conclusions

During the course of this discussion on plurilingualism and translanguaging, it was found that the increased and simultaneous interactions that occur in local, global, and virtual contexts today, both globally and in the Arabian Peninsula context in specific, have made the use of plurilingual approaches ever important than before. Hence, to conclude, it is time that language educators, especially in HEIs in countries of the Arabian Peninsula, grabbed this opportunity and accelerated the learning process by adopting plurilingualism as a resource rather than considering it as an obstacle. Given the right resources, educators can easily overcome the barriers that hamper the use of plurilingual approaches in classrooms.

Recommendations

The following are some of the recommendations that can greatly help educators in the Arabian Peninsula to bring about a shift in language education and lead them to focus on plurilingualism and plurilingual pedagogies in schools and universities of countries within the Arabian Peninsula.

First, for plurilingualism to succeed in countries in the Arabian Peninsula, it is important that educators consider plurilingualism not simply as a symbol of diversity in the classroom but rather adopt it as a common practice that is implemented across the curriculum. Second, the successful adoption of plurilingualism pedagogy in schools and universities largely depends on the extent to which instructors and program directors are willing to take the gradual shift from an English-language-only to a plurilingual approach. To do so, it is important that both language instructors and program directors work together or collaboratively with students. This is of critical importance because it is in fact the students who are ultimately going to benefit the most from the adoption of plurilingualism pedagogy in the classroom.

Third, successful adoption of plurilingualism in classrooms also depends on the kind of support and encouragement that educators or teachers receive from the administration of schools and universities when it comes to the implementation of plurilingual pedagogy and how open the teachers are to students' use of other languages apart from English in the classroom. With that being said, results of research in this area show that when teacher views are surveyed, they report minimal mixing of languages in classrooms. However, when they are observed while teaching, they are found to engage in translanguaging practices for various pedagogical purposes (Abourehab & Azaz, 2020; Alqahtani, 2022; Hillman et al., 2019; Hopkyns et al., 2018). There seems to be no opposition to the practice of mixing English and Arabic per se, but rather an expectation that only English should be used in EMI context. The teacher perceives this as the expectation of the students and, therefore, upholds this by speaking mainly English. To overcome this and help teachers break their perceived monolingual ideologies and to acknowledge the fact that the majority are using translanguaging without knowing, teachers in the Arabian Peninsula should be educated about this, and classroom-based research on these approaches should be shared with them to help them realize the effectiveness of those approaches on the learner and to use them without fear or doubt. Moreover, teachers should be trained on how to use translanguaging and plurilingualism in a methodological way to maximize their effectiveness in the language learning process.

Fourth, adopting translanguaging and plurilingualism, especially in countries of the Arabian Peninsula where English language is being considered as a threat to their native language Arabic, can help students to realize that their language repertoire is in fact one of the rich resources that they can use to learn any language, which also includes English language besides their own home language.

Finally, it is important to note that successful implementation of plurilingual pedagogical practices will not be possible, unless there occur some systemic changes in teacher education. This would involve profound changes not just in teachers' understanding of language education but also dramatic changes in education policies. While translanguaging practices undoubtedly occur within classrooms where the instructor and learners use both Arabic and English, these educational and meaningful exchanges cannot be documented for fear that they could have a negative impact on the instructor's career (Van den Hoven & Carroll, 2021; Hillman, S., Graham, & Eslami, 2019). Stakeholders in the countries of the Arabian Peninsula should be aware of this and be open to challenge the prevalent assumptions regarding preserving the language "purity" and be more flexible in accepting the use of Arabic alongside English.

References

Abourehab, Y., & Azaz, M. (2020). Pedagogical translanguaging in community/heritage Arabic language learning. *Journal of Multilingual and Multicultural Development*, 1–14. 10.1080/01434632.2020.1826496

Ahmadi, Q. S. (2017). Unwelcome? English As a medium of instruction (EMI) in the Arabian Gulf. *English Language Teaching, 10*(8), 11–17.

Alhassan, A. (2021). Challenges and professional development needs of EMI lecturers in Omani higher education. *SAGE Open*, 1–12.

Alrabah, S., Wu, S., Alotaibi, A. M., & Aldaihani, H. A. (2016). English teachers' use of learners' L1 (Arabic) in college classrooms in Kuwait. *English Language Teaching, 9*(1), 1–11.

Al-Mahrooqi, R. I. (2012). English communications skills: How are they taught at schools and universities in Oman. *English Language Teaching, 5*(4), 124–130.

Alqahtani, M. H. (2022). The Saudi 2030 vision and translanguaging in language learning in Saudi Arabia: Looking for concord in the future. *Journal of Language and Linguistic Studies, 18*, 556–568.

Baker, C. (2001). *Foundations of bilingual education and bilingualism*. Multilingual Matters.

Baker, C. (2011). *Foundations of bilingual education and bilingualism* (5th ed.). Multilingual Matters.

Baker, F. S. (2017). National pride the new school model: English Language education in Abu Dhabi, UAE. In R. Kirkpatrick (Ed.), *English language education policy in the middle East and North Africa* (pp. 279–291). Springer.

Bell, D. M. (2003). Method and postmethod: Are they really so incompatible? *TESOL Quarterly, 37*, 325–336. https://doi.org/10.2307/3588507

Bialystok, E. (2001). *Bilingualism in development: Language, literacy, and cognition*. Cambridge University Press.

Bickes, H. (2004). Bilingualismus, Mehrsprachigkeit und mentales Lexikon—Evolutionsbiologische, soziokulturelle und kognitionswissenschaftliche Perspektiven [Bilingualism, plurilingualism and mental lexicon—Perspectives from evolutionary biology, sociocultural and cognitive sciences]. *Fremdsprachen lehren und lernen* [*Learning and Teaching Foreign Languages*], *33*, 27–51.

Cenoz, J., & Gorter, D. (2013). Towards a plurilingual approach in English language teaching: Softening the boundaries between languages. *TESOL Quarterly, 47*(3), 591–599.

Coleman, J. (2013). Foreword. In A. Doiz, D. Lasagabaster, & J. M. Sierra (Eds.), *English-Medium instruction at universities: Global challenges* (pp. xiii–xixv). Multilingual Matters.

Cook, V. (2001). Using the first language in the classroom. *Canadian Modern Language Review, 57*, 402–423.

Cook, V. (1992). Evidence for multicompetence. *Language Learning, 42*, 557–591. https://doi.org/10.1111/j.l 467-1770.1992.tbOl 044.x

Cook, V. (1999). Going beyond the native speaker in language teaching. *TESOL Quarterly*, 33, 185–209. https://doi.org/10.2307/358771

Cook, V. (2002). Background to the L2 user. In V. Cook (Ed.), *Portraits of the L2 user* (pp. 1–28). Multilingual Matters.

Council of Europe. Council for Cultural Co-operation. Education Committee. Modern Languages Division (2001). Common European framework of reference for languages: Learning, teaching, assessment. Cambridge University Press.

De Houwer, A., & Wilton, A. (Eds.). (2011). *English in Europee today: Sociocultural and educational perspectives*. John Benjamins.

Dooly, M., & Vallejo, C. (2019). Bringing plurilingualism into teaching practice: A quixotic quest?. *International Journal of Bilingual Education and Bilingualism, 23*(1), 81–97. 10.1080/13670050.2019.1598933

Duarte, J., & Van der Ploeg, M. (2019). Plurilingual lecturers in English medium instruction in The Netherlands: The key to plurilingual approaches in higher education? *European Journal of Higher Education, 9*(3), 268–284.

Ellili-Cherif, M. (2014). Integrated language and content instruction in Qatar independent schools: Teachers' perspectives. *Teacher Development, 18*(2), 211–228.
Ellis, E. (2013). The ESL teacher as plurilingual: An Australian perspective. *TESOL Quarterly, 47*(3), 446–471. https://doi.org/10.1002/tesq.120
Galante, A., Okubo, K., Cole, C., Abd Elkader, N., Carozza, N., Wilkinson, C., Wotton, C., & Vasic, J. (2019). Plurilingualism in higher education: A collaborative initiative for the implementation of plurilingual pedagogy in an English for academic purposes program at a Canadian university. *TESL Canada Journal, 36*(1), 121–133.
García, O. (2009). *Bilingual education in the 21st century: A global perspective*. Wiley-Blackwell.
García, O., & Wei., L. (2015). *Translanguaging: Language, bilingualism and education*. Palgrave Macmillan.
García, O., & Otheguy, R. (2020). Plurilingualism and translanguaging: Commonalities and divergences. *International Journal of Bilingual Education and Bilingualism, 23*(1), 17–35.
Gorter, D. (2013). Multilingual interaction and minority languages: Proficiency and language practices in education and society. *Language Teaching*. https://doi.org/10.1 1017/S0261444812000481
Grosjean, F. (1985). The bilingual as a competent but specific speaker-hearer. *Journal of Multilingual and Multicultural Development, 6*, 467–477. https://doi.org/10.1080/01434632.1985.9994221
Hillman, S., Graham, K. M., & Eslami, Z. R. (2019). Teachers' translanguaging ideologies and practices at an international branch campus in Qatar. *English Teaching & Learning, 43*(1), 41–63.
Hopkyns, S., Zoghbor, W., & John Hassall, P. (2018). Creative hybridity over linguistic purity: The status of English in the United Arab Emirates. *Asian Englishes, 20*(2), 158–169.
Jaafarawi, N. (2018). *Culture Vulture Child*. DAR AL-KOTOB AL-HADITHA.
Kumaravadivelu, B. (2001). Toward a postmethod pedagogy. *TESOL Quarterly, 35*, 537–560. https://doi.org/10.2307/3588427
Lantolf, J. (2011). The sociocultural approach to second language acquisition: Sociocultural theory, second language acquisition, and artificial L2 development. In D. Atkinson (Ed.), *Alternative approaches to second language acquisition* (pp. 24–47). Routledge.
Lewis, G., Jones, B., & Baker, C. (2012). Translanguaging: Developing its conceptualisation and contextualisation. *Educational Research and Evaluation, 18*(7), 655–670.
Lüdi, G., & Py, B. (2009). To be or not to be … a plurilingual speaker. *International Journal of Multilingualism, 6*(2), 154–167. https://doi.org/10.1080/14790710902846715
Marshall, S., & Moore, D. (2016). 2B or not 2B plurilingual? Navigating languages literacies, and plurilingual competence in postsecondary education in Canada. *TESOL Quarterly, 47*(3), 472–499.
Marshall, S., & Moore, D. (2018). Plurilingualism amid the panoply of lingualisms: Addressing critiques and misconceptions in education. *International Journal of Multilingualism, 15*(1), 19–34.
Mouhanna, M. (2016). English as a medium of instruction in the tertiary education setting of the UAE: Perspectives of content teachers. [Ed.D Thesis: University of Exeter].
Mustafawi, E., Shaaban, K., Khwaileh, T., & Ata, K. (2022). Perceptions and attitudes of Qatar university students regarding the utility of Arabic and English in communication and education in Qatar. *Language Policy, 21*, 75–119.
Nor, N. M., & Ab Rashid, R. (2018). A review of theoretical perspectives on language learning and acquisition. *Kasetsart Journal of Social Sciences, 39*(1), 161–167.

O'Neill, G. T. (2016). Heritage, Heteroglossia and home: Multilingualism in Emirati families. In L. Buckingham (Ed.), *Language, identity and education on the Arabian Peninsula: Bilingual policies in a multilingual context* (pp. 13–38). Multilingual Matters.

O'Neill, G. T. (2017). Multilingualism and occluded diversities within the superdiverse condition of the United Arab Emirates: A study of the multiple language resources, practices and ideologies of young Emirati women. [Ph.D. Thesis: Macquarie University].

Paulsrud, B., Rosen, J., Straszer, B., & Wedin, A. (2017). Perspectives on translanguaging in education. In B. Paulsrud, J. Rosén, B. Straszer, & Bristol (Eds.), *New perspectives on translanguaging and education* (pp. 10–19). Multilingual Matters.

Perani, D., Abutalebi, J., Paulesu, E., Brambati, S., Scifo, P., Cappa, S. F., & Fazio, F. (2003). The role of age of acquisition and language usage in early, highproficient bilinguals: An fMRI study during verbal fluency. *Human Brain Mapping, 19*, 170–182. https://doi.org/10.1002/hbm.10110

Rasman, R. (2018). To translanguage or not to translanguage? The multilingual practice in an Indonesian EFL classroom. *Indonesian Journal of Applied Linguistics*, 7(3), 687–694.

Siemund, P., Al-Issa, A., & Leimgruber, J. R. E. (2020). Multilingualism and the role of English in the United Arab Emirates. *World Englishes, 40*, 191–204.

Solloway, A. J. (2016). English-Medium instruction in higher education in the United Arab Emirates: The perspectives of students.[Doctoral Thesis: The University of Exeter].

Steinhagen, T. G., & Said, F. (2021). "We should not bury our language by our hands": Crafting creative translanguaging spaces in higher education in the UAE. *Applied Linguistics Research and Good Practices for Multicultural and Multilingual Classrooms, 169*, 169–183.

Taha-Thomure, H. (2019). Arabic language education in the UAE. In: Gallagher, K. (ed), *Education in the UAE: Innovation and transformation*. Springer. https://doi.org/10.1007/978-981-13-7736-5_5

Van den Hoven, M., & Carroll, K. S. (2021). English-medium policy and English conversational patterns in the UAE. *World Englishes, 40*(2), 205–218.

Velasco, P., & García, O. (2014). Translanguaging and the writing of bilingual learners. *Bilingual Research Journal, 37*(1), 6–23.

Vogel, S., & García, O. (2017). Translanguaging. Oxford Research Encyclopedia of Education https://academicworks.cuny.edu/gc_pubs/402/

Wei, L. (2011). Moment analysis and translanguaging space: Discursive construction of identities by multilingual Chinese youth in Britain. *Journal of Pragmatics, 43*(5), 1222–1235.

Wei, L., & Lin, A. M. (2019). Translanguaging classroom discourse: Pushing limits, breaking boundaries. *Classroom Discourse, 10*(3-4), 209–215.

Williams, C. (2000). *Llythrennedd deuol: Trawsieithu – Pecyn datblygiad staff [Dual literacy: Translanguaging – Staff development pack]*. BBC.

Williams, C. (2002). *Ennill iaith: Astudiaeth o sefyllfa drochi yn 11–16 oed [A language gained: A study of language immersion at 11–16 years of age]*. School of Education. http://www.bangor.ac.uk/addysg/publications/Ennill_Iaith.pdf

3

ARABIC LANGUAGE TEACHER TRAINING IN THE ARABIAN PENINSULA

Great teachers don't grow on trees

Hanada Taha Thomure

Where in the world are we?

Imagine walking down the hallways in school A. The hallways are adorned with children's art and written work in Arabic and English. Arab cultural artifacts including calligraphy pieces, artistic depictions of traditional Arab jewelry, and different styles of incense burners that are on display serve as pleasurable reminders of where in the world you are. Classrooms are visible to all via large glass windows that oversee the hallways greeting the passerby and inviting them in. No one really notices you when you walk into the Arabic language arts classroom. Every child is fully engaged in the story book the teacher is reading aloud. Classroom walls are adorned with students' work, drawings, writings, and various crafts. Sight words are on the side of the word wall, reading strategies' charts are hanging from a clothesline across the room, and there is a reading corner that has a large number of Arabic children's literature books all arranged in buckets with a letter on each bucket depicting the books levels. Children ask questions about the book, share, and tell a quick story on how this book relates to them, while others ask the teacher to keep on reading. Wow, I think to myself. I want to be in this classroom enjoying learning Arabic.

Now imagine walking through school B. The hallways are wide, clean, and empty. A hint of Clorox scent seeps through and fills up the air. You walk into a classroom, and the teacher stops what they are doing and asks all the children to stand up and greet you in a nicely rehearsed and well-orchestrated chant. Children then go back to what they were doing, listening to the teacher explain the meanings of new vocabulary words using a PowerPoint presentation and a video. Three boys in the back are busy playing with pencils rolling them down the desk and trying to get a perfect roll; a couple of girls in the third row are busy checking their lunchboxes and tidying their pink pencil cases; another student is

DOI: 10.4324/9781003315971-5

adjusting the straps on his backpack; and another has his head resting on the desk struggling to stay awake. No one asks any questions while the teacher keeps on going with their monologue, and there are no activities in which children are engaged beyond listening and repeating the new vocabulary words. The walls in the class have a chart hung up with the classroom rules written in Arabic. Beyond that, no student work is on display, no word wall, no sight words, and no children's art are displayed. There is no reading corner designated and no children's books to be seen anywhere around the classroom.

Both schools are real ones in which the author observed classes, and both schools are well funded and are in wealthy Arab nations. However, one leaves school A and school B with widely and wildly different sets of feelings, thoughts, ideas, and conclusions. One leaves with probably several big questions as follows: what is it that makes Arabic language arts learning in school A so different and so exciting? What is the formula one can inject into all schools to make learning Arabic fun, effective, and rigorous all at once? How does teacher training play into it all?

This chapter will try to take a look at all those questions and will attempt to deconstruct what is behind the success story of one K-12 school in KSA whose students have consistently ranked in the top five percent of all students in KSA. What are the components needed to have a success story in Arabic language teaching and learning that has been a quest of many schools in the region?

What is the current situation in Arabic language teaching and learning?

The Progress in International Reading Literacy Study (PIRLS) is an international, standardized, reading comprehension test that fourth graders in primary schools take. The purpose of PIRLS is to measure students' ability to read in their first language and comprehend literary and informational texts using the following framework: (1) being able to access straightforward information directly from the text, (2) making explicit inferences, (3) explaining ideas presented in the text, and (4) analyzing the meanings, language, and other features presented in the text (Mullis & Martin, 2012, 2013).

Results from the 2016 PIRLS test show that out of 50 countries whose grade 4 students took the test, Egypt was ranked 49th, Morocco 48th, Kuwait 47th, Oman 46th, KSA 44th, Qatar 43rd, Bahrain 42nd, and United Arab Emirates 41st, all scoring below the international scale average of 500. Countries who scored the highest on the PIRLS 2016 test were the Russian Federation, Singapore, Hong Kong, Ireland, Finland, and Poland. Grade 4 students in those high-performing countries demonstrated a high ability to interpret, integrate, and evaluate reading comprehension skills and strategies (Mullis & Martin, 2012, 2013; Taha-Thomure, 2019). The PIRLS test administrators analyze five indicators affecting students' reading proficiency. Those are (1) home environment, (2) teacher education, (3) school resources for reading, (4) school climate, and (5) classroom instruction.

Scores achieved on the Arabic language reading comprehension on the PIRLS tests and other international tests including the Program for International Students Assessment (PISA) are one of the indicators of the schooling system the students come from. Those scores from Arab countries reflect not only the home environment that is usually poor in literacy activities but also a school culture and classroom practices that do not put Arabic literacy front and center. Those scores could also be a reflection of a teacher preservice preparation and in-service training system that has not effectively equipped Arabic language arts teachers with the knowledge, skills, and attitudes needed to teach reading and implement effective reading intervention plans when needed (Al Danan, 2010; Gregory et al., 2021; Obeid, 2010; Taha-Thomure, 2008; Wagner, 2017).

It has to be said, however, that recently and because of the unsatisfactory results students are consistently getting, many Arab countries have been trying to reform their educational system. One of the first things they usually tackle, probably because it is the most measurable and quickest to get done, is changing the textbooks. This, however, has not proven to be the magical solution everyone is looking for in Arabic language teaching and learning just because the issues are multifold and need to be looked at not only with a worm's eye view that focuses on one thing and one detail but also with a bird's eye view as well that can have a 360-degree idea of what's going on and what needs to be worked on.

The below section takes that 360-degree view and describes the factors that could be affecting the quality of Arabic language teaching and learning in most countries in the Arabian Gulf region.

The seven impediments to effective Arabic language teaching and learning

Taha-Thomure (2019) summarized the seven impediments to effective Arabic language teaching and learning as follows:

1. *Time allocated to Arabic language arts*: The first impediment is that Arabic language arts is not given the time it needs as a first language in schools. Time spent in the Arabic classroom in most schools does not exceed 45 to 50 minutes a day, which is not an international best practice when it comes to learning a first language. Literature often refers to the 90-to-120-minute literacy block where teachers have ample time to engage students not only in foundational skills they need but also in the various types of reading and writing that they ought to be immersed in (Underwood, 2018). Depriving students of the right of immersion in their first language means that students will not get the depth and breadth of knowledge needed to be proficient readers and writers in their own language (Al Farra, 2011).
2. *Rigor:* It can be said that there is a general lack of rigor in the Arabic language arts classroom due to the lack of teacher expertise and challenging and interesting curricula (Taha-Thomure, 2019). Rigor is romanticized but not

tolerated, while getting As on the report card is an expectation. There is a need for in-depth teacher preservice preparation and in-service training on the most effective literacy strategies and on how to maintain rigor throughout their classes by challenging students and at the same time offering multiple scaffolding opportunities. There is also a bigger need to educate the public at large on the value of rigor and learning even when it comes at the expense of getting high grades.

3. *Uninformed school leadership:* A third impediment to learning Arabic in many Arab countries has to do with two types of school leadership that are seen in the region (Taha-Thomure, 2019). The first type is often seen in private schools, mostly Western and uninformed about Arabic language. This leads them to frame it as "I don't know anything about the language, so I'm leaving it to the Arabic teachers." This diminishes the value of the language and sends the message that it is an afterthought, a subject that is not of importance to the administration, and that English is superior to it (Taha-Thomure, 2019). The other types of school leadership are the local principals in public schools who see themselves as "paper leaders" mainly shuffling paperwork, getting through the day doing scheduling, following up on attendance, and responding to the Ministry of Education (MoE) paperwork requests. Those principals are usually untrained and unempowered, rendering them, thus, hardly available to offer any academic help to Arabic language arts teachers (Taha-Thomure, 2019). Both types of academic leaders are uninformed in very different ways; the first are uninformed about Arabic language arts and as such create a two-tiered camp within their own schools, and the second are generally uninformed due to the lack of effective preparation and training as school leaders.
4. *Every teacher is not a teacher of reading*: Very few schools see that every teacher is a teacher of reading first and a teacher of the subject matter they teach second. This confines the presence of the Arabic language to the Arabic language arts classroom only and often times sends the message to teachers, parents, and students that Arabic is not an important language that needs all teachers working together to ensure that all children are reading by the end of grade 3 (Taha-Thomure, 2019; Tsimpera-Maluch & Taha-Thomure, 2021).
5. *Preservice teacher preparation:* A fifth impediment in teaching Arabic has to do with the quality of Arabic language arts teachers, be it because of the outdated preservice preparation programs, the ineffective in-service training they receive, or a combination of both. Teacher preparation programs are for the most part outdated, based on rote learning, with minimal field experience required (Taha-Thomure, 2017). New teachers entering the profession are not offered the opportunity of an induction year that could ease them into the system and ensure that some hand-holding, mentoring, and coaching are adopted to help them acquire the needed skills as junior teachers. This results in disenfranchised young teachers who are disappointed by a system that failed them and who tend to revert back, as a result, to old

teaching methods that require little time, effort, and preparation (Bannayan & Al Attia, 2015; Taha-Thomure, 2017, 2020).

6. *Curriculum Quality*: Most curricula currently available in schools are textbook based, grammar based, and not well aligned with the 21st century skills nor with the other subjects in school (Faour, 2012; Harb & Taha-Thomure, 2020). There is a lack of understanding of what curriculum is. In most ministries of education, the thinking is that if textbooks are changed, then the curriculum will be alright and teaching and learning will happen. There is little attention given to the importance of aligning content and performance standards with textbook design, students' linguistic profile, teacher training, teaching methodologies, and formative and summative assessments. Many ministries of education have worked hard to develop cutting edge Arabic language standards, assessments, and literature-based textbooks; however, they left off training teachers and school leaders, which has only led to more confusion and a replication of the same unsatisfactory student results (Gregory et al., 2021; Thomure & Speaker, 2018). Classrooms in almost all public schools around the Arab world lack a classroom library with enough children's literature books in it, and, accordingly, students are not given the tools and resources to interact with books and acquire reading not only as a skill but also as a habit (Taha-Thomure et al., 2020).
7. *Teacher professional development:* According to Fullan (2007), student learning depends on ensuring that every teacher is learning and developing all the time. Few teachers of Arabic in the region receive professional development, and when they do, it is mostly ineffective and irrelevant and learning is hardly ever transferred into the class (England & Taha, 2006). Curriculum development is usually overseen by curricula directorates in ministries of education who operate on a quite traditional and uninformed model of Arabic language literacy. Accordingly, Arabic language arts curricula are mostly didactic in nature, disciplinary in outlook, and miss the opportunity to engage students and teachers in learning experiences that could help them all grow and get inspired using the language.

   Schools seem to be split into two camps when it comes to teacher professional development (PD). Some schools strive to train their general body of teachers well and provide them with annual and continuous professional development opportunities; however, when it comes to training their Arabic language teachers, they find themselves mostly training them in the English language on issues that are irrelevant to the needs of Arabic teachers and are conducted in a language they do not fully understand (Taha-Thomure, 2017). Other schools (mostly public) do not have a well-designed and targeted training plan for their teachers. Instead, all teachers are provided with two to three weeks of general training throughout the year where they attend any sessions they want, including sessions on flower arranging, robotics, and cooking, which can be fun. However, this is an approach to PD that has wasted valuable time during which teachers could have been better supported via PD that is focused on content, pedagogy, and reflective practice (Allen, 2003; Coe et al., 2014; Darling-Hammond et al., 2012).

The rest of this chapter will be focused on a success story highlighting practices in a school in Saudi Arabia that has consistently ranked among the best in the kingdom on national and international Arabic literacy tests.

Methodology

Context

Dhahran Ahliyya Schools (DAS) started as a family-run, not-for-profit school in 1977 in the Eastern Province of KSA starting with 56 students and six teachers. Currently, DAS has two K–12 campuses with local student enrollment of 2,000 and over 200 teachers and staff (DAS website, 2021). The mission of the school found on their website is "to empower each student to be a compassionate, thinking, lifelong bilingual learner who makes a positive difference, locally and globally" (DAS website, 2021). The school's philosophy posted on their website as well states the following:

> We believe that excellent education touches both the hearts and minds of students, developing their intellectual, personal, emotional, and social skills to learn and work in a rapidly changing and globalizing world. Moreover, it should provide them with a sense of belonging in their own country while also an openness to their roles as citizens of the world, committed to taking action to help make their world a better place.
>
> *(DAS website, 2021)*

Methodology

A qualitative approach has been employed in this study, and that is using, namely, focus groups and interviews to solicit data from key stakeholders in the school due to the wealth of information about the nature of instruction that such a method can yield (Bogdan & Biklen, 1998). Four focus groups were conducted including parents, students, student support teachers, and administrators (Flores & Alonsa, 1995). In addition, a one-on-one interview was conducted with the head literacy coach at the school due to their wealth of knowledge and a long 40-year tenure at the school. Each focus group and interview lasted about 90 minutes. All focus groups and interviews were recorded and later transcribed. The data were then analyzed, and based on the analysis, seven major themes emerged. The researcher developed a semi-structured focus group and an interview guideline or protocol that was shared with the school beforehand. The research procedures upheld the ethical principles required of qualitative research where the participants agreed in writing to participate in the study. The researcher explained the purpose of

TABLE 3.1 Participants

Stakeholders	*Number of Participants*	*Type of Interview*
Parents	6	Focus group
Students	12	Focus group
Academic administrators/leaders	4	Focus group
Teacher trainers/literacy coaches	7	Focus group
Head literacy coach	1	Interview

the study, the focus groups and interviews were conducted with respectful attentiveness, and all identifying information was omitted (Arksey & Knight, 1999).

Participants

Focus groups and interviews were conducted over a period of two weeks. All the meetings were scheduled with the help of the school administration. All meetings were conducted online.

The above Table 3.1 summarizes stakeholders interviewed and numbers of participants *per group*.

Data analysis

Data collected from all participants were analyzed based on the guiding questions. Responses were grouped based on those guiding questions, and then the data were organized and reduced into seven main emerging themes, with each theme given a distinct title. Analysis was then done on each theme looking deeply into the ideas that participants shared on that specific idea. Finally, all the data collected were reviewed again to ensure that all ideas linked to the seven major themes were included. Below are the seven main themes emerging out of participants' stories: 1) continuous teacher training and coaching, 2) knowing what to teach and how to teach: curriculum and learning resources, 3) administrative support, 4) student reading support, 5) What do students say? 6) What do parents say? and 7) cultivating common understandings.

Findings and discussion

This section presents the main findings based on the seven main themes mentioned above:

Continuous teacher training and coaching

Research suggests that time allocated to teacher coaching inside classrooms may allow teachers to internalize the new classroom practices acquired and help them truly master the rationale and practices of the intervention introduced (Coe et al., 2014; Hindman & Wasik, 2012). Being aware of the importance of coaching, DAS has trained Arabic literacy coaches whose main focus is working with teachers and ensuring that each teacher is acquiring a set of effective strategies and skills that can be implemented in the classroom. In the interview with the head coach at the school, they mentioned that one of the main things that permeate throughout the school is a belief in change. This belief is engrained in teachers from the day they join the school so that they know that change is expected and valued and that change is a constant at the school.

The head coach interviewed for the purpose of this study has served the school for 40 years. She is a sharp, resilient, and well-read 80-year-old powerhouse who has worked with hundreds of teachers during their long tenure at the school so far. The head coach mentioned that teacher training and coaching at the school start with working with all teachers on classroom and learning management. According to the head coach, "There is a no learning that can happen without first ensuring that everyone in class knows the rules, respects the rules and is ready to learn and help others learn as well. This can only be achieved if every teacher is able to manage learning well in their classroom."

Other themes emerging from the discussions with seven literacy coaches at the school included the following:

1. Coaches in the school are trained to accept teachers as they are and help them develop and change based on common goals and not on personal preferences. Teachers come to the school without sufficient preparation in college; however, if they are hired, then the school needs to invest in them and work with them to change their classroom practices.
2. Coaches are aware that any change in classroom practices has to be informed by research, evidence, and studying what is happening in international best practices.
3. Coaches work with teachers on a standards-based instructional philosophy, where standards rather than textbooks are the driving force behind all learning. Textbooks and resources are used to ensure that the standards and performance indicators specified for each grade level are achieved by each and every student.

Coaches in the school work with the teachers but are focused on student learning as an evidence of teacher learning. They not only review lesson plans with teachers, observe classes, and co-teach alongside teachers, but are responsible, as well, for checking that the school is sincerely following the standards and curriculum in place. Coaches get continuous training on Arabic content, pedagogy, and leadership skills.

Coaches at DAS work with teachers on unpacking the standards into mini skills and strategies that students need to acquire, and they study the curriculum together in order to reach common understandings on what each performance indicator means and how it can best be achieved (Du Four, 2004).

The whole school, according to coaches' focus groups, reflects on students' results and plans professional development, instruction, and intervention plans based on those results. PD takes several forms at the school. The first is by having external international experts visit the school and conduct workshops on targeted topics that are part of the strategic vision of the school. The second form of PD happens throughout the year via workshops that are internally conducted by the supervisors, coaches, and academic leaders who all focus on strategies and skills that are part of a well-thought training agenda for that year. Another way of training is through having teachers attend conferences and come back to school to share what they have learned. In addition, the school has established a not-for-profit publishing house that translates into Arabic new and relevant research published in English on topics that are related to the work done in the school (literacy, numeracy, reading comprehension, early reading, differentiation, teacher professional development, and other topics). DAS has monthly scheduled discussion groups within the school to discuss and reflect on ideas teachers, coaches, and supervisors read in those translated best practice books.

The head coach at the school explained during the interview that teaching practices are continuously updated and revised to be in line with the needs of teachers and students and with what research and evidence from data tell them. The head coach added that they work closely with their teachers to ensure that they remain flexible and willing to be life-long learners and that they understand that using one teaching technique or method will not work for all students all the time. They added that they work with the teachers on ensuring that they have impeccable learning and classroom management skills and that they are able to support the learning of all students. Coaches work with teachers in the classroom on an almost daily basis, the head coach said. They plan lessons together, find interesting and engaging resources together, look at student results, and work together through the professional learning community in the school on coming up with intervention plans and ways to help teachers address some of the challenges they face.

Knowing what to teach and how to teach: Curriculum and learning resources

Academic leaders and the head coach at DAS emphasized that in every Arabic language arts class at DAS, students have to engage on a daily basis with reading texts that are appropriate to students' proficiency levels and writing about what they read. Coaches in the school, as well, are expected and encouraged to finesse their practices by reading and learning on a daily basis. They, in turn, take the new concepts learned to teachers they work with.

The school adopts the International Baccalaureate Program where the whole school from preK to 12 is based on that educational philosophy. Additionally, the school has adopted standards-based instruction and the total integration between the themes taught in Arabic and English language arts. This integration between the two languages, one of the supervisors mentioned, allows teachers to talk together, plan together, and share best practices and resources that can help them achieve the goals set for each theme they work on. In Arabic, they work on thematic units in addition to introducing the various literary genres starting in primary school all the way through high school (Al Hashmi et al., 2022).

Administrative support

Principals at DAS are not considered administrative leaders, but are mostly expected to be chief academic leaders who are heavily involved in all academic decisions, directions, and practices adopted in the classroom. Academic leaders are continuously following up on student progress and have weekly meetings with supervisors, coaches, and teachers to discuss classroom practices and student progress and to find ways to best help teachers and students achieve the standards and goals set for each grade level. Academic leaders agreed in a focus group they participated in that the main question that everyone asks in their school is as follows: did students learn? That question is the focal point around which the whole school revolves.

The academic leaders added that parents are considered partners at their school. Parents receive weekly communications explaining the themes their children are working on. Parents are also invited to workshops that aim at raising their awareness to the ways in which they can help their children at home. They are given tips on how to help improve their children's literacy doing fun and engaging activities. Academic leaders added that the school encourages parents to read for and with their children at home and sends them ideas and tips on how to do that.

Student reading support

The school has a dedicated unit for student academic support that includes among others four Arabic support teachers. The supervisor in charge of the unit explained that students are referred to the unit for reading intervention based on a diagnostic test that all students have to take prior to starting a new unit. If students are found below the needed standard for reading and comprehension, the teacher refers them to the intervention unit who study their portfolio and meet with the parents to ensure that they are aware of their child's reading level and ensure that they are able to support their child at home in ways that would be beneficial and targeted. An intervention plan is then designed and implemented with the child within small groups for eight weeks. The child is evaluated again after eight weeks, and the results are discussed in the presence of the grade-level supervisor, the teacher, and the parents. If the student is ready to go back to their regular class, then the intervention has succeeded, and the goals have been met. If the student is not yet reading at grade level, another intervention plan is drawn with the approval of the parents. The reading specialist in the academic support unit works with the student on a one-to-one basis or might work with two students at a time. The intervention plan usually consists of smart mini lessons that break down the needed reading skills and strategies into smaller chunks that the specialist works with the students on. Lots of visual and auditory materials are used to help engage the student with the skills needed in Arabic. Texts chosen for the intervention usually target similar themes to those used in the classroom, which helps form a connection between the intervention plan and what is happening in the classroom. Intervention might be extended until the end of the term or until the student has learned the needed skills to enable them to work at their grade level.

One of the literacy coaches interviewed mentioned that support for all students is also available via the vast number of resources and Arabic children's literature available in the school and classroom libraries. Making those resources available and accessible to all students with the expectation that all students will be readers and ensuring that there is time in the classroom dedicated to engaging in all types of reading is a message that permeates throughout the school.

What do students say?

Twelve students from various grade levels were interviewed (ranging from grade 6 to grade 12). One of the recurrent themes emerging from students' focus groups is their awareness of the importance of being proficient in Arabic language. Students said that they find the curriculum they work with at DAS interesting and filled with texts from various genres and varied topics. The curriculum is focused on reading novels and articles that can be at times challenging, but teachers are always available to help scaffold learning for students. Most students agreed that they feel they have acquired the needed skills to analyze any text that they read including translated texts. Most students interviewed said that they have a close relationship with their teachers and that their teachers were caring and communicated with them after class. Students added that teachers follow up with them to ensure that they are indeed learning and acquiring all the skills expected of their grade level. One student said that their teacher consistently suggests titles of books that might be of interest to them and that the teacher is always available to answer any questions students have. All students interviewed agreed that they feel they are indeed bilingual and that their Arabic and English skills allow them to use both languages comfortably to read, write, and analyze high-level texts. Most students mentioned that homework is not extensive nor hard, and it is focused on specific tasks or skills that they need to practice. A female student in grade 10 said, "We are proud to belong to this school and this community. We value social responsibility, serving our community and preserving our language and heritage."

What do parents say?

One theme that reemerged in focus groups with parents from the school was their satisfaction with the school for focusing on Arabic reading comprehension, communication skills, and keeping parents informed. Parents interviewed said that the school teaches Arabic in unconventional ways and does not focus on memorization and rote learning. Parents highlighted the importance of children's literature and the well-written curriculum the school uses, in addition to the clarity they have when it comes to what their children are learning and what they are expected to do to help their children with Arabic language.

Parents sounded pleased with the fact that their children are becoming indeed bilingual and proficient users of both Arabic and English. Parents mentioned that their children's teachers are well trained and know what kind of homework to send back home. They mentioned that teachers are focused on teaching reading especially in the lower grades and ensuring that all students are readers early on (Guthrie & Klauda, 2014; McCoach et al., 2006). Two parents mentioned that the school makes Arabic language a priority not only in the Arabic language classroom but also across all other subjects as well and that this was unlike any other private or international school they have seen. "The school, according to them, doesn't undermine the children's first language like other schools do," one parent said. Parents mentioned that there are classroom libraries in each classroom that the teachers actually utilize and that this has contributed greatly to their children's engagement with reading. There are reading contests being announced regularly, achievement certificates to encourage reading in addition to awards, and other incentives for reading and for encouraging their kids to orally present to an audience. Parents mentioned that they are regularly informed by the teachers about their children's progress and that teachers come to the meetings informed with evidence from their children's work. Parents added that teachers and the school administration display great flexibility and listen to their concerns with great care. Parents mentioned that their high schoolers prefer to read in English because of the vast choice of interesting resources and literature they have available to them, but that they are still proficient and capable in their first language.

Cultivating common understandings

One of the recurrent themes in the interviews we had with the literacy coaches, academic leaders, parents, and students that kept on revisiting is the notion of using a common language and having common understandings. All parties the researchers spoke to understood that the Arabic curriculum they have was a standards-driven one. Even students used words like standards and performance indicators in the focus group. All teachers took part in unpacking the standards the head coach said in the interview, and as such, they became partners in constructing and building the Arabic language arts curriculum at DAS. Moreover, academic leaders, coaches, and teachers all took part in building the Arabic language arts scope and sequence based on those content standards, which helped all of them become closely familiar with the curriculum and shared in planning it. This community work allowed them as well to speak the same jargon and have a similar understanding of the terms and approach adopted to teaching

Arabic language arts at DAS. This focus on professional learning communities (Senge, 1990) and reflective practice (England & Taha, 2006) at DAS was evident in all the focus groups and interviews conducted. Weekly professional learning community (PLC) meetings are held across every grade level in which teachers, coaches, and school leaders discuss common challenges, clarify understandings, and reflect on classroom practice.

Conclusion: Is there a formula?

When ten of the academic leaders and coaches at DAS were asked to rank their school's Arabic language arts program out of ten, the average ranking they gave was a seven. When asked why they ranked themselves as average when their Arabic language arts program is one of the best in KSA, if not in the region, the response was that they are not happy with all that they have done and that there is so much more to be done in the future. This mentality of growth and continuous development could be one of the main reasons behind the secret of this school's success. Contrast that with a primary school the researcher visited and observed less than mediocre Arabic lessons in. When the researcher asked the principal of this latter school afterward, what kind of PD do they think the Arabic language arts teachers might need, the response was "Nothing, our teachers are well trained and don't need any more PD!"

In effective schools, Arabic language is not seen as a language that is taught only at a specific time of the day, but rather it is looked at as an overarching umbrella that extends to all other subjects in the school and that everyone from staff to parents, administrators, leaders, and students are aware of. Using common themes and strategies in Arabic and English has also helped bring awareness to different ways of thinking about language arts and helped integrate best practices from both languages for the benefit of students.

One of the academic leaders at DAS said, "Success is a series of small keys you empower everyone with in schools that learn. It's a collaborative relationship where we influence all teachers around us and get influenced by them." This was a recurrent theme heard from all the people interviewed at DAS. Everyone in the school rallies around those common understandings. Understanding that student learning comes first, understanding that teaching does not necessarily mean that learning has happened, understanding that everyone in the school, including parents, is all one community with one goal that they all work toward were the key elements that colored the main story the researcher heard.

Knowledge of practice at DAS is constructed while in practice (Cochran-Smith & Lytle, 1999). Effective schools operate under the assumption that all teachers need to have knowledge, skills, and attitudes that will ensure that all students will learn and be able to succeed. Rasmussen et al. (2004) suggested that it is not necessarily the quantity of PD and its format that make teachers effective, but rather it is attention to coherence, working with research and evidence-based practices and teacher and school leaders' capacity building that need to be emphasized. Whether the DAS model can be replicated with success in another Arab context is another question that might need further research. The resources needed, amount of reskilling and upskilling needed on all levels at the schools, and the patience to see results are all challenges that will need to be available for such a model to be successful and replicable to some degree. However, many schools in the region with similar resources and dedication might be able to replicate the DAS model with the variation that any replication necessarily entails. This success story might inspire other school systems to look deeper into what type of a teacher training framework can work for them based on knowledge from the field and the challenges that face Arabic language teaching and learning. This chapter is a call to all stakeholders to consider a teacher training framework for the Arab region that is focused on both content and pedagogical knowledge and that is long term, cultivates common understandings, and is built around student support and early intervention.

References

Al Farra, S. (2011). Education in the UAE: A vision for the future. Education in the UAE: Current status and future developments. Emirates Center for Strategic Studies and Research Abu Dhabi, pp. 219–237.

Al Danan, A. (2010). The theory of teaching MSA through natural practice: Application, assessment and dissemination. *Damascus-Syria: AlBasha'er Publishing House* [Preprint].

Al Hashmi, M., Taha-Thomure, H., & AlMazroui, K. (2022). Arabic language teachers' perceptions of a standards-based educational reform. *Gulf Education and Social Policy Review, 2*(1). https://doi.org/10.18502/gespr.v2i1.10044

Allen, M. (2003). Eight questions on teacher education: What does the research say? A summary of the findings. *Education Commission of the States.* Retrieved from http://www.ecs.org/html/educationissues/teachingquality/tpreport/home/summary.pdf

Arksey, H., & Knight, P. T. (1999). Interviewing for social scientists. SAGE Publications, Ltd. https://dx.doi.org/10.4135/9781849209335

Bannayan, H., & Al Attia, H. (2015). Preparing teachers, changing lives: A position note on teacher preparations program in Jordan. Queen Rania Teacher Academy, Queen Rania Foundation.

Bogdan, R. C., & Biklen, S. K. (1998). *Qualitative research for education: An introduction to theory and methods.* Allyn & Bacon.

Cochran-Smith, M., & Lytle, S. L. (1999). Chapter 8: Relationships of knowledge and practice: Teacher learning in communities. *Review of Research in Education, 24*(1), 249–305. https://doi.org/10.3102/0091732X024001249

Coe, R., Aloisi, C., Higgins, S., & Major, L. (2014). What makes great teaching? Review of the underpinning research. Sutton Trust. Retrieved January 16, 2017.

Darling-Hammond, L., Jaquith, A., & Hamilton, M. (2012). *Creating a comprehensive system for evaluating and supporting effective teaching.* Stanford Center for Opportunity Policy in Education. Retrieved from https://edpolicy.stanford.edu/sites/default/files/publications/creating-comprehensive-system-evaluating-and-supporting-effective-teaching.pdf

Dhahran Ahliyya Schools (DAS) website. Retrieved October 23,2021, from https://www.das.sch.sa/

DuFour, R. (2004). What is a " professional learning community"? *Educational Leadership, 61*(8), 6–11.

England, L., & Taha, Z. A. (2006). Methodology in Aarabic language teacher education. In K. Wahba, Z. Taha, & L. England (Eds.), *Handbook for Arabic language teaching professionals in the 21st century* (pp. 419–436). First. Lawrence Erlbaum Associates.

Faour, M. (2012). *The Arab World's education report card: School climate and citizenship skills.* Carnegie Endowment for International Peace. Retrieved from http://carnegieendowment.org/files/school_climate.pdf

Flores, J. G., & Alonsa, C. G. (1995). Using focus groups in educational research: Exploring teachers' perspectives on educational change. *Evaluation Review, 19*, 84–103.

Fullan, M. (2007). *The new meaning of educational change.* Fourth. Teachers College, Columbia University New York and London: The Teachers College Press. Retrieved from http://mehrmohammadi.ir/wp-content/uploads/2019/07/The-New-Meaning-of-Educational-Change.pdf

Gregory, L., Taha-Thomure, H., Kazim, A., Boni, A., ElSayed, M., & Taibah, *N.* (2021). Advancing Arabic language teaching and learning: A path to reducing learning poverty in the MENA', *Washington, D.C. World Bank Group* [Preprint].

Guthrie, J. T., & Klauda, S. L. (2014). Effects of classroom practices on reading comprehension, engagement, and motivations for adolescents. *Reading Research Quarterly, 49*(4), 387–416.

Harb, M., & Taha-Thomure, H. (2020). Connecting literacy to curriculum ideologies. *Curriculum Perspectives, 40*, 27–33. https://doi.org/10.1007/s41297-020-00099-0

Hindman, A. H., & Wasik, B. A. (2012). Unpacking an effective language and literacy coaching intervention in head start: Following teachers' learning over two years of training. *The Elementary School Journal, 113*(1), 131–154. https://doi.org/10.1086/666389

McCoach, D. B., O'Connell, A., Reis, S., & Levitt, H. (2006). Growing readers: A hierarchical linear model of children's reading growth during the first 2 years of school. *Journal of Educational Psychology, 98*(1), 14.

Mullis, I. V., & Martin, M. (2013). *PIRLS 2016 assessment framework.* TIMSS & PIRLS International Study Center Lynch School of education, Boston College and International Association for the Evaluation of Educational Achievement (IEA), IEA Secretariat., p. 194. Retrieved from https://files.eric.ed.gov/fulltext/ED545242.pdf

Mullis, I. V., & Martin, M. (2012). PIRLS 2011 International Results in Reading. International Association for the Evaluation of Educational Achievement; Boston College, TIMSS & PIRLS International Study Center: ERIC.

Obeid, A. (2010). Reasons for the low performance in the teaching of Arabic language. *Tunisia: Arab Organization for Education, Culture and Science. Investing in Cutting Edge Arabic Language Education* [Preprint].

Rasmussen, C., Hopkins, S., & Fitzpatrick, M. (2004). Our work done well is like the perfect pitch. *The Learning Professional, 25*(1), 16.

Senge, P. M. (1990). *The fifth discipline: The art and practice of the learning organization.* Random House. ISBN 9780307477644

Taha-Thomure, H. (2017). Arabic language teacher education. In A. Gebril (Ed.), *Applied linguistics in the middle East and North Africa.* John Benjamins Publishing Company, pp. 267–287. https://doi.org/10.1075/aals.15.12tah

Taha-Thomure, H. (2019). Arabic language education in the UAE: Choosing the right drivers. In K. Gallagher (Ed.), *Education in the United Arab Emirates.* Springer, pp. 75–93. https://doi.org/10.1007/978-981-13-7736-5_5

Taha-Thomure, H. (2008). The status of arabic language teaching today. *Education, Business and Society: Contemporary Middle Eastern Issues*, *1*(3), 186–192. https://doi.org/10.1108/17537980810909805

Taha-Thomure, H. (2020). The status of arabic language mirrors the status of its teachers. In M. AlBatal (Ed.), *Status report of Arabic language*. Ministry of Culture & Youth.

Taha-Thomure, H., & Speaker, R. B. (2018). Arabic language arts standards: Revolution or disruption? *Research in Comparative and International Education*, *13*(4), 551–569. https://doi.org/10.1177/1745499918807032

Taha-Thomure, H., Kreidieh, S., & Baroudi, S. (2020). Arabic children's literature: Glitzy production, disciplinary content. *Issues in Educational Research*, *30*(1), 323–344. Retrieved from http://www.iier.org.au/iier30/taha-thomure.pdf

Tsimprea-Maluch, J., & Taha-Thomure, H. (2021). Shifting paradigms in Arabic pedagogy and policy in the UAE: Opportunities and challenges for teacher education. In N. Bakkali, & N. Memon (Eds.), *Teacher training and education in the GCC: Unpacking the complexities and challenges of internationalizing educational contexts*. Rowan & Littlefield. ISBN 978-1-7936-3673-7

Underwood, S. (2018). What is the evidence for an uninterrupted, 90-minute literacy instruction block. *Education Northwest*. http://educationnorthwest.org/resources/what-evidence-uninterrupted-90-minute-literacyinstruction-block [Preprint].

Wagner, D. A. (2017). Children's Reading in low-income countries. *The Reading Teacher*, *71*(2), 127–133.

4

TEACHER EDUCATION AND EMI IN THE UAE AND ARABIAN PENINSULA – PAST, PRESENT, AND FUTURE PERSPECTIVES

Kay Gallagher and Anna Dillon

Introduction

The recent focus on teacher education has arisen in large part from the analysis by national governments of comparative student performance in international achievement tests, such as PISA[1]. Scrutiny of student performance in such global tests has led to a focus on the impact of teaching on student achievement, and this in turn has led to attention to the quality of teachers and the quality of their professional preparation. It is now well established in the research literature that, student factors aside, the quality of teaching is the single most important external factor in determining student success (Barber & Mourshed, 2007). Moreover, in order to recruit high-quality teachers for schools, research also highlights that high-ability candidates need to be recruited into high-quality teacher preparation programs at universities (Darling-Hammond, 2017; Liu, 2021). The attention to teacher quality and teacher educator quality in this global knowledge economy era has been characterized as "unprecedented" (Cochran-Smith & Reagan, 2021, p. 2) in the history of education, as countries around the world seek to raise their educational performance in the belief that this will enhance national human capital and increase their global economic competitiveness.

These exigencies have put pressure on teacher education in the Arabian Peninsula, as elsewhere, and have been acutely felt in the United Arab Emirates (UAE) in particular, where the Ministry of Education acknowledges that its ongoing efforts to transform education are driven by the imperatives of participation in the knowledge economy, evidenced in statements such as the following: "The most important and significant step in the transformation of the education system is the shift to the knowledge economy" (MOE, 2021a, p. 10). Yet, results from the most recently administered PISA tests continue to show that school students in the Gulf states underperform significantly compared to

DOI: 10.4324/9781003315971-6

the global average, and the educational underachievement in the region has been linked to weak teacher preparation (Wiseman et al., 2017).

In this chapter, we examine the role of language in teacher education in the Gulf Cooperation Council (GCC) member countries – Bahrain, Kuwait, Oman, Qatar, Saudi Arabia, and the UAE – with reference also to the neighboring Yemen. To begin, an overview of the preparation of teachers for state schools in the region is provided, with reference to contemporary developments in teacher education globally. We examine in particular the development of quality in national teacher education in the UAE, as a flagship for educational development and innovation in the region. The linguistic trials faced by both teacher candidates and teachers in the field are then examined, in light of the challenges presented to teacher education by shifting curricula and changing medium of teaching and learning in schools. Then, strategies needed within teacher education to prepare teachers for bilingual education are identified for countries such as the UAE, which actively seek to develop a bilingual and biliterate national population. Finally, the chapter looks to the future and explores the affordances of a translanguaging pedagogy for teacher education in the region.

Teacher education has been characterized as a "complex and multifaceted field" (Cochran-Smith & Maria Villegas, 2015, p. 379). It is best conceived of as a continuum which begins with the recruitment of students into teacher preparation programs which focus on the development of both content knowledge and pedagogical knowledge, while also providing practical classroom experience and cultivating appropriate dispositions for teaching. It encompasses induction programs for novice teachers in the field and includes ongoing teacher appraisal. It also incorporates continuing in-service professional and career development (Darling-Hammond, 2017). That said, the primary focus of this chapter is on preservice teacher education, housed within public higher education, which prepares teachers for young learners in state school systems.

The countries of the Gulf Cooperation Council (GCC) share common educational structures and aims (Hayes & Al-Abri 2019) and recently have shared a focus on implementing qualitative improvements in education in general. Three aspects of the ongoing efforts to drive up quality in national teacher education in the region are next addressed, with particular reference to the UAE as a case in point. These are the role of accreditation, the adoption of insights from comparative education globally, and the introduction of teacher licensure.

Accreditation

Many of the GCC states are remarkably open to global influences and are keen to adopt effective international practices in order to raise quality in all spheres. In education, this is evidenced by governmental support for international accreditation for national teacher education preparation, and many federally funded teacher education providers, including Bahrain, Oman, Qatar, and the UAE, have obtained U.S.-based international accreditation from NCATE/CAEP for their teacher education programs. Moreover, national higher education accreditation, such as the UAE's *Commission for Academic Accreditation* (CAA) and Saudi Arabia's *National Center for Academic Accreditation and Evaluation* (NCAAA), is a prerequisite for any program of teacher preparation to operate in-country.

Comparative educational research

In light of the regional openness to global influences, comparative international research studies into teacher education also offer insights that are applicable in the region. A case in point is the comparative study of effective teacher preparation in the seven highest performing school systems globally[2] (Sato & Abbiss, 2021) which uncovered the following common characteristics:

- high status of teaching within the national culture;
- selectivity of teacher candidates;
- strong financial support for teacher preparation and teacher professional development programs;
- professional standards for teachers;
- teacher education as a continuum of learning and development;

In what follows, the extent to which teacher education in the region meets each one of the above characteristics is briefly examined, using the UAE as the primary point of reference.

Status

The status of teaching impacts on the status of teacher education, and in turn on the quality of applicants to teacher education programs. A number research studies into the status of teaching in the UAE have been carried out, and while these report a mixed picture, in general the status of teaching as a profession is much lower than in high-performing systems internationally. As with other aspects of education in the UAE, the diverse nature of the country's demographics results in differing perceptions among different groups. Expatriates comprise 89% of the population in the UAE, similar to Qatar with 86%, while the GCC average is 51% overall (Gulf Research Center, 2017). Among UAE nationals, the status of teaching has been found to be low among males (Dickson & Le Roux, 2012; Ibrahim & Al-Tenaiji, 2019) due to low salary and perceived unattractive working conditions. In addition, Dickson's (2013) survey of approximately 500 female Grade 12 Emirati students in Abu Dhabi about their perceptions of teaching as a career found that that they considered it to be an unappreciated job. On the other hand, more than half of the teachers surveyed in Saudi Arabia for the Organization for Economic Cooperation and Development's (OECD) global investigation into teaching, TALIS (OECD, 2019), agreed that teaching is valued in society, double the OECD average. Yet, it has been reported from Saudi

Arabia that teachers "no longer have the social status of previous time periods when they had special respect and status" (AlNahdi, 2014, p. 3).

Selectivity

Concerns have been expressed for some time about the quality of candidates admitted to and graduating from teacher education programs in the UAE (Badri & Al Khaili, 2014; Gardner, 1995). Quality improvement measures taken in the UAE since 2019 include an increase in admission scores and the introduction of an admissions interview, as discussed in more detail later in the chapter. Also, in Bahrain, the Ministry of Education implements an annual campaign to attract high-quality candidates, admitting 20% of applicants annually (BTC, 2022), and including an admissions interview as well as exam-based selection.

Financial support

Strong financial support for teacher education is another common feature of the world's highest performing educational systems, according to Sato and Abbiss (2021). Federal and local funding for teacher education programs is provided across the Gulf for undergraduate national citizens. What is lacking, however, are incentives to attract high-caliber candidates to the profession, whether national or expatriates. Some limited incentive programs have been implemented, such as the *Future Teachers* program in the UAE (MOE, 2019) which provides scholarships to study math or physics or chemistry at university for high-performing Emirati nationals and Arabic-speaking expatriates, and offers them priority in employment as schoolteachers. However, these programs focus on the development of content knowledge only and do not seem to address pedagogical content knowledge or general pedagogical knowledge. Moreover, governmental support for graduate-level studies in education is inconsistent and is not widely available in-country.

Professional standards for teachers

Another avenue to raising the bar toward international excellence in teacher quality lies in teacher licensure. This approach to standardization of quality is seen to be of special importance in the Gulf due to the diverse qualifications of teachers who arrive in the region from all around the world. As mentioned above, with 89% of the population of the UAE comprised of expatriates (Gulf Research Center, 2017), this means that it is not possible to recruit enough local teachers. Until the establishment of ADEC (Abu Dhabi Education Council) in 2005, the UAE state school system had recruited most of its non-national teachers from the Middle East and North Africa (Kippels & Ridge, 2019), but then switched instead to Anglophone countries (Gallagher, 2019). The majority of schools in the UAE are privately owned, and the vast majority of teachers in such schools are expatriates, and within the government school system, there are significant numbers of expatriate teachers also. In the UAE, there are almost twice as many teachers in private schools as in government schools (MOE, 2021b).

To ensure common standards among teachers, a national teacher licensing system was launched in 2018, and by the end of 2020, teacher licensure became a requirement for all practicing educators in the UAE, whether in the public or in the private school sector (MOE, 2021b). The examination for teacher licensure is comprised of a subject-specific test and a test of pedagogical knowledge. In Qatar, however, where teacher licensure had been introduced earlier, skepticism about the readiness of the teaching cadre for licensure has been reported (Ellili-Cherif et al., 2012).

A continuum of learning and development

The final common factor in the top educational systems globally, as uncovered by Sato and Abbiss (2021), is the belief that teacher education occurs along a continuum of learning and development and that it must continue past preservice programs. Most teachers surveyed in the UAE for the international TALIS study of teaching (OECD, 2019) reported participation in induction programs upon starting teaching; however, the lack of sustained and connected induction was noted, resulting in a recommendation that induction should be "more structured, systematic and sustained for longer periods of time" (OECD, 2020, p. 54). Moreover, it was recommended that induction should be extended to all teachers, not just novice teachers, to help reduce attrition and to hasten integration for the thousands of experienced teachers arriving from other countries, and for the many teachers switching from one school to another annually. Teacher attrition is very high, and UAE schools in particular struggle with high teacher turnover rates (OECD, 2015). Periodic reform upheavals, such as the introduction of English-medium teaching in schools in 2009, cause significant further disruption (Dickson et al., 2014).

Teacher professional development presents a similar picture. Teachers in the UAE report a high level of engagement in professional development (Litz & Scott, 2017). However, this high figure is likely due to mandatory professional development at the start of each new term (Buckner et al., 2016) when teachers choose individually from a menu of courses. But, what is missing is a thematic or coherent whole-school focus (Buckner et al., 2016). Moreover, teacher empowerment around their own professional development has been called for (Warner, 2018), and in addition, there have been calls to align it with the transformation agenda in order to be more "continuously relevant to the demands of school reforms and improvement" (Blaik-Hourani & Litz, 2018, p. 12). However, such initiatives are rare within the GCC. In Saudi Arabia, for example, relative to most TALIS countries, a smaller proportion of teachers report having undertaken professional development in the 12 months prior to the survey (OECD, 2018).

Challenges posed by English as a medium of instruction (EMI) for teacher education

Within the general context as set out above, there are particular issues surrounding language within teacher education in the region. This section explores some of the contemporary linguistic challenges for teacher candidates and teachers. Taking the UAE as the baseline case, with reference to other GCC countries as available in the literature, three main challenges posed by the dominance of English as a -medium instruction (EMI) are explored. Firstly, the linguistic context for teacher candidates upon admission is explored, in terms of university admission requirements. Next, the impact of EMI on content learning for teacher candidates is viewed through the presentation of a number of cases. Finally, one of the major challenges to teacher education in the UAE is addressed, namely the curricular context of the public school system for graduates. There is considerable fluidity in the public school system in terms of medium of instruction and curriculum.

Admission of teacher candidates – Language requirements

Teacher education in the UAE is provided primarily through the medium of English as the main medium of instruction in higher education. Qualifications in the education field are available from a number of public tertiary institutions, and Emirati students can attend free of charge at the undergraduate level. The majority of all content courses are taught through the medium of English. While it is possible to access qualifications in education from some private universities in the UAE, it is beyond the scope of this chapter to explore this. Gobert (2019) notes that in order to be competitive in the workplace, be it the education sector or any other sector, Emiratis must master the English language. This has led to issues and challenges with admissions requirements, benchmarking, and bridging the gap between high school and the university level with English language support in many cases.

In the UAE, students have historically entered programs with an IELTS band 5 which equates to a B1 CEFR level, placing them at an intermediate level, on the cusp of being an independent user. While the IELTS exam tests four skills, with students obtaining a score for each skill, the reality is that while a student may enter the program with a Band 5 overall, their score for reading or writing could well be a Band 4 (CEFR A2), while their proficiency in speaking may have earned them a Band 6, thus inflating the overall impression of their language capabilities (Dillon et al., 2021). Until quite recently many students did not receive sufficient K–12 linguistic preparation for accessing academic content through the medium of English at university level. The majority of students did not meet the threshold level of competency in English to meet admissions requirements and were required to take a pre-baccalaureate intensive English foundation program. However, in recent years, government mandates have seen the pre-baccalaureate foundation programs being phased out, with teacher candidates now entering directly from high school having already achieved the required English language score. Gobert (2019) offers a thorough overview of English language teaching in the UAE, noting that UAE public schools have started to follow international school trends by teaching the scientific subjects K–12 through the medium of English. As of 2019, Gobert stated that as part of the Emirates School Model (ESM), science, mathematics, and English were taught through the medium of English by "licensed native English speaking teachers" (2019, p. 113), whereas other subjects were taught through Arabic. However, at the time of writing in 2022 this is not the case, and the ESM has been replaced by the Emirates School Establishment. The curriculum is currently undergoing further changes, as is common in this context, and it is unknown as yet what this will mean for the future of EMI in public schools. The issue of regularly changing curriculum will be addressed later in this chapter.

Upon admission, teacher candidates are currently required to present their end-of-school test scores, the Emirates Standardized Test (EmSAT), which is a national system of standardized computer-based tests, based on UAE national standards. Admissions requirements have changed in recent years and have increased in some institutions to CEFR level B2 in the UAE, meaning that school leavers generally have, at best, pre-intermediate to intermediate levels of proficiency in the language in which they will be taught at university. The admissions requirements for teacher education are less clear in the case of Kuwait where applicants must meet "specified benchmarks" (Tryzna & Al-Sharoufi, 2017, p. 86) in a standardized English test.

In keeping with global trends, the teaching of English as a school subject has over time been introduced in state schools at an increasingly younger age. In Bahrain, Oman, Qatar, and Kuwait, it starts in Grade 1 (Barnawi & Al-Hawsawi, 2017), and also in KSA since 2021. In the UAE, English language teaching starts in kindergarten. Within the Gulf overall, students in the UAE consistently outperform neighboring countries in English proficiency (Green, 2020). In a systematic review of the research into English teaching and learning in KSA, Alsowat rather baldly notes that "Saudi students are at the bottom of the list in English proficiency compared to their counterparts all over the world" (Alsowat, 2017, p. 32).

In any discussion of English language admissions criteria for teacher candidates, the full linguistic repertoire of students must be considered. Gulf Arabic-speaking teacher candidates also face a linguistic challenge in terms of the diglossic nature of Arabic as there are great differences between the spoken and written versions of the Arabic language. While spoken Arabic derives from the region, country, and dialect of the region within the country where it is spoken, written Arabic is much more standardized. Moreover, within written Arabic, there are two types: Modern Standard Arabic (MSA), which is used in newspapers, magazines, books, government documents, and for business transactions, and Classical Arabic, which is the language of the Qur'an and classical Arabic literature (Dillon et al., 2020). The profile of teacher candidates being admitted to EMI programs includes these multiple versions of Arabic, and while one might expect that Gulf Arabic-speaking teacher candidates would have higher levels of Modern Standard Arabic as Arabic is their mother tongue, that is not necessarily the case. Emirati students tend to have lower than expected levels of literacy in MSA. Students tend not to be prepared with the skills to read quickly, and for understanding (Dillon et al., 2021). Taha-Thomure (2019) discusses the evidence from two cycles of the Progress in International Reading Literacy (PIRLS) test, which show that UAE-based students' achievement in reading in Arabic as a native language is below the international average and that the results of standardized national tests of Arabic reading proficiency show that higher order reading comprehension skills are poorly developed among students in the UAE.

Impact of EMI on content learning

The leaders of GCC states have shown a willingness to go above and beyond in terms of pushing their citizens forward so that they may benefit from career and academic opportunities in a globalized world. One development in this arena is the provision of EMI programs, with English adopted as the language of teaching in higher education since the late 1980s in the UAE. However, the decision to adopt EMI does not come without complications. Macaro et al. (2018) note that while there is a wealth of EMI research on teacher and student attitudes and perceptions, there is a lack of research on the actual impact of EMI on content learning. This has implications for teacher education in that language competence and language awareness are crucial elements in teacher education in general, but especially so for early years educators in the bilingual and multilingual context of the GCC.

Content teachers in higher education in the UAE have expressed concern that students' comprehension may be compromised due to low levels of English language proficiency (Mouhanna, 2016). The English language admissions criteria mentioned above mean that, in reality, many students struggle with reading skills and comprehension, processing, and textual practices. The difference between CEFR level B1 and B2 is quite significant, in terms of readiness for academic participation. For example, level B1 indicates that learners can produce simple connected text on topics which are familiar or of personal interest, while level B2 indicates that learners can produce clear, detailed text on a wide range of subjects and explain a viewpoint on a topical issue giving the advantages and disadvantages of various options. Level B2 is much more indicative of an ability to engage with academic writing and critical thought in an additional language. It is not surprising that teacher candidates can appear ill equipped to deal with the language complexities needed to study in English since the reality is that an EMI setting uses "the English language to teach academic subjects in countries or jurisdictions where the first language of the majority of the population is not English" (Macaro et al., 2018, p. 37). Trenkic and Warmington (2019) suggest that while minimum language requirements to study in an EMI setting may be enough for students to complete their program of study, it may not be sufficient to realize their full academic potential. Therefore, it is of great importance to support the development of content-specific academic language within EMI programs. Gulf Arabic-speaking intermediate learners of English must be provided with appropriate scaffolding so that they can access course content through their mother tongue as well as through the target language. One experimental study conducted in the UAE (Dillon et al., 2021) which provided teacher candidates with the opportunity to access a piece of text in either English, Arabic, or English and Arabic indicates that learners benefit most from accessing textual content through the target language (English) when it is presented alongside a similar version in their native language (Arabic).

In the Yemeni context, on the other hand, Muthanna and Karaman (2011) report that English language teacher candidates were seeking more courses taught through English than through Arabic, as they felt that this would improve their preparation as English teachers. Similarly, Tryzna and Al-Sharoufi (2017) note that there are many opportunities for the improvement of English language teacher education in Kuwait, especially considering that the majority of coursework is completed through the medium of Arabic. Students in that context would rather have their coursework be completed through the medium of English.

Curriculum change

Teacher education is contextualized by school and societal needs, or the aspirations of the government at the time. In contexts where economic needs and populations are changing drastically, curriculum reform tends to take place on a regular basis. Kippels and Ridge (2019) provide an in-depth review of curriculum reforms in the UAE, where several reforms have taken place in a short period of time. While curriculum reforms can lead to educational innovation, they can also make it challenging for teacher education providers to tailor their programs to the specific future needs of teacher candidates at any given time. For example, in the UAE, curriculum reform has involved incorporating the English language as a medium of instruction at varying levels. Curriculum must be tailored to meet the needs of society, and therefore teacher candidates who enter the workforce having completed a course of study in teacher education must be prepared to teach in accordance with ministry requirements, especially with regard to the medium of instruction of various subjects.

It is also worth noting that alongside the fluidity of medium of instruction in various public schools, a wide variety of curricula are in place in GCC countries, as the labor market model relies heavily on expatriate workers who often bring their families to live with them. This means that across the GCC a wide variety of schools are available, including public schools (usually for citizens of the country only) following the national curriculum of the country, charter schools following either the national curriculum or an imported one, and private schools following a variety of national curricula (British, International Baccalaureate, Indian, French, German, and so on), serving mainly the expatriate population. In the UAE alone, at least 13 different curricula are offered in the early childhood sector alone (Dillon, 2019). The situation is similar in Kuwait (Tryzna & Al-Sharoufi, 2017), another country where the curriculum is fluid and ever changing to meet the needs of society.

Future directions for bilingual teacher education

In the context of the UAE, where sociolinguists have noted that "English and Arabic are used at high levels of proficiency by both Emiratis and non-Emiratis, [pointing] to the development of a bilingual society" (Siemund et al., 2021, p. 202), bilingualism in Arabic and English is targeted as a school graduate skill (MOE, 2021c). In this section, we make recommendations for future possible directions in the preparation of bilingual teachers for those countries such as the UAE, which seek bilingualism as an educational goal. By bilingual education, we follow the definition provided by Christian and Genesee (2001) as *education involving two languages as media of instruction*. By *bilingual teacher education*, we mean a teacher preparation program where candidates study two or more languages, learn content knowledge through the medium of two or more languages, learn how to integrate the teaching of content and language, and learn about bilingualism and multilingualism.

We believe that bilingual teacher education is necessary in order for candidates to teach effectively in bilingual school systems upon graduation, particularly in bilingual early years home room classrooms. Support for bilingual teacher education is informed by the research which concludes that positive learning outcomes accrue for all students in bilingual education, including young learners, and that there is "no evidence for harmful effects of bilingual education and much evidence for net benefits in many domains" (Bialystok, 2018). In fact, research over 50 years shows that teaching school subjects through a target language results in benefits such as academic achievement, language and literacy development, and enhanced cognitive skills (Williams-Fortune, 2012).

Having identified earlier in this chapter the need for improvements in teacher candidates' proficiency in English, we now suggest two particular strategies that are needed within bilingual teacher education in the Gulf to help produce a bilingual and biliterate society. These are innovation in mother tongue teacher education in Arabic and education in implementing language across the curriculum.

Arabic language teacher education

Young learners in state schools in the Gulf are developing their knowledge and skills in their native language, Arabic, while at the same time, beginning to learn English. However, age-appropriate literacy in the first language, Arabic, is not securely attained by children in the Gulf, according to data from international tests of reading achievement for the Gulf countries. Around one-third of the children in Bahrain, UAE, Qatar, KSA and Oman and half of the children in Kuwait are reported to suffer from "learning poverty," defined as being unable to read and understand an age-appropriate text in their mother tongue by age ten (World Bank, 2021, p. 15). Moreover, within the UAE, wide variation is reported in student literacy standards according to the type of school – private or public – and the type of curriculum offered. Students attending private UK or IB curriculum schools in Dubai, for example, achieve well above the international average in reading in their first language, while the attainment of students attending both public and private schools offering the local Ministry of Education curriculum falls "substantially below the international average" according to the Knowledge and Human Development Authority, the Dubai educational authority for private schools (KHDA, 2018, p. 12).

One key factor that is believed to influence these below-global average results among Arabic-speaking children attending state or private schools offering the state school curriculum is the quality of Arabic language teacher preparation. The World Bank report highlighting learning poverty in the Arab world observes that "very few university teacher preparation courses include Arabic pedagogy studies" (World Bank, 2021, p. 10), leading to a recommendation to "revisit Arabic language teacher education programs (preservice) and teacher professional development programs (in-service) to add Arabic language pedagogy studies, extensive practical experience with students, and effective planning for student learning" (World Bank, 2021, p. 14). The preparation of teachers focuses on content knowledge of the Arabic language, but not on pedagogical content knowledge (i.e., how to teach Arabic), and as a result, "teachers might be proficient in Modern Standard Arabic (MSA) but are not trained in language pedagogy" (Tsimpera-Maluch & Taha-Thomure, 2021). A discussion of the pedagogical and curricular reforms needed in teacher education to lift literacy levels in Arabic is beyond the scope of this chapter, but clear recommendations for the UAE and other Gulf countries may be found in the literature, especially in Taha-Thomure (2019) and in Tsimpera-Maluch and Taha-Thomure (2021).

A recent positive development with regard to raising the profile of Arabic has been the introduction of content courses taught through the medium of Arabic in teacher education preparation programs in the UAE. In 2020, new guidelines for teacher preparation programs in federally funded early childhood teacher education were introduced, requiring that 20% of preservice undergraduate degree courses be taught through the medium of Arabic. While this will not in itself improve the pedagogical practices of future teachers, it does signify a recognition of the importance of maintaining and developing candidates' proficiency in Arabic. On the other hand, in Kuwait, the opposite situation prevails, and it has been observed that future teachers of English are insufficiently prepared to teach English in Kuwait because they "complete an overwhelming majority of the coursework in Arabic, including crucial pedagogical subjects such as teaching methodologies, with only four courses mandatory in English" (Tryzna & Al-Sharoufi, 2017,

p. 85). Better alignment between teacher preparation programs and the future context of practice upon graduation is required, and teacher education in the Gulf needs to become less generic and more targeted towards the linguistic contexts of classrooms.

Language across the curriculum

It has been argued that language and content integration should constitute the heart and soul of immersion teacher education (Peltoniemi & Bergroth, 2020), and in this regard, we welcome Morton's construct of LKCT, "language knowledge for content teaching" (Morton, 2018, p. 275). An important aspect to the preparation of bilingual teachers for a bilingual and biliterate population is the inclusion of courses in language across the curriculum in teacher preparation programs. A language-across-the-curriculum perspective assumes that the development of students' language proficiency – whether in the first language or in a target language – is the responsibility of all teachers, not just language teachers. In this regard, we suggest that teacher education in the Gulf region has much to learn from Europe where CLIL (Content and Language Integrated Learning) has been implemented for many years as a strong version of language across the curriculum. Defined as "a dual-focused educational approach in which an additional language is used for the learning and teaching of content and language with the objective of promoting both content and language mastery" (Marsh et al., 2010, p. 11), CLIL is practiced in many schools in Europe, and student teachers are exposed to it during their studies (Lopez, 2011). Indeed, a clear framework for a CLIL curriculum in teacher preparation is provided in *The European Framework for CLIL Teacher Education* (Marsh et al., 2010). Just as the CEFR (Common European Frame of Reference) has been incorporated into the English state school curriculum in the UAE, the CLIL Framework for Teacher Education deserves similar attention within preservice teacher preparation and teacher professional development programs.

Moreover, Beacco et al. (2016, p. 102) urge that "pre-service training courses focusing on the language dimension should be offered to all teachers, and not only to future language specialists, and that such courses should be made mandatory in the long run." In fact, a study in Spain on the impact of teacher education in CLIL methodology found that it had an observed impact on teacher practices, with those who were educated in CLIL practices utilizing a wider range of approaches and materials in the classroom than those who were not (Alcaraz-Mármol, 2018).

Affordances of translanguaging pedagogy in teacher education

While teacher candidates in Gulf countries could benefit from the previously mentioned language and content integration, and varying degrees of bilingual education, depending on the particular goals of teacher education programs, it is important to explore the affordances of a translanguaging pedagogy within EMI programs. EMI programs traditionally encourage students to draw upon the target language. This includes, at the programmatic level, course outlines, course learning outcomes, and program learning outcomes, and at the pedagogical level, student–student talk and teacher–student talk. Assignments tend to be produced monolingually. However, even in contexts where assignments are produced in English, and teacher talk might be possible in English only, due to many of them being Anglophone with limited or no knowledge of Arabic, it is possible to develop a translanguaging pedagogy in teacher education, just as it is possible in higher education overall. Pedagogical translanguaging entails the teacher planning teaching and learning activities while intentionally finding ways to draw on the linguistic resources of learners (Cenoz & Gorter, 2017).

Young children in bilingual and multilingual educational settings tend to fluidly support each other by drawing on their linguistic repertoires to translate as needed and to paraphrase in the language they feel most comfortable with, depending of course on the classroom context. These practices activate the resources that learners have in the linguistic repertoire (Cenoz & Gorter, 2017). However, as learners get older, they tend to become socialized in monolingual practices and intentionally hold back from translanguaging practices (Parra & Proctor, 2022). Often, this can be because translanguaging is not perceived by learners as an accepted practice in classrooms, due to traditional perspectives on EMI that have tended to link the separation of languages with learner success and to mistakes made in the target languages being associated with linguistic confusion (Cenoz & Gorter, 2017). Parra and Proctor (2022) discuss harnessing the "corriente," which translates directly from Spanish as the current of the flow of the river, and tapping into the "translanguaging corriente" (p. 2) in order to engage with classroom language practices and strategies that contribute to a translanguaging pedagogy. The authors see the "corriente" as a metaphor for the flow of language within the classroom. Strategically integrating learners' linguistic repertoires into classroom practices can ensure that bilingual learners have opportunities to participate actively and expand opportunities for their language and literacy practices. This softening of boundaries between languages takes all of the linguistic resources of the learner into consideration (Cenoz & Gorter, 2017). Within the "corriente," Parra and Proctor (2022) propose three distinct parts of a continuum of translanguaging pedagogy – listening, where teachers accept the full linguistic repertoire available to learners; channeling, where teachers not only accept but also promote the use of multiple languages within the classroom; and flowing, where teachers actively promote and plan for translanguaging in teaching and learning. Similarly, Cenoz et al. (2022) and Iversen (2020) distinguish between spontaneous and pedagogical translanguaging. Cenoz et al.'s (2022) study showed that where teachers implemented a translanguaging pedagogy, learners' anxiety about learning through a second language was reduced, and teachers felt less guilty about using more than one language in the classroom. Interestingly, Iversen's study showed that teacher candidates in Norway were uncertain about their ability to intentionally include additional languages other than Norwegian during their school placements. Similarly, from a more local context, Al-Bataineh and Gallagher's (2021) study showed that when a group of teacher candidates in the UAE were encouraged to shuttle between Arabic and English in the development of a children's storybook, they displayed paradoxical and ambivalent attitudes toward this practice.

It is worth exploring how a monolingual teacher education program in an EMI context in the Gulf may benefit from tapping into the "corriente" at various levels and what specific strategies could be used. Engaging with a translanguaging pedagogy surely affords the stakeholders to consider translanguaging from a social justice perspective, where the linguistic funds of knowledge of all stakeholders are acknowledged and valued. While the monoglossic orientation toward content teaching in EMI contexts has allowed for some code-switching as a default but not well-tolerated practice, spontaneous and intentional translanguaging across the continuum can offer learners the opportunity to construct knowledge in a way that opens up opportunities to learn, rather than constraining those opportunities (Probyn, 2019). Even in multilingual European contexts, where much research has been conducted in relation to CLIL across the education continuum, a pedagogy which tended to neglect the multilingual component has traditionally been implemented in teacher education (Portolés Falomir & Martí, 2018).

If the Arabic language is regularly heard as part of natural classroom discussion in teacher education, and learners appear to enjoy and benefit from explaining concepts, skills, or knowledge to each other using their mother tongue, then it is time to listen to that lived reality and challenge those monolingual ideologies that have not typically valued the ability of learners to draw from their linguistic repertoires. It will also be of benefit to have instructors intentionally listen to, observe, and document how learners use their communicative resources to engage with texts in the teacher education classroom. It is critical to learners to see that their bilingual/multilingual practices are valued and appreciated. It is also important for instructors to open up spaces where supports are provided to learners to access the curriculum, whether they are texts in a second language (Dillon et al., 2021), specific glossary lists with conceptual explanations of education-related vocabulary that may be provided to learners (as described in an unpublished study by Qureshi and colleagues), or simply scaffolding and differentiating instruction for learners through modeling translanguaging if they happen to speak the languages of the learners themselves, as well as the target language (Durán & Palmer, 2014).

Parra and Proctor (2022) note that it may seem challenging for students to engage in translanguaging if instructors do not speak the language(s) of their students, as is the case in many EMI programs in the UAE, where the majority of faculty members are hired from non-Arabic speaking countries. Therefore, they advise instructors to be creative in channeling the "corriente" by seeking support from appropriate community members – in this case, other students and peers, teaching assistants who do speak the languages(s) of their students, and online resources such as translators. Learners in EMI settings often find it challenging to engage in academic writing, particularly paraphrasing and summarizing (Myers et al., 2021). In order to address this issue, teacher candidates could be encouraged to paraphrase using strategies such as note-taking from the original source text, mind mapping these notes using their main language, and taking time to interpret these notes back into the target language by engaging with those community and online supports. This will lead them to have some time to deepen their conceptual understanding and synthesize their writing in their own words, without always feeling forced to engage in metacognitive thought through the target language. Think-aloud protocols, where learners are afforded the opportunity to verbalize their thoughts while completing a task using their full linguistic repertoire, can have an important part to play in this intentional translanguaging pedagogy (Cenoz & Gorter, 2017). These strategies, as part of a planned and intentional translanguaging classroom, open up a translanguaging space where students can "develop their confidence and agency" (Parra & Proctor, 2022, p. 14) where their diverse linguistic repertoires are harnessed as part of their funds of knowledge. When engaging with academic texts in the target language, it can also be helpful to draw on multimodal forms of non-traditional "text," such as videos or podcasts available in students' home languages, to support understanding. Holistically, Cenoz et al. (2022) found in their study that more opportunities for language learning in teacher education programs can be created through candidates drawing on their full linguistic repertoires. For a catalog of practical plurilingual and translanguaging strategies and activities that can be used by teacher educators and teachers in the Arabian Gulf states, see Coelho and Steinhagen, this volume.

Conclusion

Parra and Proctor (2022) advise that approaching teaching and learning with the translanguaging continuum in mind, flowing between the awareness level and the level of planned translanguaging spaces, will help to provide an experience that is more socially just for bilingual students. It also provides a space where learners can experience less anxiety about their learning through an additional language and allows teachers to feel less guilty about students drawing on their linguistic funds of knowledge. However, as shown in Al-Bataineh and Gallagher's (2021) study, teacher candidates' linguistic ideology can play a large part in the acceptability of translanguaging as a practice. At a basic level, the goal of teacher education is to prepare candidates to work with learners to ensure their academic success, as well as their holistic development. If the linguistic repertoires of learners in classrooms are to be harnessed to enhance learning, then certainly teacher education has a crucial role to play in shaping teacher candidates' perspectives toward translanguaging (Portolés Falomir & Martí, 2018). However, this area has not received much attention in the Gulf region to date.

Furthermore, instructors within EMI contexts could benefit from significant professional development programs to gain knowledge and skills in navigating the translanguaging pedagogy that could be implemented at the higher education level for teacher candidates (Lasagabaster, 2022).

Notes

1 PISA is the Programme for International Student Assessment, administered by the Organization for Economic Cooperation and Development (OECD), which tests 15-year-olds' ability in reading, mathematics, and science.
2 These top-performing national school systems were identified, based on student performance in standardized international tests, as Alberta and Ontario in Canada, New South Wales and Victoria in Australia, Shanghai in China, Finland, and Singapore.

References

Al-Bataineh, A., & Gallagher, K. (2021). Attitudes towards translanguaging: How future teachers perceive the meshing of Arabic and English in children's storybooks. *International Journal of Bilingual Education and Bilingualism*, *24*(3), 386–400.

Alcaraz-Mármol, G. (2018). Trained and non-trained language teachers on CLIL methodology: Teachers' facts and opinions about the CLIL approach in the primary education context in spain. *Latin American Journal of Content & Language Integrated Learning*, *11*(1), 39–64. http://dx.doi.org/10.5294/laclil.2018.11.1.3

AlNahdi, G. (2014). Educational change in Saudi Arabia. *Journal of International Education Research*, *10*, 1–6. https://doi.org/10.19030/jier.v10i1.8342

Alsowat, H. (2017). A systematic review of research on teaching English language skills for Saudi EFL students. *Advances in Language and Literary Studies*, *8*(30), 30–45.

Barber, M., & Mourshed, M. (2007). *How the world's best-performing school systems come out on top*. McKinsey & Company.

Badri, M., & Al Khaili, M. (2014). Migration of P-12 education from its current state to one of high quality: The aspirations of Abu Dhabi. *Policy Futures in Education*, *12*(2), 200–220.

Barnawi, O., & Al-Hawsawi, S. (2017). English education policy in Saudi Arabia: English Language education policy in the Kingdom of Saudi Arabia: Current trends, issues and challenges. In R. Kirkpatrick (Ed.), *English Language education policy in the middle East and North Africa*. Springer, pp. 199–222. https://doi.org/10.1007/978-3-319-46778-8_11

Beacco, J., Fleming, M., Goullier, F., Thürmann, E., & Vollmer, H., with contributions by Sheils, J. (2016). *The language dimension in all subjects – A handbook for curriculum development and teacher training*. Council of Europe. ISBN: 978-92-871-8232-6

Bialystok, E. (2018). Bilingual education for young children: Review of the effects and consequences. *International Journal of Bilingual Education and Bilingualism*, *21*(6), 666–679. https://doi.org/10.1080/13670050.2016.1203859

Blaik-Hourani, R., & Litz, D. (2018). Perceptions of the school self-evaluation process: The case of Abu Dhabi. *School Leadership & Management*, *36*(3), 247–270. https://doi.org/10.1080/13632434.2016.1247046

Buckner, E., Chedda, S., & Kindreich, J. (2016). Teacher Professional Development in the UAE: What Do Teachers Actually Want? Shaikh Saud Bin Saqr Al Qasimi Foundation for Policy Research. Retrieved from https://publications.alqasimifoundation.com/en/teacher-professional-development-in-the-uae-what-do-teachers-actually-want

Buckner, E. (2017). *The status of teacher and professional satisfaction in the United Arab Emirates.* Al Qasimi Foundation for Policy Research. Retrieved from http://www.alqasimifoundation.com/en/publication/69/the-status-of-teaching-and-teacher-professional-satisfaction-in-the-united-arab-emirates

BTC (2022). Bahrain Teachers' College. Relationship to 2030 Goals. Retrieved from http://www.btc.uob.edu.bh/btc-beyond-bahrain-2030

Cenoz, J., & Gorter, D. (2017). Translanguaging as a pedagogical tool in multilingual education. In J. Cenoz, D. Gorter, & S. May (Eds.) (3rd ed.), *Language awareness and multilingualism. Encyclopedia of language and education.* Springer, pp. 309–321.

Cenoz, J., Leonet, O., & Gorter, D. (2021). Developing cognate awareness through pedagogical translanguaging. *International Journal of Bilingual Education and Bilingualism,* 1–15. https://doi.org/10.1080/13670050.2021.1961675

Cenoz, J., Santos, A., & Gorter, D. (2022). Pedagogical translanguaging and teachers' perceptions of anxiety. *International Journal of Bilingual Education and Bilingualism,* 1–12. https://doi.org/10.1080/13670050.2021.2021387

Christian, D., & Genesee, F. (2001). (Eds.) *Bilingual education.* TESOL Publications, p. 1.

Cochran-Smith, M., & Maria Villegas, A. (2015). Studying teacher preparation: The questions that drive research. *European Educational Research Journal, 14*(5), 379–394. https://doi.org/10.1177/1474904115590211

Cochran-Smith, M., & Reagan, E. (2021). "Best practices" for evaluating teacher preparation programs. *National Academy of Education.* Retrieved from https://naeducation.org/wp-content/uploads/2021/09/NAEd-EITPP-Paper-Cochran-Smith-and-Reagan.pdf

Darling-Hammond, L. (2017). Teacher education around the world: What can we learn from international practice? *European Journal of Teacher Education, 40*(3), 291–309. https://doi.org/10.1080/02619768.2017.1315399

Dickson, M. (2013). School improvements in Abu Dhabi, UAE – asking the "expert witnesses." *Improving Schools, 16*(3), 270–282.

Dickson, M., & Le Roux, J. (2012). Why do Emirati males become teachers and how do cultural factors influence this decision? *Learning and Teaching in Higher Education: Gulf Perspectives, 9*(2), 1–16. Retrieved from http://lthe.zu.ac.ae/index.php/lthehome/article/view/111

Dickson, M., Riddlebarger, J., Stringer, P., Tennant, L., & Kennetz, K. (2014). Challenges faced by Emirati novice teachers. *Near and Middle Eastern Journal of Research in Education, 4.* http://dx.doi.org/10.5339/nmejre.2014.4

Dillon, A. (2019). Innovation and transformation in early childhood education in the UAE. In K. Gallagher (Ed.), *Education in the United Arab Emirates.* Springer. https://doi.org/10.1007/978-981-13-7736-5_5

Dillon, A., Chell, G., Moussa-Inaty, J., Gallagher, K., & Grey, I. (2021). English Medium instruction and the potential of translanguaging practices in higher education. *Translation and Translanguaging in Multilingual Contexts,* 7(2), 153–176.

Dillon, A. M., Hojeij, Z., Perkins, A., & Malkawi, R. (2020). Examining the text quality of English/Arabic dual language children's picture books. *International Journal of Bilingual Education and Bilingualism, 23*(8), 888–901.

Durán, L., & Palmer, D. (2014). Pluralist discourses of bilingualism and translanguaging talk in classrooms. *Journal of Early Childhood Literacy, 14*(3), 367–388.

Ellili-Cherif, M., Romanowski, M., & Nasser, R. (2012). All that glitters is not gold: Challenges of teacher and school leader licensure licensing system in Qatar. *International Journal of Educational Development, 32*(3), 471–481.

Gallagher, K. (2019). Challenges and opportunities in sourcing, preparing, and developing a teaching force for the UAE. In K. Gallagher (Ed.), *Education in the United Arab Emirates: Innovation and transformation*. Springer. ISBN 978-981-13-7735-8

Gardner, W. (1995). Developing a quality teaching force for the United Arab Emirates: Mission improbable. *Journal of Education for Teaching, 21*(3), 289–302.

Gobert, M. (2019). Transformation in English language education in the UAE. In K. Gallagher (Ed.), *Education in the United Arab Emirates: Innovation and transformation* (pp. 113–126). Springer. ISBN 978-981-13-7735-8

Green, S. (2020). *Scaffolding academic literacy with low-proficiency users of English*. Palgrave Macmillan.

Gulf Research Center (2017). *Percentage of Nationals and Foreign Nationals in GCC Countries populations*. Retrieved from https://gulfmigration.org/media/graphs/Graph1_09_05_2017.pdf

Hayes, A., & Al-Abri, K. (2019). Regional solidarity undermined? Higher education developments in the Arabian Gulf, economy and time. *Comparative Education, 55*(2), 157–174.

Ibrahim, A., & Al-Taneiji, S. (2019). Teacher satisfaction in Abu Dhabi public schools: What the numbers did not say. *Issues in Educational Research, 29*(1), 106–122.

Iversen, J. Y. (2020). Pre-service teachers' translanguaging during field placement in multilingual, mainstream classrooms in Norway. *Language and Education, 34*(1), 51–65.

KHDA. (2018). *Creating stronger readers today for a brighter tomorrow: Results from Dubai's participation in PIRLS and ePIRLS* 2016. file:///Users/z9299/Downloads/KHDA%202018_Creating%20Stronger%20Readers.pdf

Kippels, S., & Ridge, N. (2019). The growth and transformation of K–12 education in the UAE. In K. Gallagher (Ed.), *Education in the United Arab Emirates*. Springer. https://doi.org/10.1007/978-981-13-7736-5_3

Lasagabaster, D. (2022). Teacher preparedness for English-medium instruction. *Journal of English-Medium Instruction, 1*(1), 48–64.

Litz, D., & Scott, S. (2017). Transformational leadership in the educational system of the United Arab Emirates. *Educational Management Administration & Leadership, 45*(4), 566–587. https://doi.org/10.1177/1741143216636112

Liu, W. C. (2021). *Singapore's approach to developing teachers: Hindsight, insight, and foresight*. Taylor & Francis.

Lopez, E. (2011). *CLIL teacher training across Europe: Current state of the art, good practices and guidelines for the future*. Málaga. [Unpublished report].

Macaro, E., Curle, S., Pun, J., An, J., & Dearden, J. (2018). A systematic review of English medium instruction in higher education. *Language Teaching, 51*(1), 36–76.

Marsh, D., Mehisto, P., Wolff, D., & Frigols Martin, M. (2010). *European framework for CLIL teacher education: A framework for the professional development of CLIL teachers*. European Centre for Modern Languages.

MOE (2019). Future Teacher Scholarships. Retrieved from https://www.moe.gov.ae/En/MediaCenter/News/Pages/Future-Teacher-Scholarships.aspx

MOE (2021a). Six Years of Achievement: 2015-2020. Retrieved from https://www.moe.gov.ae/En/AboutTheMinistry/Documents/MOE%20BOOK.pdf.

MOE (2021b). About the Ministry. Retrieved from https://www.moe.gov.ae/En/AboutTheMinistry/Documents/MOE%20BOOK.pdf, 67–68.

MOE (2021c). MOE Education System 2020-2021. Retrieved from https://www.moe.gov.ae/En/ImportantLinks/Documents/matrix/MOEducationSystem2020-2021.pdfBilingual

Morton, T. (2018). Reconceptualizing and describing teachers' knowledge of language for content and language integrated learning (CLIL). *International Journal of Bilingual Education and Bilingualism, 21*(3), 275–286. https://doi.org/10.1080/13670050.2017.1383352

Mouhanna, M. (2016). English as a medium of instruction in the tertiary education setting of the UAE: The perspectives of content teachers. [PhD, University of Essex]. Retrieved from https://ore.exeter.ac.uk/repository/bitstream/handle/10871/23758/MouhannaM.pdf?sequence=1

Muthanna, A., & Karaman, A. C. (2011). The need for change in teacher education in Yemen: The beliefs of prospective language teachers. *Procedia-Social and Behavioral Sciences, 12*, 224–232.

Myers, T., Buchanan, J., Balanyk, J., & Nicoll, T. (2021). ESAP-in-EGAP. In C. MacDiarmid, & J. J. MacDonald (Eds.), *Pedagogies in English for academic purposes: Teaching and learning in international contexts*. Bloomsbury, pp. 137–152.

OECD. (2015). Better Skills, Better Jobs, Better Lives: A Strategic Approach to Education and Skills Policies for the United Arab Emirates. Retrieved from https://www.oecd.org/education/A-Strategic-Approach-to-Education-and%20Skills-Policies-for-the-United-Arab-Emirates.pdf

OECD (2019). TALIS 2018 Results (Volume I): Teachers and School Leaders as Lifelong Learners. https://doi.org/10.1787/1d0bc92a-en

OECD (2020). Teaching in the United Arab Emirates – 10 lessons from TALIS. Retrieved from https://www.oecd.org/education/talis/Teaching_in_the_UAE-10_Lessons_from_TALIS.pdf

OECD (2018). TALIS 2018: Saudi Arabia. Retrieved from https://gpseducation.oecd.org/CountryProfile?primaryCountry=SAU&treshold=5&topic=TA

Parra, M. O., & Proctor, P. (2022). The translanguaging pedagogies continuum. *Journal of Education*. https://doi.org/10.1177/00220574211053587

Peltoniemi, A., & Bergroth, M. (2020). Developing language aware immersion teacher education: Identifying characteristics through a study of immersion teacher socialisation. *International Journal of Bilingual Education and Bilingualism*. https://doi.org/10.1080/13670050.2020.1757613

Portolés Falomir, L., & Martí, O. (2018). Teachers' beliefs about multilingual pedagogies and the role of initial training.

Probyn, M. (2019). Pedagogical translanguaging and the construction of science knowledge in a multilingual South African classroom: Challenging monoglossic/post-colonial orthodoxies. *Classroom Discourse, 10*(3–4), 216–236.

Sato, M., & Abbiss, J. (2021). International insights on evaluating teacher education programs. National Academy of Education Committee on Evaluating and Improving Teacher Preparation Programs. National Academy of Education. Retrieved from https://naeducation.org/wp-content/uploads/2021/11/3rd-pp-for-NAEd-EITPP-Paper-8-Sato_Abbiss.pdf

Siemund, P., Al-Issa, A., & Leimgruber, J. (2021). Multilingualism and the role of English in the United Arab Emirates. *World Englishes, 40*, 191–204. https://doi.org/10.1111/weng.12507

Taha-Thomure, H. (2019). Arabic language education in the UAE. In K. Gallagher (Ed.), *Education in the UAE: Innovation and transformation*. Springer. https://doi.org/10.1007/978-981-13-7736-5_5

Trenkic, D., & Warmington, M. (2019). Language and literacy skills of home and international university students: How different are they, and does it matter? *Bilingualism: Language and Cognition, 22*(2), 349–365.

Tsimpera-Maluch, J., & Taha-Thomure, H. (2021). Shifting paradigms in arabic pedagogy and policy in the UAE: Opportunities and challenges for teacher education. In Bakili, N. & Memon, N. (Eds.), *Teacher training and education in the GCC: Unpacking the complexities and challenges of internationalizing educational contexts*. Rowan & Littlefield. ISBN 978-1-7936-3673-7

Tryzna., M., & Al-Sharoufi, H. (2017). English Language education policy in Kuwait. In R. Kirkpatrick (Ed.) *English language education policy in the middle East and North Africa*. Springer, pp. 77–92. https://doi.org/10.1007/978-3-319-46778-8_11

Warner, R. (2018). Education policy reform in the UAE: Building teacher capacity (49). Retrieved from http://www.mbrsg.ae/getattachment/872091c8-05f3-418b-84a9-48294717ebbb/Building-Teacher-Capacity

Williams-Fortune, T. (2012). What the research says about immersion. In *Chinese language learning in the early grades: A handbook of resources and best practices for Mandarin immersion* (pp. 9–13). Asia Society. ISBN 978-1-936123-28-5

Wiseman, A., Davidson, P., & Brereton, J. (2017). Teacher quality in gulf cooperation council (GCC) countries: translating global discourse to national education systems. In M. Akiba & G. LeTendre, G. (Eds.), *International handbook of teacher quality and policy* (pp. 218–238). Routledge. https://doi.org/10.4324/9781315710068

World Bank (2021). Advancing Arabic Language Teaching and Learning: A Path to Reducing Learning Poverty in the Middle East and North Africa. World Bank. Retrieved from https://www.worldbank.org/en/region/mena/publication/advancing-arabic-language-teaching-and-learning-path-to-reducing-learning-poverty-in-the-middle-east-and-north-africa

PART 2

Empirical research on plurilingual education in the Arabian Peninsula context

5

FROM BINARIES TO PLURALITY

Emirati college students' perspectives on the plurilingual identities of English users and expatriate teachers

Melanie van den Hoven and Sarah Hopkyns

Introduction

Since the outset of higher education in the Arabian Peninsula about five decades ago, imported English-medium teachers from around the world have been a visible presence at university campuses in this region where Arabic is the official language. In 2021, the inaugural Arab University Rankings adopted a world-wide measurement of a university's international reputation (THE, 2021) and adapted it to promote teaching and research priorities as dominant indicators for the region. Within these calculations, the presence of international teachers, defined as nationalities that differ from the country where the institution is based, constitute a favorable metric for enhancing international perspectives. Universities offering English medium instruction (EMI) with foreign academics are thus well set up to compete in international ranking systems. The rationale is that productive teachers generate widely cited English language research publications as well as international research collaborations. This development further underscores the contributions of expatriate teachers in English-medium campuses in the region, which should be scrutinized against internationalization processes of higher education, neoliberal language policies (Barnawi, 2022), and prevailing issues of language, culture, and identity (Al-Issa & Dahan, 2011; Hopkyns, 2020).

Despite the value of expatriate teachers and long-standing recognition of English users as having "multicultural identities" (Kachru, 1992, p. 357), descriptions of the plurilingual identities of imported academics are not common. Expatriate teachers in the Arabian Peninsula with their inherent diversity are often categorized by binary constructions such as expatriate or local, native or non-native English speaker, and also English teacher or content teacher. Such labels warrant scrutiny for underlying constructions of in-group and out-group

DOI: 10.4324/9781003315971-8

membership. Naming practices reveal in-group and out-group orientations and normalize "us" and "them" designations in daily talk. For instance, social stratification according to the *kafala* system segregates residents demographically and legally by citizenship status (Lian et al., 2019). Labels of expatriate–local refer to relevant designations for access to particular resources, such as government schools and real estate. Similarly, native–non-native English speaker labels, originating in English Language Teaching (ELT) discourses, refer to proficiency in the language. The dichotomous labels, however, have lost relevance as World Englishes and Plurilingual Pedagogy increasingly document the ways English and other languages mix and merge in *lingua franca* communication. In addition, English language teachers are often differentiated from English-medium content teachers by employment contracts and associated benefits. These acts of naming reflect stances toward people, language, and social interaction in educational domains.

EMI classrooms in the UAE are robust sites of intercultural contact. It is in these domains where such labels circulate even though they may originate in the broader society. In the UAE, expatriates outnumber nationals by more than five to one (Boyle, 2011), due to the post-oil boom attracting transnational workers to the region. Although nationals play increasingly visible roles in higher education, most teachers are from abroad and represent an array of cultural and linguistic identities. Teacher identities then represent intercultural dimensions of classrooms as superdiverse contact zones with "unique configurations of diversity" (Garces-Bacsal et al., 2021, p. 1). Greater understanding of the adoption of English to diverse linguistic ecologies, including English-medium domains in the Arabian Peninsula, has been one outcome of recent World Englishes research (Elyas & Mahboob, 2021). In addition, as shown by the focus in this book, plurilingual approaches to teaching are gaining relevance for promoting learning environments where students' languages are viewed as a resource (Galante et al., 2022).

A missing theme to date, however, is the ways in which educational contexts in the Arabian Peninsula regard the linguistic profiles of expatriate teachers as a resource. This study addresses this gap by exploring the meanings attributed to English users, expatriates, and expatriate English-medium teachers. Doing so, however, necessitates engaging with competing constructions of belonging within an English-using professional community, the diversity of linguistic profiles in the UAE, and "multiple layers of Othering" (Garces-Bacsal et al., 2021, p. 1).

This chapter builds on an emergent recognition of linguistic pluralism in the UAE (Hopkyns & van den Hoven, 2022; van den Hoven & Carroll, 2017) to explore the conceptions of English users via students' accounts of their own plurilingual identities in relation to UAE residents in general, and, in particular, the EMI teachers in their midst. Our chapter begins with a survey of changing labels for expatriates who come as economic migrants to the region, finding some evidence of a spatial turn toward greater recognition of ethnolinguistic diversity of residents in the Arabian Peninsula (Buckingham, 2017). Our review of labels for English users challenge binary notions of native and non-native

English speakers within educational discourses and position English users in the region within the international spread of English. Also, we situate our professional experiences within an ethnographic approach to gathering data and draw on social constructionism (Berger & Luckmann, 1971) as a lens for interpreting student accounts of intercultural interactions with expatriates during a particular phase of socialization in higher education. Based on the findings, we propose concrete strategies for ways in which policy makers, educational leaders, and teachers can promote greater linguistic awareness and, in so doing, fulfill expected outcomes of the internationalization of higher education in the region.

Labels for English users in multicultural settings in the Arabian Peninsula

Our interest in names and labels for English users falls is aligned with recent World Englishes scholarship for the attention to the social history of the English language, the people who use it worldwide and within globalized contexts, and the consequences of its use (Seargeant, 2012). A central argument put forth in World Englishes scholarship is that the meaning of English as a single "coherent conceptual entity" (Seargeant, 2010, p. 97) is contested. Labels and meanings given to the conceptual entities of English and English users are based on the selection and exclusion of certain features and highlight particular concepts of language use and "presuppositions about human agency and society" (Seargeant, 2010, p. 109). In today's globalized era, *lingua franca* communication in a language such as English is seldom a problem in itself. Rather, individual users of English may experience problems related to "communication and intelligibility, to identity and cultural politics, or to professional concerns such as education" (Seargeant, 2012, p. 14). By asking questions about labels for English-using residents in the Arabian Peninsula, we examine relationships between English speakers and the particular implications of using English with others.

Concern with perspectives of the identities of the region's multilingual and multicultural residents is relatively recent. Nominations of incoming expatriates in the Arabian Peninsula by those who were there before them show attention to shifting ways of constructing difference, not originally based on language use. Subsequent expressions of "we" and "us" in the regional literature link to accounts of conviviality and belonging in *lingua franca* communities (Blommaert, 2013). Our discussion of labels then narrows to situated language ideologies in the UAE and names for English users during a distinct era of societal bilingualism in Abu Dhabi.

"Us" and "them" categories in the Arabian Peninsula

As in other global cities, waves of migration characterize many cities in the Arabian Peninsula, evoking strong community attachments by citizens and residents alike (AlMutawa, 2020; Gardner, 2011; Walsh, 2014). The oil-rich environment has hosted relationships between nationals and expatriates in more or less productive arrangements for decades. Early scholars characterize the relationship by "politeness" (Kapiszewkski, 2001, p. 177), more evident under times of economic growth. Over the past two decades, expatriates themselves have been linked to different agendas carried by a colonial footprint, aspirations for economic mobility, and, more recently, opportunities for lifestyle migration. Expatriates in the region have always characterized themselves by diversity albeit with different features of diversity selected.

Early descriptions of the UAE workforce used socioeconomic differences as categories to subdivide expatriates into two groups. Non-citizens are distinguished as resident expatriates or workers, as seen in the following:

> resident expatriates...[and their] smaller cultural subgroups [who are] separate and distinct, ... social and ethnic groups [residing] side by side ... temporary workers ... [and] expatriate community groups [of] all nationalities.
>
> *(Davidson, 2005, pp. 268–271)*

However, all non-citizens in the UAE workforce are temporary residents even though some residents stay for a few years and others for decades. The short-lived contributions have been framed as "cultural contamination" (Davidson, 2005, p. 262) in part because "expatriates" and "workers" reside in segregated communities which "dwarf the local Emirati populations" (p. 281). The physical segregation of different types of residents by dwelling underscores "us" and "them" orientations, perhaps explained by constraints that living separately has on intercultural engagement. The features held to the light are ratio of non-citizen to citizen, ethnicity, and socioeconomic class.

Subsequent references delineate incoming groups by specific nationalities bearing political or economic interests. While traditionally most migrants to the UAE come from South East Asian countries such as India, Bangladesh, and Pakistan, recent waves of migrants from Russia, China, Brazil, Japan, South Korea, and France have come into focus (Fulton & Sim, 2018). Metaphorical language capturing the macro forces shaping the political structure of transnational relationships appears. For instance, a recent iteration of "friends with benefits" (Fulton, 2019, p. 33) describes the strategic alliance between two nations. Despite the greater array of nationalities in focus, a tendency to present nation as a homogeneous actor is detected, which downplays diversity within transnational groups. A warning for teachers then is to closely scrutinize commonly used labels for tacit assumptions of essentialism which promote seeing other nationals as having a "unitary ethnic group identity" (Matsuda, 2012, p. 61).

To this end, recent site-specific ethnographic studies show greater awareness of ethnolinguistic diversity and hybridity within transnational groups. One notable ethnographic study of British migrants in Abu Dhabi, Dubai, Doha, Manama, and Muscat highlights the perspectives of English-speaking transnational migrants and their sense of belonging to their respective cities (Walsh,

2014). This study establishes the kinds of touchpoints British expatriates rely on to establish us–them relationships, such as what Britishness means relationally to "Arabness" (Walsh, 2014, p. 14). In so doing, attention to "place-specific heterogeneity" (Walsh, 2014, p. 1) becomes especially important given distinct national histories of migration flows and ratio of migrants to nationals. Another ethnographic study showing a similar spatial turn is Cook's (2021) analysis of top-down migration policies and urban planning for associated impact on communicative behaviors of linguistically diverse expatriates in Ras Al Khaimah, UAE. Cook (2021) refers to the *kafala* system to explain divisions of "desirable" and "undesirable" migrants. The methodological approach relies on language stories of seven middle-class foreign residents with work visas, who navigated two cafés to show patterns of community segregation. The study critically discusses how experiences of social inequity are enacted within the UAE's multilingual spaces where "nationality and race determine job and salary offers" (p. 8).

In a further study, AlMutawa (2020) describes cafés within Dubai malls as sites of belonging and conviviality for enabling citizens and non-citizens "to see other members of society, interact with them directly or indirectly, people-watch, chit-chat, and keep up-to-date with the community" (p. 45). Expatriates seen within these interactional zones are labeled "long-term inhabitants" (p. 46) and credited for participation in these civic spaces. Exclusion by racial and class profile, rather than a strictly linguistic one, is highlighted as important for "boundary maintenance" (AlMutawa, 2020, p. 49), enabling Emirati women, like AlMutawa, to feel safe and secure.

This brief overview of the regional literature offers situated perspectives of in-group and out-group membership, showing that constructions of "us" and "them" have shifted across time and space. At different times, the features of nationality, socioeconomic class, and gender are used to explain how the diverse constellations of residents in the Arabian Peninsula interact with each other.

Naming English users in educational domains

The majority of names for English in everyday talk signal how English users are treated in educational domains (Seargeant, 2010). Labels like "native English-speaker teacher" (NEST) and "non-native English speaker teacher" (NNEST) have long been common in ELT and EMI discourses. Despite decades of criticisms of such terms by scholars in the field of applied linguistics (Aneja, 2016; Aslan & Thompson, 2017; Higgins, 2003; Medgyes, 1992; Rampton, 1990), the binary division between the labels NEST and NNEST remains, as Cook (2016) puts it, a "ghost in the machine" (p. 187). Such labels are influenced by linguistic norms associated with "inner circle" countries where English has long been spoken as a first language (Kachru, 1992). Teachers from inner circle countries have also been labelled "BANA teachers," meaning "British, Australian and North American teachers" (Holliday, 2002). Using a BANA-centre and periphery framework, English users in the Arabian Peninsula are positioned in the periphery, outside of the main locus of action; yet, in fact, a percentage do connect to inner circle countries whether by birth, education, or acquired residency, for instance.

Of some concern, the label "native speaker" is circulated and reinforced by appearance in job advertisements regionally and globally. For example, Mahboob and Golden (2013) analyzed 77 ELT job advertisements in Asia and the Middle East and found that 87 percent had requirements relating to nationality or "native" speaker status. More recently, Hopkyns (2022) noted that although ELT job advertisements rarely used the native speaker label in job headings, they may feature wording in the criteria list specifically requiring passports from inner circle countries, or native speaker applicants. Binary labels such as NEST and NNEST divide English teachers into essentialized groups, disadvantaging the latter group. NEST and NNEST distinctions also appear in the UAE literature base (King, 2013; McLaren, 2011), underpinning critiques of the "foreign presence at university faculty level" (Lootah, 2011, p. 37) as well as reported discriminatory ELT hiring practices. However, labels like EMI users (Troudi & Jendli, 2011) and English-speaking monolinguals (Belhiah & Elhami, 2015; McLaren, 2011) may infer binaries such as Arabic-medium users or English-speaking bilinguals, but they are not common. Of note, such labels avert explicit reference to nationality yet signal a pejorative orientation to the exclusive use of English among residents.

In this regard, the shifting balance from "Arabic mostly" to "English often" is significant for meanings given to English speakers in an Arabic-speaking region. The UAE, which has traditionally been classified as an expanding-circle country (Kachru, 1992), moved from using "English as a foreign language" (EFL) (Syed, 2003) to "English as a Second Language" (ESL) (Karmani, 2005), suggesting a shift away from Arabic for daily life toward English for use both inside and outside the classroom. As the focus on English proficiency has increased in intensity both in the UAE and globally, new labels invoking an international community of lingua franca communicators have appeared. Such labels include "English as an international language (EIL)" (Dahan, 2007), "English as a lingua Franca (ELF)" (Boyle, 2011), and "English as a global language/Global English" (Al-Issa & Dahan, 2011; Hopkyns, 2014). These labels serve to decenter English from a norm-dependant center rendering dichotomous labels of NEST and NNEST of limited value.

The study

Social context of the study

The teacher training college in which the study takes place is an interactional space where policy is not just top-down but also enacted. Founded in 2009 by a high-profile Singaporean university, the college was established to integrate Emirati preservice teachers into English-medium teaching as per Abu

Dhabi's educational vision (Moussly, 2009). A key element of the new vision was "developing the students' Arabic and English literacy" (ADEC, 2013), but the college singularly developed Emiratis as English-medium teachers (EMTs) and not Arabic-medium teachers (AMTs). During this time, discourses signaled a broader push toward societal bilingualism. In this dynamic, young Emiratis became the new face of English users in the Emirates' government primary schools amid increasing concerns of the "marginalisation of Arabic" (Gallagher, 2011, p. 66). Policy documents of this era guided the communication of the curriculum reforms and used the labels of ESL, EFL, and EIL as synonyms to justify the implementation of EMI in Abu Dhabi schools (Badri & Al Khaili, 2014). In addition, the labels of EMT and AMT circulated as a naming practice associating novice Emirati teachers as agents in the bifurcation of language use.

Although the original vision lost steam when the cross-border affiliation with Singapore collapsed, the college environment remained a sole provision for enskilling Emiratis as EMTs. Accordingly, the college hosted intercultural interaction in English among students and expatriate teachers from over 25 different nationalities. The site also hosted a spectrum of mixed-method and qualitative studies, showing a range of labels accounting for ethnolinguistic diversity and varieties of English. For instance, a matched-guise study using descriptors of correctness, pleasantness, and understandability sought student perspectives on accents of educated speakers of English. Six regional labels for English speaker varieties were used, nominated as "Gulf, North American, UK, Non Gulf Arab, Oceanic, and a South Asian" (Kennetz et al., 2011, pp. 150–151). Another study reported that English and Arabic were considered primary languages in Abu Dhabi but "Indian," "Persian," "Filipino," and Korean were also identified as languages belonging to the linguistic ecology (van den Hoven & Carroll, 2017).

Although coursework included modules in dual language instruction, the environment did not openly embrace plurilingual teaching practices in English and Arabic. Yet, one study of bilingual academics reported the use of the mother tongue instruction but found documenting this practice to be taboo, out of concern for negative repercussions from administrators (Carroll & van den Hoven, 2017). Another study showed that students readily incorporated translanguaging into their "college English" (van den Hoven & Carroll, 2020). These findings suggest at once that teachers and students hold differing perspectives regarding the plausibility of using both English and Arabic for learning.

Methodology

The study takes an ethnographic approach to explore the labels Emirati college students give to English users in Abu Dhabi's rich linguistic context. The research design featured three phases of data collection. Each phase featured the use of different ethnographic tools for different purposes: focus group interviews, participant observations, and in-depth individual interviews. This chapter primarily relies on interview data to show "us" and "them" constructions and labels for Emiratis and expatriate residents, including English-medium teachers.

The three main research questions are as follows:

RQ1) What labels do Emirati college students use for their linguistic identities?
RQ2) What labels do Emirati college students use for linguistic identities of expatriates, including English-medium teachers?
RQ3) How do these labels account for the ethnolinguistic diversity within Abu Dhabi's rich linguistic context?

These research questions emerged from professional engagement as teachers and researchers in the Abu Dhabi setting, where both researchers are residents. When researchers are also participants in the research setting, ethnography as a research method can enable "making sense of our surroundings" (Hammersley, 1998, p. 2) and support an engagement with the setting in which researchers play a part, which "yields empirical data about the lives of people in specific situations" (Spradley, 1979, p. 13). Our interview questioning drew out descriptions anchored in daily practices in order to focus talk on lived experiences with real people. To put it more succinctly, we followed Spradley's (1979) guidance: "don't ask for meaning, ask for use" (p. 97).

The findings shared in this chapter originate from a larger study featuring over 12 hours of transcribed talk with 16 participants over two years of data collection. Among these, 12 participated in four focus group discussions. A year later, a total of ten individual interviews were conducted with six of the original focus group members, as shown below in Table 5.1.

Selected extracts originate from transcribed talk with 16 Emirati college students who took part in focus groups and individual interviews (see Table 5.2). All 16 students belonged to the same incoming cohort, who were among the first

TABLE 5.1 Research design

Tool	*Timeline*	*Data Collected*
1. Focus group discussions	3rd year of a 4-year program	• four transcripts • 12 participants • 3.5 hours of interview data
2. Participant observations	1st semester of the 4th year	• 55 ethnographic field notes

3. In-depth individual interviews	After 2nd semester of the 4th year	• ten transcripts
		• ten participants
		  • six original focus group members
		  • four new participants
		• 9.5 hours of interview data

TABLE 5.2 Participant profiles

Social Profile	*Linguistic Profile*
• 16 female students at an Abu Dhabi teacher training college; • all lived with family members in Abu Dhabi city and suburbs; • all were single at the time of first interviewing • by the end, three were married but one was separated	• all spoke Local Arabic as a mother tongue; • all learned English as a foreign language in primary and secondary school; • all reported exposure to languages other than English and Arabic in daily life (e.g., Hindi, Urdu, Farsi, and Tagalog)

wave of Emirati EMTs. The participants consisted of a homogenous group in the sense that all were graduates from Abu Dhabi government schools. Expected protocols of ethics clearance and use of pseudonyms were applied to ensure anonymity of the students. Details of the social and linguistic profiles are shared in Table 5.2.

Although the interviews were conducted mostly in English, participants were informed they could use their full linguistic repertoires during the interviews. Many participants used Arabic and English flexibly, particularly when demonstrating linguistic repertoires practiced at the site. Holmes et al. (2013) argue that flexible communicative exchanges are multilingual processes and explain that that mixing languages can be used strategically by researcher and researcher participants. Accordingly, the interviews became a situated space to not only talk about but also demonstrate linguistic repertoires.

A deductive and inductive approach of thematic analysis (Braun & Clarke, 2006) was used to code data into themes according to interactant type and phase of socialization (Berger & Luckmann, 1971). Six extracts have been selected to exemplify the quality of social interactions with a range of English users. In asking about face-to-face interactions, we sought to provide theoretical insights reflecting "typification of one's own and other performances" (Berger & Luckmann, 1971, p. 89). In other words, we sought descriptive accounts of interactant type and reported linguistic performances, including details about frequency, intensity, and degree of commitment to using English or Arabic. To this end, codes developed into themes showing positions taken in relation to the following: English use (i.e., as bilinguals who needed support, agents of language maintenance, or agents of language shift); English users, including expatriate teachers and other residents (i.e., as in-group or out-group members); as well as accounts of language performances, including quality of descriptions about ethnolinguistic diversity.

Findings and discussion

The findings highlighted ways Emirati students in an English-medium teacher training college described English users in the UAE, including themselves and their teachers. Three key themes were identified, as shown in in Figure 5.1.

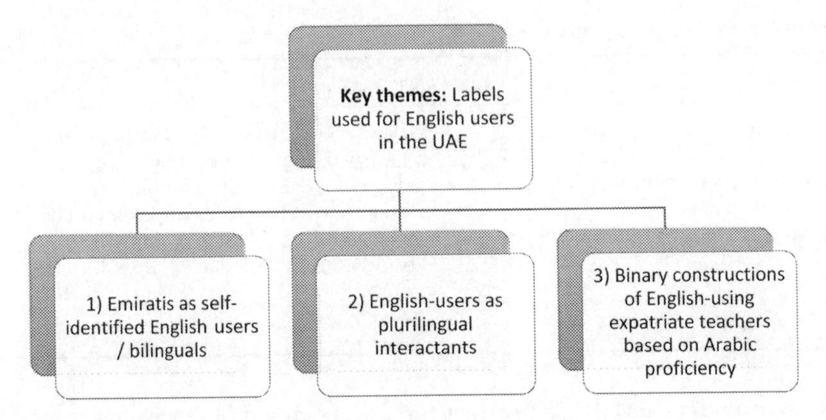

FIGURE 5.1 Key themes: labels used for English users in the UAE

Theme 1: Emiratis as self-identified bilingual English users

Throughout the interviews, the Emirati participants often referred to themselves as bilingual English users. As bilinguals, several accounts specified a capacity to think and speak in English and Arabic and mediate for non-bilinguals. In Interview 1, Hibah refered to herself as a bilingual with proficiency in English and Arabic. Hibah's use of "we" shows she included herself within a group of bilingual peers.

Extract 1

> We think in English. [...] I think in English. [...] I am good at English and I am good at Arabic as well
>
> *(Hibah, Individual Interview 1)*

Khaloud from Interview 4 described her skillset as a novice English-medium teacher, which entailed modeling English use for the next generation of bilinguals. She admitted her shock upon observing students' capacity to interpret content from a teacher–parent interview for their parents. Extract 2 highlights her "moment of awareness" (Kohler, 2015, p. 136) that her students could mediate between "two cultural and linguistic frames of reference" (p. 143), being the teacher's explanation in English recast as reported speech into Arabic for non-English-speaking parents.

Extract 2

> Most of them, they are comfortable in English. They even translate the Eng - when we met their parents in the meeting, some of them translate for their parents. That was AMAZING *(with emphasis)* for me. That shocked me. She said and translated for her. 'The teachers say like this' and 'She mentioned like this', 'She means like this'.
>
> *(Khaloud, Individual Interview 4)*

This theme exemplifies Emirati self-perceptions as bilingual English users who mediated between thinking and speaking in two languages. Extracts 1 and 2 show that this practice was affiliated with two generations. The extracts also signal a sense of agency invoked by the participants when describing the significance of their students' linguistic behaviours in relation to broader patterns of societal bilingualism. Khaloud's narration provides her firsthand account when discovering her students had developed a capacity to mediate for members of an older generation who could not speak English.

Theme 2: English users as plurilingual interactants

Several participants described encounters with expatriates in public domains. These accounts showed a readiness to decide on the spot to use either Arabic or English for *lingua franca* communication. When asked to specify with whom they decided to use English, various labels appeared showing a fuzzy conception of "foreigner." Probing revealed that out-group membership categories were based on lack of Arabic proficiency. This finding is consistent with an earlier study where English is used "with foreign people who don't speak Arabic" (van den Hoven, 2014, p. 72). Other illustrations of "foreign" and "foreign speakers" showed fuzzy categories of social groups (Smart, 2003), loosely connected to difference.

In the following extract, Iman initially reported that English was used with foreigners but subsequently alluded to diversity using the word "different" to qualify both language spoken and place of origin.

Extract 3

> "foreign speaker[s] … different speakers from different countries"
>
> *(Iman, Focus Group 2)*

Extract 3 shows "foreigners" nominated as English speakers Iman met in public spaces. In this way, she signaled an emergent awareness of plurilinguals within wider society but also her limited range of vocabulary for ethnolinguistic diversity.

In Extract 4, Saeeda explained that the public domain featured the use of English as an international language and refered to Asians as a subgroup of English-using expatriates.

Extract 4

> Asian people [… since] they all, *yani,* all, it's international, *yani,* as you know, language so everybody talking in English. And if we want anything we talk in English with them, everywhere.
>
> *(Saeeda, Individual Interview 2)*

Frequent interactions with Asian speakers of English reified its value as an international language and, arguably, an Asian language as well (Kachru, 1998; Kirkpatrick, 2011). Saeeda's account shows she self-identified as an Emirati English user within interactional spaces hosting international English speakers. She later elaborated that interactions with non-Asians, such as Egyptians, could occur in English or Arabic; however, English was used with Egyptians in particular transactional zones, such as fast food restaurants.

Extracts 3 and 4 are shared to signal an emergent awareness of the plurilingual expatriates with the use of generic descriptive words, such as foreign, international, and different. These extracts show constructions of outsiders as interactants from Asia as well as from Egypt who use English as a *lingua franca*. However, the quality of the descriptions does not demonstrate rich intercultural knowledge of other English-speaking residents in their midst.

Theme 3: Binary constructions of English-using expatriate teachers based on Arabic proficiency

There were no references to expatriate teachers showing associations with cultural forms of contamination (Davidson, 2005). Participants spoke well of their teachers in ways that showed respect and familiarity, such as by identifying them by title and first name (e.g., Dr. Melanie or Dr. Sarah). There were no references showing teachers ranked as better or worse in terms of nationality. Furthermore, there were no references to "native or non-native" English speaker in any of the transcripts. As summed up by Saeeda, teachers are a respected group of English users, valued for professional service.

Extract 5

> [They prepare] "everything for us."
>
> *(Saeeda, Individual Interview 2)*

Extract 6 shows a general satisfaction with the quality of intercultural interactions in the college. It also shows groupings based on profession.

Extract 6

> I see the foreign. First time I went - I sit with foreign - like teachers, the administrators, how they communicate. I seem - they are more serious … [than] in schools
>
> *(Fatma, Individual Interview 8)*

In Extract 6, Fatma described her first exposure to English users at the college. Despite her accurate use of professional roles, her vocabulary for the identities of expatriates is limited to "the foreign." There were no other classifications of teachers in our data set based on citizenship, subject matter expertise, or gender.

Follow-up questions pursuing details of the "foreigners" encountered in educational and other domains showed the use of two categories. Binary constructions of foreigners with Arabic proficiency and foreigners without Arabic proficiency appeared in several transcripts. Both groups of foreigners are cast as out-group members, who co-exist within a shared speech environment where English or Arabic supported *lingua franca* communication. However, Arabic was the first choice for *lingua franca* communication, and if non-Arabic speaking status was determined, English became the default choice.

Labels used showed classifications into two categories of English-medium teachers: 1) bilingual, Arab and Arabic, or 2) foreign and English. Several accounts featured labels of English-medium teachers refering to bilinguals as Arabs and Arabic speakers, but foreigners were non-users of Arabic with no other linguistic profiles identified (e.g., Portuguese or Romanian). This conception of "foreign" delineated non-Arab social groups and is similar to reports shared in Bristol-Rhys's (2010) ethnographic study on Emirati women. These labels also resonate with binary constructions of linguistic profiles of Abu Dhabi school teachers established in a local English newspaper at this time as either "Arab" for AMTs or "Westerner" for EMTs (Pennington, 2015). In our data set, the plurilingual identities of English-medium teachers were based primarily on their proficiency in Arabic rather than proficiency in English or other languages.

Implications

Our study explored Emirati students' use of labels to describe a range of English users. As Emiratis, the participants self-identified as bilingual users but the plurilingial identities of other expatriate non-Arabic users evoked no similar labels. This finding offers theoretical insights for processes of "othering" in UAE classrooms (Garces-Bacsal et al., 2021). Our study challenges assumptions of in-group and out-group membership based on English proficiency to highlight the first choice of Arabic for *lingua franca* communication.

Labels for the plurilingual identities of people living in Abu Dhabi were limited to bilingual English users, "foreigners," and international users of English. Asians and Egyptians were the only English-using expatriates nominated in terms of place of origin. Firsthand encounters using English in malls, cafés, and educational domains among a range of different people who could not use Arabic appeared as rationales for the use of English as a default *lingua franca*. Participants cast English-medium teachers as belonging to their educational worlds, suggesting familiar and respectful relational bonds, but there were no illustrative examples of rich vocabulary for their teacher's linguistic profiles.

Given the merit of international teachers in Arab University Rankings, educational zones can be reconceptualized as preparatory sites for developing lifelong communicative practices with an array of transnational migrants. While the intercultural interactions among students and teachers were described in warm and professional tones, there was little evidence of curiosity in knowing how to describe the plurilingual identities of their teachers. An apparent satisfaction with binary classifications linked to Arabic–English dichotomies appeared.

These findings can be discussed within arguments in favor of the development of intercultural competencies within UAE classrooms. By prioritizing critical language awareness as an outcome of learning, then the plurilingual identities of all members of Arabian Peninsula educational settings can be cast as a resource for learning. As suggested by Galante et al. (2022), the value of a plurilingual approach to teaching is the promotion of critical awareness of societal multilingualism, relatability, and empathy. Similarly, Nickerson (2015) argued that intercultural competencies, such as communication effectiveness in diverse multilingual and multicultural teams, should be the forefront of the curriculum given the overall diversity in UAE workplaces. However, as warned by Garces-Bacsal et al. (2021), ways of speaking about "intercultural others" can appear as essentialism and teachers must first be sensitive to the use of ready-made stereotypes.

One takeaway is attending to the multilayering of diversity within resident and citizen population groups. The disproportionate ratio of expatriate teachers to national teachers in the UAE could be viewed favorably for enhancing meaningful conversations about cross-cultural and linguistic differences beyond national paradigms. Accounts of *lingua franca* communication in English and Arabic in Arabian Peninsula contexts and daily encounters of societal multilingualism are adequate justifications for framing expatriate teachers as a resource for greater linguistic awareness.

Limited term contracts, however, position expatriate teachers as mobile academics. Policy makers and administrators can orient to the aims of plurilingual pedagogy by starting with prioritizing intercultural learning as a lifelong benefit. While patterns of contractual employment for international academics will continue to see mobile educators on a "brain train" (Knight, 2009, p. 116), educational leaders in the region can view mobile academics as a "brain gain" for the local context. One way this can be achieved is by recognizing the linguistic repertoires of all the members of the educational domain. Another way is to capitalize on students' apparent interest in various languages they recognize as belonging to the region (i.e., Hindi, Urdu, Farsi, and Tagalog/Filipino), and other languages they want to learn out of cultural interest, such as Korean (van den Hoven & Carroll, 2017).

Expatriate teachers themselves can also promote greater linguistic awareness and respect for ethnolinguistic diversity via recommended tasks for classroom-based learning (Galante et al., 2022). In addition to language research assignments, teachers can also host elective language awareness sessions and other linguistic diversity events as per the tradition of Dubai's Global Village. Teachers can also sponsor language clubs by inviting connections with other community members. Such initiatives operationalize an under-realized dimension of intercultural awareness in UAE classrooms and ultimately promote "we" orientations showing how "they" belong to "us" when viewing all residents in the Arabian Peninsula as community members in a shared linguistic ecology.

Conclusion

This chapter reviewed "us" and "them" orientations and shared labels assigned to a range of English users in an Abu Dhabi educational context. Our study targeted Emirati students' perspectives of expatriate teachers in an EMI context in Abu Dhabi, where Emiratis as host nationals interacted with teachers of different nationalities. While the literature used categories of social class, gender, and nationality to describe foreign residents, our study shared findings which highlighted references to languages used for *lingua franca* communication. We shared extracts showing that perspectives of plurilingual identities in the Arabian Peninsula were shaped primarily in terms of Arabic proficiency rather than English. Our findings align with broader critiques of the limited value of labels for native or non-native English speakerhood in the World Englishes literature base in ways that, ultimately, reinforce the vitality of Arabic for *lingua franca* communication.

However, in establishing the ways linguistic profiles come to the foreground, the findings also reinforce the gains that can be made with respect to plurilingual pedagogy regarding critical awareness of societal multilingualism (Galante et al., 2022). This chapter then contributes to the literature by documenting a gap in linguistic awareness as seen by an over-reliance on binary constructions when describing intercultural others. We showed that these Emirati students have positive associations of their intercultural interactions with expatriate teachers but lacked adequate vocabulary to describe their plurilingual identities, often relying on generic descriptors or binary constructions of Arab versus foreign. The chapter reinforced the value of recognizing mobile academics as a resource for greater linguistic awareness and provided some practical recommendations for ways to promote an internationalizing outlook. In sum, we argue in favor of the value of daily experiences of *lingua franca* communication among a wide range of language speakers. This can be achieved by recasting teachers in English-medium classrooms as a resource for critical language awareness in ways that allow more talking time about the specific and complex linguistic profiles among Arabic and English users in the region.

References

ADEC. (2013). Curriculum Improvement. Retrieved from https://www.adec.ac.ae/en/Education/KeyInitiatives/Curriculum-Improvement/Pages/default.aspx

Al-Issa, A., & Dahan, L. S. (2011). Global English and endangered Arabic in the United Arab Emirates. In A. Al-Issa & L. S. Dahan (Eds.), *Global English and Arabic: Issues of language, culture, and identity* (Vol. 31, pp. 1–22). Peter Lang.

AlMutawa, R. (2020). "Glitzy" malls and coffee shops: Everyday places of belonging and social contestation in Dubai. *Arab Studies Journal, 28*(2), 44–75.

Aneja, G. A. (2016). Rethinking nativeness: Toward a dynamic paradigm of (Non)Native speakering. *Critical Inquiry in Language Studies, 13*(4), 351–379. https://doi.org/10.1080/15427587.2016.1185373

Aslan, E., & Thompson, A. S. (2017). Are they really "two different species"? Implicitly elicited student perceptions about NEST s and NNEST s. *TESOL Journal, 8*(2), 277–294.

Badri, M., & Al Khaili, M. (2014). Migration of P–12 education from its current state to one of high quality: The aspirations of Abu Dhabi. *Policy Futures in Education, 12*(2), 200–220.

Barnawi, O. Z. (2022). Branding in transnational English medium instruction-oriented universities in the Arabian Gulf: Implications for language policy. *Eurasian Journal of Applied Linguistics, 8*(1), 58–72.

Belhiah, H., & Elhami, M. (2015). English as a medium of instruction in the Gulf: When students and teachers speak. *Language Policy, 14*, 3–23.

Berger, P., & Luckmann, T. (1971). *The social construction of reality*. Penguin.

Blommaert, J. (2013). *Ethnography, superdiversity and linguistic landscapes*. Multilingual Matters.

Boyle, R. (2011). Patterns of change in English as a lingua franca in the UAE. *International Journal of Applied Linguistics, 21*(2), 143–161.

Braun, V., & Clarke, V. (2006). Using thematic analysis in psychology. *Qualitative Research in Psychology, 3*(2), 77–101.

Bristol-Rhys, J. (2010). *Emirati women: Generations of change*. Hurst.

Buckingham, L. (2017). *Language, identity and education on the Arabian Peninsula: Bilingual policies in a multilingual context*. Multilingual Matters.

Carroll, K., & van den Hoven, M. (2017). Translanguaging within higher education in the United Arab Emirates. In C. M. Mazak, & K. Carroll (Eds.), *Translanguaging practices in higher education: Beyond monolingual ideologies* (pp. 141–156). Multilingual Matters.

Cook, V. (2016). Where is the native speaker now? *TESOL Quarterly, 50*(1), 186–189.

Cook, W. (2021). A tale of two cafés: Spatial production as de facto language policy. *Current Issues in Language Planning*, 22(5), 535–552.

Dahan, L. (2007). English as an international language in the Arabian Gulf: Student and teacher views of the role of culture. In S. Midrij, A. Jendli, & A. Sellami (Eds.), *Research in ELT contexts* (pp. 158–172). TESOL Arabia.

Davidson, C. (2005). *The United Arab Emirates: A study in survival*. Lynne Rienner Publishers.

Elyas, T., & Mahboob, A. (2021). World Englishes in the Middle East and North Africa (MENA): Wiley Online Library.

Fulton, J. (2019). Friends with benefits: China's partnership diplomacy in the Gulf. *Shifting Global Politics and the Middle East*, 34(1)33–38.

Fulton, J., & Sim, L.-C. (2018). *External powers and the Gulf monarchies*. Routledge.

Galante, A., Chiras, M., & Zeaiter, L. (2022). Plurilingual guide: Implementing critical plurilingual pedagogy in language education. Plurilingual Lab Publishing. Retrieved from https://www.mcgill.ca/plurilinguallab/files/plurilinguallab/plurilingual_guide.pdf

Gallagher, K. (2011). Bilingual education in the UAE: Factors, variables and critical questions. *Education, Business and Society: Contemporary Middle Eastern Issues, 4*(1), 62–79.

Garces-Bacsal, R. M., Tupas, R., Alhosani, N. M., & Elhoweris, H. (2021). Teachers' perceptions of diversity and 'others' in United Arab Emirates (UAE) Schools. *Pedagogy, Culture & Society*, 1–19. https:/doi.org/10.1080/14681366.2021.2011774

Gardner, A. M. (2011). Gulf migration and the family. *Journal of Arabian Studies, 1*(1), 3–25.

Hammersley, M. (1998). *Reading ethnographic research*. Longman.

Higgins, C. (2003). "Ownership" of English in the outer circle: An alternative to the NS-NNS dichotomy. *TESOL Quarterly, 37*(4), 615–644.

Holliday, A. (2002). The struggle against 'us' - 'them' conceptualizations in TESOL as the ownership of English changes. In Z. Syed, C. Coombe, & S. Troudi (Eds.), *Critical reflection and practice: Selected papers from the 2002 international conference*. TESOL Arabia.

Holmes, P., Fay, R., Andrews, J., & Attia, M. (2013). Researching multilingually: New theoretical and methodological directions. *International Journal of Applied Linguistics, 23*(3), 285–299.

Hopkyns, S. (2014). The effect of global English on culture and identity in the UAE: A double-edged sword. *Learning and Teaching in Higher Education: Gulf Perspectives, 11*(2).

Hopkyns, S. (2020). *The impact of global English on cultural identities in the United Arab Emirates: Wanted not welcome*. Routledge.

Hopkyns, S. (2022). A global conversation on native-speakerism: Towards promoting diversity in English language teaching. In K. Hemmy & Balasubramanian (Eds.), *World Englishes, global classrooms: The future of English literary and linguistic studies*. Springer.

Hopkyns, S., & van den Hoven, M. (2022). Linguistic diversity and inclusion in Abu Dhabi's linguistic landscape during the COVID-19 period. *Multilingua, 41*(2), 201–232.

Kachru, B. (1992). *The other tongue: English across cultures* (2nd ed.). University of Illinois Press.

Kachru, B. (1998). English as an Asian language. *Links & Letters, 5*(1998), 89–108.

Kapiszewkski, A. (2001). *Nationals and expatriates – population and labour dilemmas of the Gulf cooperation council States*. Garnet.

Karmani, S. (2005). Islam, English, and 9/11. *Journal of Language, Identity, and Education, 4*(2), 157–172.

Kennetz, K., van den Hoven, M., & Parkman, S. (2011). Arab students' attitudes towards varieties of English. *Teaching and learning in the Arab world* (pp. 139–159). Peter Lang.

King, M. J. (2013). Championing Indian TESOL teachers in the Arabian Gulf. *Journal of ESL Teachers and Learners, 2*, 163–170.

Kirkpatrick, A. (2011). English as an Asian lingua Franca and the multilingual model of ELT. *Language Teaching, 44*(02), 212–224.

Knight, J. (2009). New developments and unintended consequences: Whither thou goest, internationalization. In R. Bhandari & S. Laughlin (Eds.), *Higher Education on the Move: New Developments in Global Mobility* (pp. 113–125). Institute for International Education.

Kohler, M. (2015). *Teachers as mediators in the foreign language classroom*. Multilingual Matters.

Lian, K. F., Hosoda, N., & Ishii, M. (2019). Introduction: Migrants in the Middle East and Asia *International labour migration in the middle East and Asia: Issues of inclusion and exclusion* (Vol. 8, pp. 1–13). Springer Nature.

Lootah, M. S. (2011). Assessing educational policies in the UAE *Education in the UAE: Current status and future developments* (pp. 27–52). The Emirates Center for Strategic Studies and Research.

Mahboob, A., & Golden, R. (2013). Looking for native speakers of English: Discrimination in English language teaching job advertisements. *Age, 3*(18), 21.

Matsuda, A. (2012). Teaching English as an international language. In A. Matsuda (Ed.), *Principles and practices of teaching English as an international language* (pp. 1–14). Multilingual Matters.

McLaren, P. B. (2011). *English medium in the United Arab Emirates: Serving local or global needs?* (Doctor of Education). University of Exeter, Exeter.

Medgyes, P. (1992). Native or non-native: Who's worth more? *ELT Journal, 46*, 340–349.

Moussly, R. (2009, November 22 2009). No one wants to teach. *Gulf News*. Retrieved from https://gulfnews.com/general/no-one-wants-to-teach-1.530676

Nickerson, C. (2015). Unity in diversity: The view from the (UAE) classroom. *Language Teaching, 48*(02), 235–249.

Pennington, R. (2015, August 23, 2015). ADEC gives a warm welcome to 500 Arab staff. *The National*. Retrieved from http://www.thenational.ae/uae/education/adec-gives-a-warm-welcome-to-500-arab-staff

Rampton, M. B. H. (1990). Displacing the 'native speaker': Expertise, affiliation, and inheritance.

Seargeant, P. (2010). Naming and defining in World Englishes. *World Englishes, 29*(1), 97–113.

Seargeant, P. (2012). *Exploring World Englishes: Language in a global context*. Routledge.

Smart, A. (2003). Sharp edges, fuzzy categories and transborder networks: Managing and housing new arrivals in Hong Kong. *Ethnic and Racial Studies, 26*(2), 218–233.

Spradley, J. P. (1979). *The ethnographic interview*. Holt, Rinehart and Winston.

Syed, Z. (2003). TESOL in the Gulf. *TESOL Quarterly, 37*(2), 337–341.

THE. (2021). Arab University Rankings 2021: methodology. Retrieved from https://www.timeshighereducation.com/world-university-rankings/arab-university-rankings-2021-methodology

Troudi, S., & Jendli, A. (2011). Emirati students' experiences of English as a medium of instruction. In A. Al-Issa, & L. Dahan (Eds.), *Global English and Arabic: Issues of language, culture, and dentity* (pp. 23–48). Peter Lang.

van den Hoven, M. (2014). The use of English for education in the Arab world. In K. Bailey, & R. Damerow (Eds.), *Teaching and learning English in the Arabic-speaking world* (pp. 65–82). Routledge.

van den Hoven, M., & Carroll, K. (2017). Emirati pre-service teachers' perspectives of Abu Dhabi's rich linguistic context. In L. Buckingham (Ed.), *Language, identity and education on the Arabian Peninsula: Bilingual policies in a multilingual context* (pp. 39–58). Multilingual Matters.

van den Hoven, M., & Carroll, K. (2021). English-medium policy and English conversational patterns in the UAE. *World Englishes, 40*(2), 205–218.

Walsh, K. (2014). Placing transnational migrants through comparative research: British migrant belonging in five GCC cities. *Population, Space and Place, 20*(1), 1–17.

6

PLURILINGUAL PEDAGOGY IN HIGHER EDUCATION IN THE UAE

Student voices in an academic writing course

Daniela Coelho

Introduction

The United Arab Emirates (UAE) is a country with a population consisting of approximately 85% of expatriates, i.e., roughly 15% are locals (World Population Review, 2020). Such multicultural community brings into the country a variety of cultures and languages, with 58% of non-UAE nationals being South Asian (e.g., Indian, Bangladeshi, and Pakistani), 17% being Asians (e.g., Filipinos), and 8.5% from Western origin (e.g., American and English) (World Population Review, 2020). The official language is Arabic; however, given the population diversity, English, Hindi, and Urdu are quite present in the daily lives of residents (World Population Review, 2020). There is no need for a foreign visitor or resident of the UAE to speak or understand Arabic since English is utilized as the *lingua franca* in the country (Siemund, Al-Issa & Leimburger, 2020 citing Barnawi, 2017). Often, Emiratis need to resort to English in shops, cafés, and restaurants as staff does not speak Arabic.

There is a certain "linguistic dualism" (Findlow, 2006) present in the UAE with Arabic usually associated with tradition, religion, cultural authenticity, and localism, while English appears linked with modernity, internationalism, business, and material status (Findlow, 2006). English is regarded as the language of globalization that will make current students become more marketable and skilled to embrace the future highly competitive marketplaces (Kennetz & Carroll, 2018). This has resulted in a national language policy that has been intensifying the presence of English in school and higher education curricula (Baker, 2017) on a quest to promote bilingualism among its citizens (Al Hussein & Gitsaki, 2018). The great majority of higher education institutions follow an English-medium instruction (EMI) model with mainly only Arabic, Islamic, or law courses being delivered in Arabic. Therefore, as stated by Al Hussein and

DOI: 10.4324/9781003315971-9

Gitsaki (2018), "in present day UAE, English language proficiency has become for Emiratis a prerequisite to pursuing higher education in their own country" (p. 103 & 104).

In this current scenario, the prevalence of underperformance in English among local students is another issue (Baker, 2017) as it may compromise academic progress. Finding methodologies that support these students and foster success in EMI contexts has become a concern of some present day educators in the UAE. Scholars and educators are calling for more research on pedagogical methods that enhance motivation and learning (Baker, 2017 citing Lambelet & Berthele, 2015). In the current applied linguistics and language education field, the *multilingual turn* (May, 2014) opened room for discussions on approaches that go beyond the traditional monolingual outlook and embrace plurilingualism. Pedagogies such as the *plurilingual approach* (also referred to as *translanguaging* – see introduction to this volume for clarification of terms) seem to be receiving attention from teachers who have multilingual classes, including in the UAE. Adopting a plurilingual pedagogy in teaching and learning means creating a learning environment where the cultural and linguistic repertoires of the students are welcome and seen as a resource for learning. It builds on the learners' previous language knowledge to support and enhance learning of another language and "highlights synthesis of language and cultural resources and competence, rather than just the idea of many or multiple [languages]" (Lau & Van Viegen, 2020, p. 12). In fact, the *English as an International Language (EIL) National Unified K-12 Learning Standards Framework* (Ministry of Education, 2014) encourages the use of Arabic in the learning of English:

> To master English, students will have to be able to make comparisons between Arabic and English languages and to accommodate them automatically. (…) As students start using English, they should be allowed—and even encouraged—to augment their speaking and writing with Arabic words and phrases because the goal is to communicate with others and get feedback on their efforts.
>
> *(p. 19)*

Research on plurilingual practices in K-12 educational contexts have recently been flourishing, while such studies in higher education are still limited, specifically in the Arab states of the Gulf (Hillman et al., 2019). Similarly, while plurilingual/translanguaging practices are gaining popularity, students' attitudes and perspectives regarding such pedagogical methodologies are often disregarded (Rivera & Mazak, 2017). Canagarajah (2011) highlighted that "it is important for teachers to learn from them [learners] rather than impose their own views of how code-meshing works. Additionally, we cannot generalize for all students and impose a one-size-fits-all pedagogy" (p. 415). Imposing pedagogical strategies that do not produce engagement and interest from the students may potentially hinder learning from the start (Rivera & Mazak, 2017).

With this in mind, this research study aims to gather student opinions on the plurilingual practices encouraged in an academic writing course delivered in a private UAE university throughout three terms with three different student cohorts. This study's research questions are the following:

- What are the perceptions of HE students in the UAE on the use of plurilingual pedagogy in their academic writing course mainly in terms of their receptivity and motivation?
- What are the affordances of such approach for their learning in the students' opinions?

Plurilingual pedagogy in other language writing: Teacher and student reports

Before describing the uses and benefits of plurilingual pedagogy in teaching and learning, it is worth inviting our reader to revisit the introduction to this volume for a clear understanding of similarities and differences between plurilingual pedagogy and translanguaging, since, for the purpose of this particular chapter, plurilingual pedagogy will be the preferred term, but translanguaging may sometimes arise in our discourse as a synonymous term. Our understanding is that they can be used interchangeably, but when referring to a specific research study, we will apply the same term used by the study's author.

In current literature, plurilingual pedagogy/translanguaging is said to present several benefits. Wei (2018) postulates that translanguaging has the ability to *transform* individuals' cognition and social structures as well as to *transcend* "socially constructed language systems and structures to engage diverse multiple meaning-making systems and subjectivities" (p. 27). García and Kleyn (2016) also mention this "going beyond" concept in which bilinguals and multilinguals start envisaging their language repertoire as one single linguistic system, as opposed to separate named languages, that fosters learning. Wei (2018) states that translanguaging also brings about *transdisciplinary* consequences since it encourages synergy between linguistics, psychology, sociology, and education.

Moody et al. (2019) listed four other benefits of translanguaging practices in classrooms based on García's work. One of them is that they support student learning especially when they are involved in complex tasks, and secondly, they facilitate the use of analytical and explanatory skills in those same tasks. In addition, translanguaging fosters a classroom environment where all languages known by the students are at the same level, and it contributes to students feeling valued as they are allowed to use their full linguistic repertoires to participate in class and to develop personal learning strategies. This concurs with Cummins's (2007) perspective that whenever other languages are used as a "cognitive and linguistic resource" (p. 238), they can work as a scaffolding system that improves performance in other languages.

Payant (2019) seems to be in agreement with Cummins's claim as she highlighted that breaking the monolingual bias has had a positive impact in the language learning process of the students she surveyed. These students reported advantages at the level of language functions, i.e., by drawing comparisons or making translations while learning grammatical structures or vocabulary, they became more proficient in those topics. Benefits were also identified in the discourse-level functions with students' first language (L1)/home language or other languages being used while generating ideas or negotiating content. Task-related functions were also recognized as ones in which other languages can be helpful, especially in understanding instructions or planning the task. Similarly, Hillman et al. (2019) explained that scaffolding tasks, such as translating a word or brainstorming in L1/home language, leveraged deeper learning because the students are applying their full linguistic repertoire to engage in such tasks.

Other advantages related to social aspects have been pointed out as well. For instance, Hillman et al. (2019) reported that the use of other languages, namely the students' L1/home language, builds good relationships between the teacher and students as it may "cultivate a shared identity, and create a positive classroom climate" (p. 43). In the same way, teachers resort to students' L1/home language to clarify topics and even for disciplinary reasons which may have positive impacts on classroom management. In agreement, based on the students' opinions, Payant (2019) announced advantages at the level of social functions as well. Examples of these could be supporting a peer in better understanding a topic or building or maintaining classroom social relationships.

As far as writing in particular is concerned, teacher and student voices have acknowledged a number of reasons for the accountability of plurilingual practices in the classroom. To begin with, when students were allowed to shift between languages, their writing pieces analyzed by Chen et al. (2019) presented better quality because students were able to generate more ideas and plan their writing better. Enriched content, professional writing, and better language were some of the elements of the quality mentioned above by Chen et al. (2019). Seltzer (2020) accounts for this *connectedness* in writing when students are allowed to translanguage:

> Asking students to talk through their linguistic choices, to discuss how they might have translanguaged in their writing (even if the piece is rendered in one named language), and to explain their choices in relationship to their audience shifts the writing process from a disconnected, product-driven school task to an authentic, meaningful practice.
>
> *(Seltzer, 2020, p. 202)*

Velasco and García (2014) argued that translingual practices are not only evident but natural in bilinguals and multilinguals' writing process, and often applied for rhetorical engagement and effectiveness. Cooperation between languages during writing was also deemed important and instinctive in bilingual and multilingual writers by Tullock and Fernandez-Villanueva (2013) who noticed the use of other languages as a strategic choice. In their study, Weijen et al. (2009) obtained similar results. They reported that even though writers used L1/home language with varying purposes and levels, their L1/home language was undoubtedly somehow ubiquitous in the second language writing, and that the presence of L1/home language was more important for weaker writers. In a similar manner, Adamson and Coulson (2015) detailed advantages for the lower proficiency students, stating that in-class L1/home language use decreased anxiety and allowed for extended time allotted for the tasks themselves.

Gunnarsson et al. (2015) describe foreign language writing as a *multilingual event* spontaneously arising. Therefore, they believe shuttling between languages should be allowed, especially when generating and organizing ideas as these seem to have been the functions in which *plurilingualizing* exposed more advantages according to students in their study. Cognitive gains were the most noted benefits to students in the study carried out by Carstens (2016). Translanguaging allowed these students to understand complex concepts "to differentiate between related concepts, and to express conceptual content" (Carstens, 2016, p. 218).

Bearing this in mind, the applied linguistics, language education, and second language acquisition communities seem to be more attentive to the potentialities of such approaches, and even though many voices still may arise in favor of a monolingual approach, particularly in the fields of general English teaching and EMI, the plurilingual shift appears eminent and already widely applied in certain contexts. In a world where globalization brought about more possibilities of studying abroad and the proliferation of EMI in some areas of the world, such as the UAE, Galante et al. (2019) reinforce the fact that in English for Academic Purposes (EAP) settings neglecting the presence of other languages or even other *Englishes* in a classroom should not be overlooked. A "differentiated pedagogy that is linguistically and culturally inclusive" (Galante et al., 2019, p. 123) has a special place and impact in EAP classrooms, so openness from teachers would hopefully be expected.

Nevertheless, and as mentioned previously in this chapter, the imposition of such pedagogy in classrooms where students may not be receptive to *plurilingualizing* may compromise learning and engagement (Canagarajah, 2011; Rivera & Mazak, 2017). Listening to students' voices is crucial in the process of implementation of any new pedagogy, method, or technique so that the lessons learned from the students' experiences contribute to shape improved future teaching and learning practices (Coelho & Ortega, 2020). This was a guiding principle in our research study and the one that shaped the methodology and purpose of our research.

Research study context and methodology

In order to understand student perspectives on the use of plurilingual pedagogy, a sample of students taking an academic writing in English Level 1 course in a private university in the UAE was selected. All the students involved were taking the course with the author of this chapter in different sections. The main goal of this course is to prepare students to become good academic writers in order to face the challenges of attending an EMI university. In the first four weeks of the course, the topics covered concern grammatical issues, such as type of sentences, conjunctions, punctuation, and common sentence errors. From then on, the focus moves to paragraph structure and essay writing. Students are asked to write mostly compare and contrast essays and opinion essays. The average size of each section was 25 students at the time, and the majority were segregated (separate female and male sections) with only a few mixed ones. Students placed in Level 1 of this course were usually identified as lower proficiency students after taking a placement test, and upon completion of Level 1, they would have to attend Level 2. Students with higher proficiency in English academic writing would go straight to Level 2 which is a mandatory course for all learners in this university. Level 1 students usually range from students who only need to slightly brush up their writing skills to be able to progress to Level 2 to students who had serious issues with spelling, punctuation, and even capitalization.

Underachievement in English in the UAE is widely discussed in the literature (e.g., Baker, 2017) and has prompted immediate action by the government with the implementation of more presence of English in Arabic curriculum schools. Given the frequent poor performance in English of these students attested by placement tests, as their teacher, the author of this study has been adamant about changing her pedagogical methodologies in order to find better ways to mitigate lower performance and generate genuine engagement and interest in the English classes. Due to her familiarity with plurilingual pedagogy and her ability to function in more than four different languages, and after approval from the Institutional Review Board, an action research plan was designed and implemented by the researcher[1]. Creswell (2012) highlights the fact that action research aims primarily at fostering change and improvement of a given context that has shown some issues which can be done through the application of a new methodology. Following this tenet, the researcher prepared her lessons in such a way that plurilingual pedagogy could emerge in several instances of her teaching; however, no specific rigid plurilingual tasks were planned. Therefore, throughout three terms, these students attended their regular academic writing classes fully delivered in English and aiming to develop English, but in an environment where other known languages were welcome as they saw fit.

Some of the most prominent plurilingual methods encouraged in these classes were as follows:

- translation of terms;
- comparison between languages;
- explanations from colleagues in Arabic or other languages;
- brainstorming in Arabic or other languages;
- planning writing tasks in Arabic or other languages;

- group discussions and peer feedback in Arabic or other languages;
- translanguaging done by the teacher (Arabic, French, and Spanish) to explain certain words/topics or draw comparisons.

After each term came to an end, a survey was distributed among the students taking this course. The questionnaire was first piloted in February 2019 and adjusted so as to have more open-ended questions that would allow the researcher to have a better view of the reasons why students chose certain answers. The improved version was distributed to students throughout the subsequent three terms. In total, the teacher taught around 80 students, but, unfortunately, only 31 responses from participants were gathered since taking part in this study was completely voluntary. Nevertheless, it is believed that the answers from these 31 students will already help draw an initial picture of HE students' perceptions of plurilingual pedagogy in academic writing.

Apart from the usual demographic question related to age groups, it was important to include questions related to nationality and languages spoken so as to provide a general sociolinguistic profile of the students in this study (see Annex 1). The remaining questions aimed to gauge perceptions in three main areas:

- comfort with and receptivity to the plurilingual pedagogy;
- motivation for learning with the plurilingual pedagogy;
- academic success enhancement due to plurilingual pedagogy.

A Likert scale was used with 1 representing "strongly disagree" and 4 "strongly agree." All these questions were followed by a "Why?" question so they could justify their choices on agreeability.

Participants' profile

The great majority of students taking academic writing in English Level 1 are usually freshmen or first year students; therefore, it would be expected that the majority would be in the younger age group. At the time the data were collected, most of the students were between 17 and 20 years old, with nine out of the 31 students in the 21–25 range and only three over 26 years old.

As for their nationalities, as shown in Figure 6.1, the majority of the students came from countries where Arabic is the official language or is widely spoken, such as the Emirates, Jordan, Morocco, Iraq, Syria, Palestine, Yemen, and Egypt. Five other non-Arabic-speaking nationalities were in our sample of students: Bangladeshi, Indian, Cameroonian, Mauritian, and Turkish. It is interesting to notice that both Cameroon and Mauritius have English as one of the official languages.

Regarding their first or home language, 78% of the respondents identified Arabic as their only first language (see Figure 6.2).

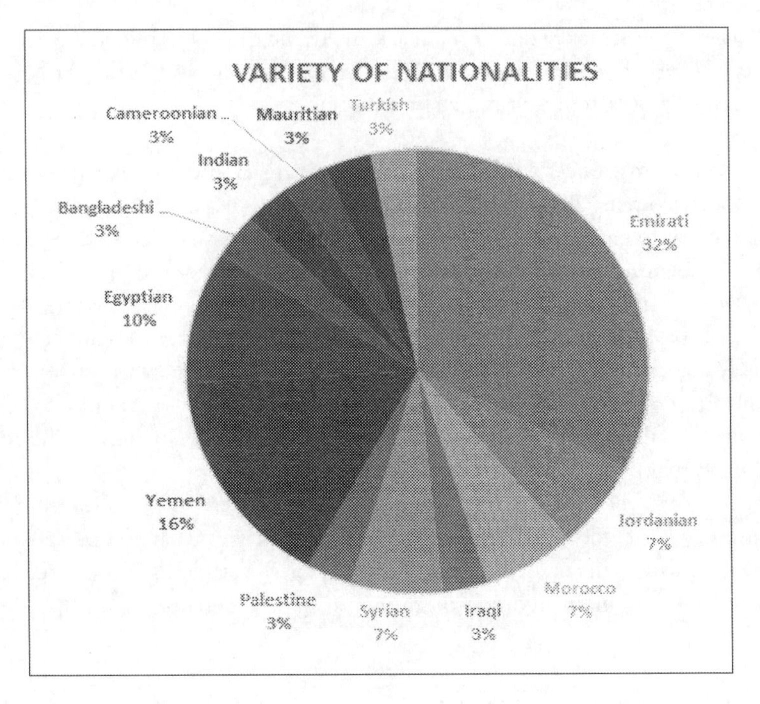

FIGURE 6.1 Nationality of students surveyed

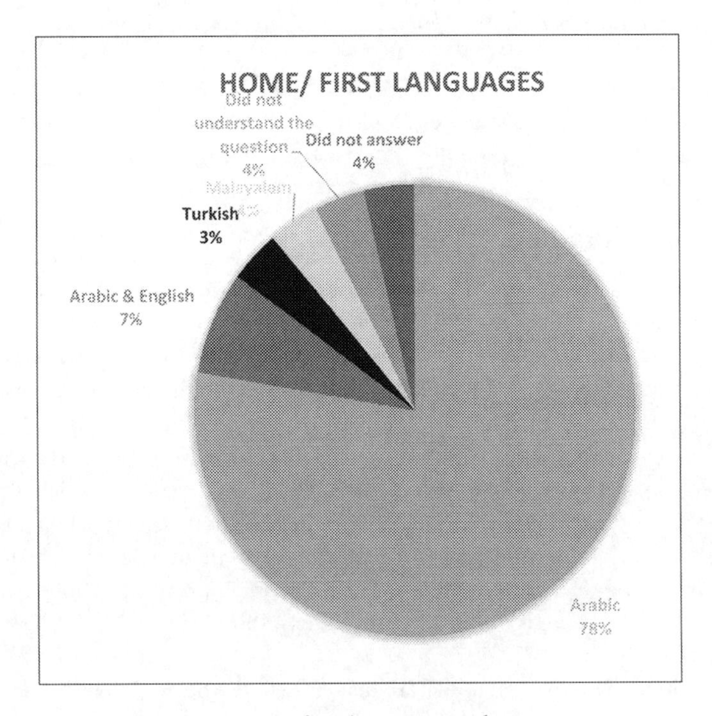

FIGURE 6.2 First/home languages of students surveyed

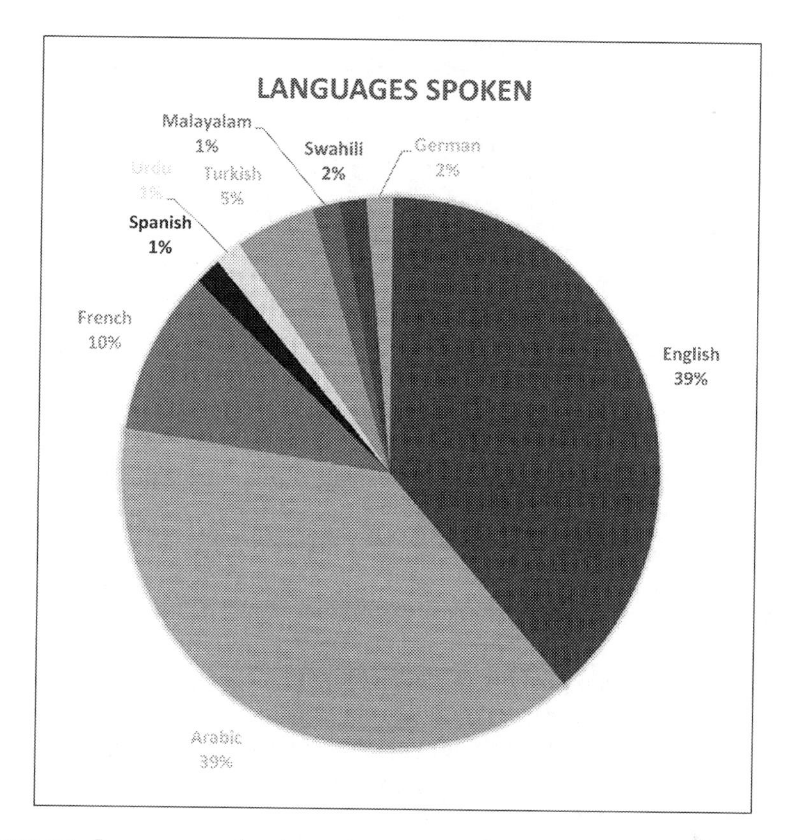

FIGURE 6.3 Languages spoken by students surveyed

Seven percent claimed they had two first languages, Arabic and English, possibly due to the pervasive presence of English in the country both in social and in academic life. Turkish and Malayalam were also represented here with 3% and 4%, respectively. Surprisingly, 8% of the students claimed they did not understand the question or simply did not answer.

When enquired about what languages they spoke, English and Arabic were the most predominant languages with equal percentage of 39% each (see Figure 6.3); however, French was quite well represented as well, and languages such as Spanish, Urdu, Turkish, Malayalam, Swahili, and German appeared too.

It becomes clear that the group of respondents in this study presents a relatively varied linguistic repertoire that goes beyond the official language in the UAE, Arabic, and the *lingua franca* in the country, English.

Results and discussion

As detailed in Annex 1 and described in the methodology section, the first area in which we wanted to collect students' opinions was on their level of receptivity to and comfort with plurilingual pedagogy practices fostered by the teacher

TABLE 6.1 Reasons for agreement with statement 1

Reasons for Agreeing with Statement #1	*Number of Times Mentioned*
Because it is easier to understand the meaning of words/ develop vocabulary.	6
Because it is helpful.	4
Because it makes me feel the teacher is not discriminating.	2
Because I would like to learn a new language.	2
Because it helps avoid misunderstandings	1
Because it shows that the teacher wants to help us understand.	1

during class. In a scale from 1 to 4, respondents had to express their agreement with the statement "I felt comfortable when my teacher encouraged me to use Arabic (or my home language or other languages) in the English class." Around 65% of the respondents chose 4 (strongly agree), and *circa* 25% opted for 3 (agree) with only 6.5% of students stating they disagreed with the practice and around 3% (corresponding to one student) saying they disagreed strongly.

While the great majority was in agreement with the statement, it is important to note the almost 10% on the disagreeing side. To explore this further, a list of reasons for the agreeing and disagreeing side is presented in Tables 6.1 and 6.2.

Table 6.1 shows the reasons presented for why they agreed that using plurilingual pedagogy made them feel comfortable and therefore receptive to such practices. Four respondents claimed plurilingual tasks were helpful in general; however, the remaining students detailed other reasons. Six respondents highlighted how applying a plurilingual stance contributed to specifically vocabulary development which corroborates with Carstens's (2016) study results. Two students stated that using other languages in class represents a way to learn other languages as well, and the same number of students claimed it created a non-discriminatory environment, which was an unexpected answer for the researcher. There was one mention to steering clear of misunderstandings in general, and one mention to the use of plurilingualism by the teacher as an effort on her part to foster understanding.

In general, the majority of the students were receptive to plurilingual tasks with most reasons focusing on better understanding but with brief mentions to opportunities to be exposed to other languages and to a classroom atmosphere that respects linguistic repertoires.

TABLE 6.2 Reasons for disagreement with statement 1

Reasons for Disagreeing with Statement #1	*Number of Times Mentioned*
Because "I would like to have a chance to know the world in Arabic but also speak English in all classes."	1
Because not allowing other languages improves English.	1
Because translating can interfere with English skills.	1

Nonetheless, the 10% who did not seem comfortable with plurilingualism in the classroom stated openly that they would prefer to use English in classes. They presented reasons usually put forward by supporters of the monolingual approach or "target-language only" policy: translation and the use of other languages may interfere with the development of English language skills.

Motivation for learning was the other focal point of our research questions. Comfort in engaging with certain pedagogical methods does not necessarily mean definite motivation for learning, hence our question on how much they agreed with the following statement: "I felt more motivated in the English classes because my teacher does not mind that I use Arabic (or my home language or other languages) for language learning purposes." Here, responses changed slightly but still with more agreeing than disagreeing voices.

In comparison with the previous question, fewer respondents strongly agreed that it was more motivating for their learning to use plurilingual approaches with around 42% stating they agreed. Still, 87% on the agreeing side speaks to the potential motivational features of such pedagogy in the English academic writing classes of these students. Thirteen percent showed disagreement, and this percentage is slightly higher on the disagreement side when compared with the comfort question.

As in the first question, reasons for the level of agreement were requested. Table 6.3 shows the reasons for those who agreed with the statement. Despite the initial claim that motivation is not necessarily generated by the level of comfort students feel with certain methods, the truth is the most popular reason presented by respondents in this question was that they felt more motivated because they felt comfortable at the same time. There seems to be a sense that creating an atmosphere where they feel unworried about using other languages may generate more motivation as well. This was mentioned in Adamson and Coulson (2015) when they highlighted the fact that using L1/home languages in classes decreased anxiety. Similarly, there is an understanding that such approaches may

TABLE 6.3 Reasons for agreement with statement 2

Reasons for Agreeing with Statement #2	*Number of Times Mentioned*
Because it makes me feel comfortable.	5
Because I already know the meanings of words which were translated into Arabic/home languages.	3
Because ALL students will understand.	2
Because the teacher makes an effort to find the meaning in Arabic even if she does not know it.	1
Because it developed Arabic language.	1
Because I can do better.	1
Because I'm allowed to think in Arabic/home language for the "main things" ("to say our ideas") and then use English for "the details."	1
Because it is beneficial.	1

motivate learning since the knowledge of word meanings makes students feel more positive about their understanding of concepts and terms needed to master the subject. There are also mentions to general understanding on the part of all students as an appreciation for an inclusive practice that allows students of different linguistic abilities and repertoires to understand classes. This might have a direct connection with one mention to plurilingualism being beneficial in general and being a promoter of academic success ("I can do better"). One student expressed interest in being able to shift between languages depending on the task or skill they needed to work on ("main ideas" and "details") in their writing. There was reference to an appreciation for the teacher's effort to find meanings in Arabic so students understood the class topics even if she did not know the terms in Arabic. This has also been reported in Hillman et al. (2019), with L1/home language use regarded as the creator of a good student/teacher relationship in class. Finally, one interesting reason was that using Arabic would help develop Arabic too.

The great majority of the students who regard plurilingual pedagogy as creator of motivation highlight reasons related to comfort, better understanding of topics, and inclusive learning.

For the 13% that disagreed with feelings of increased motivation when a plurilingual approach was applied, the reason is unanimous and rather redundant even though only two out of four students in the disagreement side detailed the reason: "because I feel more motivated if I use English." There seems to be a strong connection between "target-language only" and motivation for these students.

Some students had mentioned in their reasons that the use of plurilingual practices in the classroom made them feel they could perform better in the course. The third area of focus of this study falls exactly on academic success, i.e., besides motivation and comfort, the purpose was to know if the plurilingual practices had a positive impact on their learning in practical terms and, if so, in which areas. Respondents were asked to show their level of agreement with the following statement: "I believe the use of Arabic (or my home language or other languages) helped me learn better in the English classes."

Approximately 77% of the respondents agreed with the statement, out of which 48.4% strongly agreed. It is evident that for these students learning was enhanced through plurilingual practices. On the disagreeing side, nevertheless, we have around 23% who do not see academic benefits in the use of plurilingual tasks in class. This represents almost one quarter of the respondents, meaning that even though comfort and motivation when involved in plurilingual activities were significant for the majority of the surveyed students, slightly fewer students felt that such methodology had a practical impact on their academic success.

The reasons expressed for agreement with the statement are presented in Table 6.4. Strong connections were made between the ability to translate words and learning better in the classes, with this reason appearing nine times in the students' justifications. Translation is here seen as a powerful method to facilitate

TABLE 6.4 Reasons for agreement with statement 3

Reasons for Agreeing with Statement #3	*Number of Times Mentioned*
Because I can translate the meanings of words.	9
Because it helps understanding.	6
Because my first language (Arabic) is easier for me, so it supported the learning of English.	3
Because it facilitates learning for me.	2
Because it is beneficial.	1

learning because it enables the understanding of fundamental vocabulary as it was described in Hillman et al.'s (2019) study as well. General understanding of topics covered was also mentioned six times in the students' answers as a factor that contributed directly to enhanced learning. In addition, engaging in plurilingual tasks in this course was regarded as a means to facilitate learning in general two times, and the use of the first language (with specific mention to Arabic in most cases) as a support language was mentioned three times. Students seemed to see L1/home language use as conducive to better learning. There was one general and rather vague mention to plurilingual practices being simply beneficial.

Regarding the reasons for disagreement with the statement, not all students presented a reason, but some justifications were gathered in Table 6.5. The top reason was that students did not feel their learning was positively impacted because they already were quite proficient in English. This seems to be in concert with Weijen et al.'s (2009) study results because they too noticed higher achieving students did not seem to resort much to other languages in the learning process. One student expressed her/his preference in using only English as the method to achieve "perfection" in the language, meaning that she/he believes her/his learning advances more when using "target-language only" practices. One interesting justification was that the Arabic language was not understood or spoken by one of the students. Even though the researcher's classroom practices encouraged the use of any language known by the students in class, it is perceptible that, given that the majority of the students were Arabic speakers, this language might have been the language emerging more often in the plurilingual tasks. There could be a potential feeling of discomfort with or even disapproval

TABLE 6.5 Reasons for disagreement with statement 3

Reasons for Disagreeing with Statement #3	*Number of Times Mentioned*
Because I already have good knowledge of English.	2
Because using only English helps me write the "perfect grammar."	1
Because I do not understand or speak Arabic.	1
Because I can compare and understand.	*1*

of a practice that could be making this student feel left out; however, the student might have not understood that all languages were welcome.

Finally, curiously, one student mentioned a reason that does not seem to support his/her disagreement with this pedagogy: "because I can compare and understand." It seems unclear what kind of comparison is being referred to in this statement, but it appears that it could be comparisons between languages. If that is the case, this indicates that such practice seems to be positive for this student's learning.

Conclusion

The student cohorts of many universities in the UAE can be quite diverse culturally and linguistically. In the case of our study in particular, the student population was from 13 different countries and presented a diversified linguistic repertoire. Other than Arabic, French, Spanish, and Swahili were some of the languages known by the students. In fact, almost 20% of the students surveyed said they spoke three different languages and 13% claimed they could function in four different languages. According to plurilingual pedagogical principles, such linguistic wealth cannot be neglected in current superdiverse multilingual classes, especially in the English for Academic Purposes courses in EMI models (Galante et al., 2019). With this in mind, and considering the several advantages of translanguaging methods in academic writing mentioned by previous authors (e.g., Adamson & Coulson, 2015; Carstens, 2016; Chen et al., 2019; Seltzer, 2020; Velasco & García, 2014; Weijen et al., 2009), an action plan was designed aiming to incorporate plurilingual practices in the academic writing in English Level 1 course while class delivery in English was ensured at the same time. Due to calls for more student input on how to learn (Canagarajah, 2011; Coelho & Ortega, 2020; Rivera & Mazak, 2017), the main objective of this study was to understand the impact of such methodologies in these students' receptivity to the approach, motivation to learn, and advancement of learning according to the students themselves. This was accomplished via distribution of a survey collecting students' level of agreement with certain statements after they were exposed to plurilingual practices and tasks for one full term in the course mentioned previously.

In order to answer the first research question of this study, we will address comfort/receptivity and motivation separately. Around 90% of students surveyed confirmed enjoyment and openness to the plurilingual practices fostered in classes. The main reasons pointed out for such comfort refer to *better understanding* and *support in learning*, with some mentions to a *non-discriminatory climate*. For these students, it appears that *understanding* is directly correlated with feeling less anxiety (thus more comfort) in learning events, and the plurilingual strategies implemented seem to have worked in favor of that. Therefore, despite the 10% of "nay-sayers" claiming that the use of other languages would interfere with the development of English skills, the three student sections surveyed regarded plurilingual pedagogy through a positive lens.

Regarding motivation, 87% of the students agreed that the inclusion of plurilingual activities made classes more motivating. The leading reason was that these activities generated comfort, making students feel less anxious, which, in turn, fostered interest in learning and, consequently, motivation. This relation between comfort and motivation could also be connected to the fact that students constantly mentioned *understanding* as an important reason behind openness to plurilingual practices. The ability to grasp the topics better with the support of plurilingualism resulted in engagement and willingness to learn for the students. There is no doubt that all of us will feel more in tune with the class if we understand the topic covered completely. Inclusivity was also part of the reasons mentioned by a couple of students. They envisaged plurilingual tasks as a way to not leave anyone out in the learning process, because *everyone* was able to, again, *understand* the topics. However, 13% of the respondents claimed they did not feel more motivated for learning due to the use of other languages in learning. For these students, motivation had a direct connection with English-only practices.

The last research question intended to probe whether plurilingual practices helped students learn English writing better. Roughly 77% agreed that *plurilingualizing* supported their learning. The primary justification for this agreement was that the possibility of translating fostered understanding, thus opening room for more academic success. This focus on *understanding* is a constant in students' answers throughout the different questions. Disagreement was of course also present with the main reason presented relating to the fact that their level of proficiency in English was good enough; therefore, no support from other languages was required. This might actually indicate that these students might see plurilingual practices as only necessary for lower ability students.

Overall, it can be concluded that the majority of the students enrolled in this academic writing course responded positively to the application of plurilingual pedagogies and envisaged them as motivating and conducive to enhanced learning. Listening to these students' perspectives could be a starting point to more open discussions on and possibly a de-stigmatization (Carroll & van den Hoven, 2017) of plurilingual approaches in certain contexts in the UAE. While English continues to be the language of instruction in EMI models, allowing for short instances when other languages can be utilized to support learning could become a future teaching practice if the students are receptive.

These study results may indicate the need for a reflection on potential local language policy adjustments based on multicultural and multilingual student voices.

Limitations and recommendations

This research study has a number of limitations to take into account. To begin with, the generalization of the results obtained in this study to the whole UAE context is not advisable. Only 31 respondents studying in one university participated; such small sample could not represent the country's higher education population. Therefore, subsequent studies with students taking academic writing courses in several universities and colleges in the UAE would be required to accomplish true representation of UAE higher education students' perceptions on this matter.

Secondly, despite the belief that plurilingualism may lead to better in-class learning for the surveyed students, there is some vagueness in how and in which areas this advancement of learning happened. Further to the collection of students' perceptions, gathering information on student progress and overall performance in writing with discrimination of areas where improvement was most significant would have provided better insights into the real potentialities of plurilingual practices with these students as far as learning and academic success are concerned.

Finally, when a student mentioned their unfamiliarity with Arabic, it raised questions on how to better implement plurilingual practices in multilingual classes in order to accommodate diversified backgrounds. It is evident in this student's voice that she/he might have felt excluded when Arabic arose in the plurilingual tasks because she/he could not understand it. While the teacher encouraged the use of all languages represented in this class, languages that other students in class might not know either (e.g., Swahili, French, or Spanish) but which supported the learning of those who knew them, it might not have been clear for this student that she/he, too, could have resorted to other languages known and not feel restricted by the use of Arabic. Nevertheless, this calls for more open discussions, research studies, and experiments that explore the practical application of such approach in multilingual classes. Although benefits have been highlighted and students may appear receptive to plurilingual pedagogy, it is imperative to implement it without compromising inclusivity, as this may contribute to disengagement instead of working as a catalyst of learning.

Note

1 This research study was supported by the Office of Research and Sponsored Programs of Abu Dhabi University through an Action Research and Teaching and Learning Grant.

Bibliographic references

Adamson, J., & Coulson, D. (2015). Translanguaging in English academic writing preparation. *International Journal of Pedagogies and Learning, 10*(1), 24–37.

Al Hussein, M., & Gitsaki, C. (2018). Foreign language learning policy in the United Arab Emirates: Local and global agents of change. In C. Chua, & S. Kheng (Eds.), *Un(intended) language planning in a globalising world: Multiple levels of players at work* (pp. 97–112). De Gruyter.

Baker, F. S. (2017). National pride and the new school model: English Language education in Abu Dhabi, UAE. In R. Kirkpatrick (Ed.), *English Language education policy in the middle East and North Africa. Language policy, 13* (pp. 279–300). Springer.

Canagarajah, S. (2011). Codemeshing in academic writing: Identifying teachable strategies of translanguaging. *Modern Language Journal, 95*, 401–417.

Carstens, A. (2016). Translanguaging as a vehicle for L2 acquisition and L1 development: Students' perceptions. *Language Matters, 47*(2), 203–222.

Carroll, K. S., & van den Hoven, M. (2017). Translanguaging within higher education in the United Arab Emirates. In C. M. Mazak, & K. S. Carroll (Eds.), *Translanguaging in higher education: Beyond monolingual ideologies* (pp. 141–156). Multilingual Matters.

Chen, F., Tsai, S., & Tsou, W. (2019). The application of translanguaging in an English for specific purposes writing course. *English Teaching & Learning, 43*(1), 65–83.

Coelho, D., & Ortega, Y. (2020). Pluralistic approaches in early language education: Shifting paradigms in language didactics. In S. Lau, & S. Van Viegen (Eds.), *Plurilingual pedagogies: Critical and creative endeavors for equitable language (in) education* (pp. 145–160). Springer.

Council of Europe (2021). A framework of reference for pluralistic approaches to languages and cultures. https://carap.ecml.at/

Creswell, J. W. (2012). *Educational research. Planning, conducting, and evaluating quantitative and qualitative research*. Pearson.

Cummins, J. (2007). Rethinking monolingual instructional strategies in multilingual classrooms. *Canadian Journal of Applied Linguistics/Revue Canadienne de Linguistique Appliquée, 10*(2), 221–240.

Findlow, S. (2006). Higher education and linguistic dualism in the Arab Gulf. *British Journal of Sociology of Education, 27*(1), 19–36.

Galante, A., Okubo, K., Cole, C., Elkader, N., Carozza, N., Wilkinson, C., Wotton, C., & Vasic, J. (2019). plurilingualism in higher education: A collaborative initiative for the implementation of plurilingual pedagogy in an English for academic purposes program at a Canadian university. *TESL Canada Journal, 36*(1), 121–133.

García, O., & Kleyn, T. (2016). Translanguaging theory in education. In O. García, & T. Kleyn (Eds.), *Translanguaging with multilingual students. Learning from classroom moments* (pp. 9–33). Routledge.

Gunnarsson, T., Housen, A., van de Weijer, J., & Kallkvist, M. (2015). Multilingual students' self-reported use of their language repertoires when writing in English. *Apples – Journal of Applied Language Studies, 9*(1), 1–21.

Hillman, S., Graham, K., & Eslami, Z. (2019). Teachers' translanguaging ideologies and practices at an international branch campus in Qatar. *English Teaching & Learning, 43*(1), 41–63.

Kennetz, K., & Carroll, K. S. (2018). Language threat in the United Arab Emirates?: Unpacking domains of language use. *International Journal of the Sociology of Language, 254*, 165–184.

Lau, S. M. C., & Van Viegen, S. (2020). Plurilingual pedagogies: An introduction. In S. Lau, & S. Van Viegen (Eds.), *Plurilingual pedagogies: Critical and creative endeavors for equitable language (in) education* (pp. 3–22). Springer.

May, S. (2014). Introducing the "Multilingual Turn". In S. May (Ed.), *The multilingual turn: Implications for SLA, TESOL and bilingual education* (pp. 1–6). Routledge.

Ministry of Education (UAE) (2014). *English as an International Language (EIL)* National Unified K-12 Learning Standards Framework.

Moody, S., Chowdhury, M., & Eslami, Z. (2019). Graduate students' perceptions of translanguaging. *English Teaching & Learning, 43*(1), 85–103.

Payant, C. (2019, March 5). *Plurilingual Approaches to Language Instruction from the Language Learners' Perspective* [Video]. YouTube. https://www.youtube.com/watch?v=gVH7fetfwOc

Rivera, A. J., & Mazak, C. M. (2017). Analyzing student perceptions on translanguaging: A case study of a Puerto Rican university classroom. *How, 24*(1), 122–138.
Seltzer, K. (2020). Translingual writers as mentors in a high school "English" classroom. In S. Lau, & S. Van Viegen (Eds.), *Plurilingual pedagogies: Critical and creative endeavors for equitable language (in) education* (pp. 185–204). Springer.
Siemund, P., Al-Issa, A., & Leimgruber, J. R. E. (2020). Multilingualism and the role of English in the United Arab Emirates. *World Englishes, 40*(2), 191–2044.
Tullock, B. D., & Fernandez-Villanueva, M. (2013). The role of previously learned languages in the thought processes of multilingual writers at the Deutsche Schule Barcelona. *Research in the Teaching of English, 47*(4), 420–441.
Velasco, P., & García, O. (2014). Translanguaging and the writing of bilingual learners. *Bilingual Research Journal, 37*(1), 6–23.
Wei, L. (2018). Translanguaging as a practical theory of language. *Applied Linguistics, 39*(1), 9–30.
Weijen, D., Bergh, H., Rijlaarsdam, G., & Sanders, T. (2009). L1 use during L2 writing: An empirical study of a complex phenomenon. *Journal of Second Language Writing, 18*, 235–250.
World Population Review (2020, January 19). United Arab Emirates Population 2020. https://worldpopulationreview.com/countries/united-arab-emirates-population

ANNEX 1

Demographic questions

1. How old are you? – Choose the appropriate age range.
    - 17–20
    - 21–25
    - 26–30
    - Above 30
2. What nationality are you?
3. Write all the languages you speak/know on the line below.
4. Which would you say is your first language?

Study questions

Please read the questions below and choose ONE answer only.

On the scale presented for each question below, 1 means you DO NOT AGREE at all with the statement and 4 means you AGREE entirely.

1. I felt comfortable when my teacher encouraged me to use Arabic (or my home language or other languages) in the English classes.
    - 1 strongly disagree
    - 2 disagree
    - 3 agree
    - 4 strongly agree

Why?

2. I felt more motivated in the English classes because my teacher does not mind that I use Arabic (or my home language or other languages) for language learning purposes.

    - 1 strongly disagree
    - 2 disagree
    - 3 agree
    - 4 strongly agree

Why?

3. I believe the use of Arabic (or my home language or other languages) helped me learn better in the English classes.

    - 1 strongly disagree
    - 2 disagree
    - 3 agree
    - 4 strongly agree

Why?

7

EXPANDING COMMUNICATIVE REPERTOIRES THROUGH PLURILINGUAL PEDAGOGIES IN INTERNATIONAL BRANCH CAMPUS CLASSROOMS IN QATAR

Sara Hillman, Dudley Reynolds, and Aymen Elsheikh

Introduction

The internationalization and "Englishization" of higher education have become a phenomenon across the world and are intricately linked to neoliberal ideologies, policies, and practices (Barnawi, 2018; Phan, 2017; Phan & Barnawi, 2015). As part of this phenomenon, there has been an exponential growth of English as a medium of instruction (EMI) in national universities (Macaro et al., 2018) and English-medium international branch campuses (IBCs), with their parent institutions largely based in the United States and United Kingdom (De Costa et al., 2021). In many of these institutions, EMI may be interpreted as English only and local languages ignored (Sahan & Rose, 2021). This is often motivated by neoliberal and political agendas, pushing for monolingual practices in the classroom (see Sahan & Rose, 2021; Sahan et al., 2022). In English-medium IBC contexts, the use of local and indigenous languages may be viewed as not fulfilling contractual obligations with home institutions or funding institutions to offer equivalent degree programs or as going against the conceptualization that IBCs should mirror their home campuses as much as possible in terms of curricula, academic rigor, reputation, and tradition (Graham et al., 2021).

While EMI and IBC institutions of higher education continue to spread around the world, there has simultaneously been an ideological and multilingual shift happening in applied linguistics, moving away from monolingual pedagogies and English-only policies in the classroom to multilingual/translingual/plurilingual pedagogies (see Cenoz & Gorter, 2013; Conteh & Meier, 2014; Kubota, 2016; Losey & Shuck, 2022; Ollerhead et al., 2018; Piccardo, 2013; Raza et al., 2021; Tian et al., 2021). While the various prefixes (multi-, trans-, and pluri-) overlap in the literature in various ways, Ollerhead et al. (2018) describe

DOI: 10.4324/9781003315971-10

how multilingualism "denotes several different languages co-existing in a given physical location or social context, [while] the term 'plurilingualism' accounts for the ways in which individuals' linguistic repertories overlap and intersect and develop in different ways with respect to languages, dialects, and registers" (p. 1). Both translingual and plurilingual pedagogies see learners' ability to draw on multiple resources for effective communication as an asset rather than a deficit. Research on plurilingual pedagogy has also shown how "creating space in classrooms for students to use all of their communicative knowledge has numerous benefits, not the least of which is supporting students' writing development in English" (Losey & Shuck, 2022, pp. 3–4). As part of this shift, the English instructors' goal is no longer to help students be monolingual English speakers and follow native speaker models, but to become more multilingual (Raza et al., 2021) and to expand their communicative repertoires – this includes all the linguistic and semiotic resources and other means of communication that students use to function in the various communities in which they participate (Rymes, 2010). Semiotic resources refer to the "totality of semiotic resources that people use when they communicate (such as speech, image, text, gesture, sign, gaze, facial expression, posture, objects, and so on)" (Kusters, 2021, para. 1). Contrary to monolingual ideologies, this does not have to come at the expense of developing students' English skills. Tian et al. (2021) describe how we can "value, leverage, and even sustain students' home/community languages, cultures, and identities while expanding their repertoire to include 'English' features" (Tian et al., 2021, p. 10).

In this chapter, we first discuss some of the monolingual biases of U.S.-based IBCs in the State of Qatar, the context in which the three authors of this chapter teach. Arabic is the only official language of Qatar, but English is widely used as a lingua franca among Qatar's diverse residents and as a medium of instruction for higher education in IBCs and some national university programs (Hillman & Ocampo Eibenschutz, 2018). All three of us are applied linguists and English teachers who teach English writing courses and other core elective content courses, such as intercultural communication. Though there is a contractual agreement between our home campuses and Qatar Foundation (QF) (the organization funding the IBCs where we work) to teach in English and home campuses need to approve our courses, we all have some agency in the way we design our courses and how they are delivered (see Reynolds, 2021a for an example of this). After a discussion of the monolingual biases in the IBCs, we each reflect on ways we have shifted ideologically away from the monolingual mindset to implement plurilingual pedagogy which empowers our students who communicate using multiple languages, varieties, modalities, and semiotic resources. Specifically, we each share examples of writing assignments we have transformed over time to better tap into our students' full linguistic and semiotic repertoires, with the goal being not only to improve their writing skills in English but also to expand their full communicative repertoires.

IBC classrooms in Qatar and monolingual biases

In the interest of increasing the percentage of Qatari nationals in the workforce and moving away from its dependence on hydrocarbons to build a more knowledge-based economy, Qatar has made education one of its highest priorities. As part of this priority, QF, a state-led, non-profit organization focused on education, research, and development, has established many prestigious, English-medium IBCs. QF describes the IBCs as offering a "global education in a Middle Eastern setting" (Qatar Foundation, 2022, para. 1). According to the Cross-Border Education Research Team (2020), there are 11 IBCs total in Qatar, most of them branches of U.S.-based universities. The leadership and faculty of the IBCs often come from the home campuses, and as mentioned earlier, IBCs are supposed to offer an equivalent curriculum to their home campus programs (Graham et al., 2021). Qatari nationals make up somewhere between 35 and 80% of the student body population of individual IBCs that are part of QF, with the remaining population being mostly expatriate resident students and international students from other parts of the Arab world, Iran, Europe, and South Asia.

Although QF has announced a "commitment to preserving and celebrating the richness of the Arabic language and promoting its enduring relevance to the world" (Qatar Foundation 2020, para. 3), this has not necessarily been applied in IBC classrooms. Monolingual biases in Qatar's IBCs have been reported in a handful of previous studies by us as well as other applied linguist scholars who have worked in the IBCs (e.g., Graham & Eslami, 2020; Graham et al., 2020; Graham et al., 2021; Hillman et al., 2019, 2021; Kane, 2014; Nebel, 2017; Pessoa & Rajakumar, 2011; Reynolds, 2021a). First, the fact that IBCs are English medium acts as a gatekeeper, excluding many local citizens and residents who may not be able to score high enough on standardized English proficiency tests required for admissions to the IBCs (Jenkins, 2014; Reynolds, 2021a). Additionally, Graham et al. (2021) describe how "monolingual and monocultural norms of the Western home campus are often directly imported into the local context without a critical examination of their appropriateness" (p. 2). Furthermore, Graham and Eslami (2020) describe strong monolingual ideologies at IBCs and describe how "EMI seems to suggest a clear principle—only English will be used" (p. 9). When instructors at one IBC were asked if they use Arabic during instruction, a survey respondent wrote, "[University name] is an American university; English is the official language" (Hillman et al., 2019, p. 49). Another instructor responded during an interview regarding the same question, "They came here, it's all English, so they should expect that everybody speaks English" (p. 50). Kane (2014) describes how the faculty at an IBC medical college were discouraged from using Arabic. However, Hillman et al. (2019) also showed how instructors' monolingual biases did not always mean that only English was used in IBC classrooms. They explain that "how this policy is interpreted and implemented in the local processes of teaching appears to be more complex and nuanced" (Hillman et al., 2021, p. 245), and we still know little overall about the language policies and pedagogical practices enacted in IBC classrooms. Tensions between monolingual policies and ideologies and actual multilingual practices in EMI campuses have been documented in a number of other studies around the world, such as found in Jenkins and Mauranen's (2019) volume on linguistic diversity in EMI campuses.

From the perspective of students, Pessoa and Rajakumar (2011) state that IBC students have a desire to feel confident in both English and Arabic, and yet "students in English-medium universities have very limited exposure to written Arabic and voiced their concerns about their ability to conduct themselves academically and professionally in Arabic" (p. 160). Kane (2014) reports similar concerns from medical IBC students who need Arabic for clinical settings in Qatar but struggle to use Arabic after receiving all their medical training through EMI. Furthermore, IBC students have also expressed strong emotions about the impact of EMI on their cultural and linguistic identities, such as feeling shame that their English is better than their Arabic or being shamed by their family or members of their community for mixing English with Arabic (Hillman, 2022). Hillman et al. (2021) report that their IBC student participants were generally positive toward the idea of using Arabic along with English at their IBC. The researchers found that "students viewed Arabic use as a right and a way to maintain and celebrate their identity" (p. 246), and some felt that it was helpful when instructors, for example, translated key disciplinary vocabulary into Arabic.

While Hillman et al. (2021) and Nebel (2017) discuss how some faculty are engaged in plurilingual pedagogy at IBCs, many students are still not invited to draw on their various linguistic and cultural resources within IBC classrooms in Qatar. For many IBC instructors, their focus is more on teaching the content, which is delivered only through English, or if it is an English class, they are focused on developing students' writing skills in English. Pedagogical approaches at IBCs tend to still reinforce monolingual ideologies and do not work to expand students' multilingual capabilities and their full communicative repertoires. In the next section, we each describe how our ideologies about teaching English or EMI content courses have shifted and how we have incorporated a more plurilingual approach or "plurilingual stance" (Ollerhead et al, 2018) into our own classrooms through either minor tweaks or more significant changes to our course writing assignments.

Dudley's plurilingual writing assignment in a first-year writing course at CMUQ

In fall 2020, after 13 years of teaching Carnegie Mellon University in Qatar (CMUQ)'s first-semester, first-year writing course with multiple iterations of course themes and writing assignments, I introduced a novel tweak to the final major writing assignment: I encouraged students to include sources they could understand in languages other than English. I had never told students they could <u>not</u> use sources in languages other than English; I had simply never discussed the possibility. Over the years, very few students had ever used, or even asked if they could use, non-English sources. The assumption of both faculty and students at this IBC was that the language of an "English" course would be English.

Most CMUQ students enter the university with advanced literacy skills in multiple languages. CMUQ's class of 2021 comprised 95 students representing 23 nationalities, and almost all reported being multilingual (*CMU-Q Class of 2021*, 2021). Approximately 40% of each CMUQ class are Qatari citizens. If they studied in a government-funded high school, then the primary language of instruction was Arabic. If they studied in a private school, then the primary language of instruction was probably English, but they would have been offered religion and social studies courses in Arabic. Another approximately 40% of students are expatriate Qatar residents who have studied in schools that follow the national curricula of their home countries or an international curriculum such as International Baccalaureate®, GCE A-level, or Advanced Placement. The language of instruction in these schools is often English dominant but with some courses taught in other languages. The final group of students are classified by CMUQ as "international students," with the majority from Europe, Asia, and Africa. These students are more likely to have had a significant portion of their prior schooling in languages other than English, but they also have had the opportunity to learn and practice English to a degree that allows them to meet CMUQ's admission standards: 102 on the TOEFL iBT, 7.5 IELTS (Carnegie Mellon University, 2021).

Given the likelihood that CMUQ students' pre-university education had involved learning in multiple languages, it is strange that the university should be assumed to be an English-only environment. However, as has been well discussed in the literature, neoliberal public policies trumpeting the need for competitiveness (Phan & Barnawi, 2015; Reynolds, 2019) have propelled IBCs and other manifestations of transnational higher education to promote themselves as pathways to socially empowering command of English (Reynolds, 2021a, 2021b). Within the university, the implicit goal of commanding English merges with monolingual ideologies of what that would mean (Blommaert & Rampton, 2012; Gogolin, 1997), ideologies that pit the learning of English against the use of other languages. My class was also labeled as an "English" class, and all the assigned readings were in English. The combined force of ideology and experience had been sufficient to suppress even a question about whether sources in languages other than English could be used.

In the fall of 2020, however, I had just finished authoring a research report on how educational systems around the world were adapting to the forces of migration and globalization by promoting multilingualism (Reynolds, 2019), and I was feeling increasingly uneasy about my own complicitness in the promotion of English at the expense of other languages. When other faculty teaching the composition course suggested that we change our major paper to one where students would need to apply course readings to the analysis of a case, I saw an opportunity. The course theme was the role of civil society in promoting social development and human welfare, and students were to choose a particular civil society organization or type of organization as the case for their paper. We also made clear to students that in order to talk authoritatively about their case, they would need sources.

When I introduced the assignment in class and the need for a case, I began by encouraging the students to choose an organization that they found interesting and for which they could find information about its activities. I then suggested that it would be fine if the sources were in a language other than English, drawing on ideologies and pedagogy of scholars working in multilingual composition (e.g., Hesson et al., 2014; Horner et al., 2011). This caught some of the students by surprise, and so I used this as a "teaching moment." We talked about what would make having studied at an English-medium university useful to them in the future. I told them about conversations I had had with alumni who had to use English but also Arabic in the workplace and use both languages multimodally or who had been hired by international companies because of their competences in languages other than English. We also talked about language loss and what happens when we stop using a language that we may have studied previously.

After the introduction of the assignment, we asked the students to submit proposals identifying the organization they had chosen for the case and how they could create an argument around it. They also had to list sources they would be using to document their information. Many of the international students chose organizations from their home countries, and many of the Qatari chose organizations from Qatar. The expatriate residents sometimes chose organizations from Qatar and sometimes from the country of their citizenship. As might be expected, some students proposed what was probably the first organization that showed up when they entered "civil society organization" in an internet search engine. My feedback for these students was again to encourage them to choose an organization that had more relevance to issues that mattered to them. When it came to listing sources, many students still seemed to default to sources in English, if, for example, the organization had a website in English. A number, however, took my advice and listed sources in languages other than English. This created another teaching moment, with also a focus on semiotic resources; we discussed citations and how to cite non-English sources.

It is difficult to assess definitively the impact of allowing non-English sources. As I write up the change a year and a half later, however, I can say that I still remember papers where students got excited about their topic because they were learning things about their own countries that they did not know and creating arguments that felt meaningful to them. This past fall, when I taught the course again, I repeated my encouragement to find opportunities to work in multiple languages when writing. Again, the papers that stand out for me now are ones where students had a deeper knowledge of their organization and its geopolitical context; knowledge that was often gathered from a language other than English.

Sara's plurilingual writing assignment in a foundation English course at TAMUQ

The first year that I taught our lowest level of foundation English students at Texas A&M University at Qatar (TAMUQ) back in 2015, I started with a reflective essay in which I asked students to "Describe your relationship with writing." I would provide my students with some possible topics to focus on, such as follows:

- *How do you feel about writing?*
- *How has your relationship with writing changed over the years?*
- *How do you feel when you write in English?*
- *How does writing relate to your identity and culture?*
- *What has your experience with writing been like?*
- *What are your strengths and weaknesses with regard to writing?*
- *What strategies do you employ when writing?*
- *What are your future goals with regard to writing?*

At TAMUQ, students are required to have a minimum overall band score of 6.0 to be fully admitted, but they need a 7.0 to enroll in their first-year rhetoric and composition course. Students who only score 6.0 or 6.5 are required to take an in-house English placement test and may spend from one to three semesters in foundation English courses before they can enroll in most of the required courses for their major (Hillman et al., 2021). Since TAMUQ's inception, the foundation English program has been intricately linked with the percentage of Qatari national students admitted into the branch campus. Meeting TAMUQ's English language entry requirements can be challenging for students who attend Arabic-medium schools, and approximately 70% of incoming Qatari national students at TAMUQ place into the foundation English program each year. Thus, the students we teach in foundation English classes are mostly bilingual Arabic–English Qatari nationals.

When I assigned students the reflective essay, most students' essays would only focus on how they struggle to write in English and they never explored, for example, any writing they do in Modern Standard Arabic or even colloquial Arabic, or how they might draw on certain resources from both Arabic and English when writing, and so forth. Because it was by name a foundation *English* class, it seemed that any other forms of knowledge they had that were not related to English, they did not consider when drafting their essays. They also never used any Arabic in their essays, not even a few transliterated words.

After teaching this class that first year, I began to read a lot about the multilingual and plurilingual turn in language teaching though (Cenoz & Gorter, 2013; Conteh & Meier, 2014; Kubota, 2016; Losey & Shuck, 2022; Ollerhead et al., 2018; Piccardo, 2013; Raza et al., 2021; Tian et al., 2021) and attended many conference sessions on this topic. As I grew as a researcher and teacher, I started to reflect more on how my students' relationship with writing was not just about

English and how writing about their experiences only through English did not likely express their lived experiences. Gustavo Pérez Firmat, a famous Cuban American writer, wrote in a dedication to his volume of poetry entitled *Bilingual Blues* that writing in English about not belonging to English already falsified what he wanted to tell his readers. He questioned how he could explain to his audience that he does not belong in English through the medium of English. Like Firmat's view of "translingualism as an impossible necessity" (Kellman, 2003, p. 293), I felt that my students needed to be able to draw on their full linguistic repertoires to be able to reflect on their relationship with writing in a way that moved beyond monolingual biases.

Thus, in the second year that I taught this course, I began to transform this assignment into a plurilingual literacy narrative, and more recently, it has developed into a semester-long project that I continue to tweak. Students are first introduced to pluri-/translingual mentor texts (Machado & Flores, 2021); these serve as models for ways of sharing perspectives and emotions *about* writing in different named languages and *through* translingual practice (Canagarajah, 2013b; Horner et al., 2011). I start by reading a poem aloud to students called "Laila Shikaki, Bilingual" (Shikaki, 2013). Below is an excerpt of the poem in which the author describes her feelings toward using Arabic versus English to express herself:

> *naeeman* I say when my best friend shows me pictures of her new haircut,
> or I talk to my mother who just left the shower.
> when baba comes home, mama says, *yaeteek il afya*,
> and when I see a worker at the office I say the same thing.
> but in English I'm tongue tied,
> and I have to say good afternoon or have a good night,
> but I want to say *yaeteek il afya*,
> as in may God give you more strength,
> as in I appreciate what you are doing.
> but in English it sounds flat,
> no emotion. just simple words written and read.
> yet when it comes to Arabic love words, I am silenced.
> *bahibak* is too much to handle.
> I like you sounds better to a friend and a potential lover.
> I miss you sounds less commitment-filled than *ishtaqtilak*
> and poetry read in Arabic reads heavier on my heart,
> and words written in English sound easier on my tongue.

We first have an oral discussion about the poem, and then students do an in-class writing, responding to questions such as follows:

- *What is Laila Shikaki expressing in this poem?*
- *How does she make meaning?*
- *Do you ever mix languages together like this poem?*
- *How do you feel about mixing languages?*
- *How do you use different languages to express yourself and make sense of the world?*

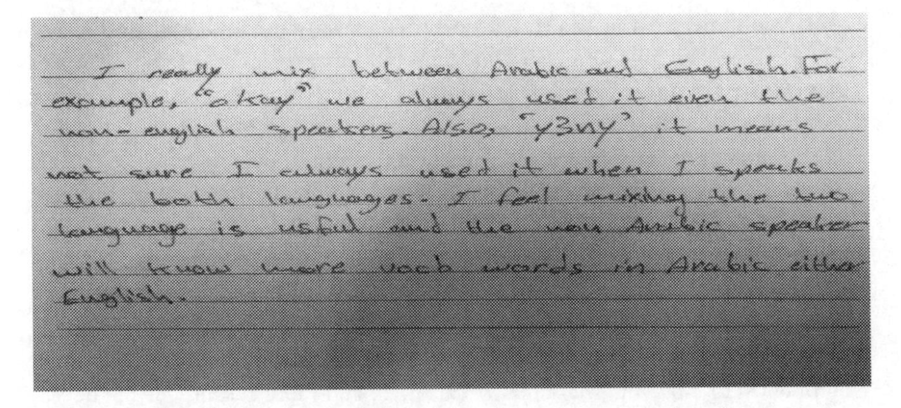

FIGURE 7.1 Example of student's in-class writing about mixing languages

Figures 7.1 and 7.2 show some examples of students' in-class writings about mixing languages and using different languages to express themselves. In Figure 7.1, the student writes, "I really mix between Arabic and English" and "I feel mixing the two language is useful." In Figure 7.2, the student writes, "I feel each language has its unique meaning and way of expressing emotion, relating to the poem I fully support the idea of using English does not fully express emotions [like] Arabic does."

After we read this poem, I have students read other examples of translingual mentor texts like the introduction to *Cuando era puertorriqueña* by the author Esmeralda Santiago in which she describes how, "I have found myself in limbo between Spanish and English, wanting to say something that I, caught up in a frustrating linguistic void, could not express" (Kellman, 2003, p. 131) and Rosario Ferré's reflection on being bilingual in Puerto Rico and the differences she feels when writing in Spanish versus English (Ferré, 2003, p. 137). We also read Gabriel Okara's reflection on writing in Nigerian English to express African

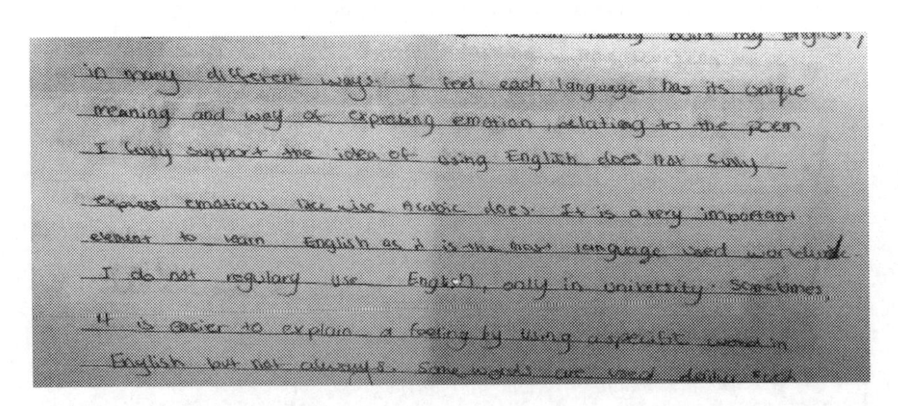

FIGURE 7.2 Example of student's in-class writing about using different languages to express herself

experiences and how he uses "the idioms of his own language in a way that is understandable in English" (Okara, 2003, p. 187), and other unpublished literacy narratives from bilingual Arabic–English teachers and students.

Students then write their own translingual literacy narratives (an idea adapted from Canagarajah, 2020), exploring their emotions about learning or using the languages they know. Students are told in the assignment guidelines, "You should feel free to use both Arabic and English (or other languages) in your writing if it helps to communicate an idea better. Not everything has to be translated into English. You should also feel free to use nonverbal signs and symbols, color, or different font sizes, if it helps to express meaning better. For example, you can use emojis, memes, or pictures if you want." In other words, students are encouraged to "negotiate diverse languages and semiotic resources in the composing process" (Canagarajah, 2020) if it helps them to better express their literacy journeys and feelings about named languages. Students receive feedback on their literacy narratives from me and their peers and usually revise it at least two times. The revision process not only helps them to develop their English features in writing but also pushes them to think about how best to express meaning through a variety of linguistic and semiotic resources.

The last thing that students do is present their written narratives through a multimodal video, which allows them to draw on diverse resources beyond just words. This multimodality allows them to use "photos, symbols, other graphics, text, audio, and video in producing and consuming meaning" (Losey & Shuck, 2022, p. 7), thus also helping to expand their semiotic repertoires. In the end, students have a multilingual, multimodal product of their literacy journeys that captures so much more of their lived experiences than what students used to produce in my original reflection paper assignment, which was biased toward their experiences just with English literacy.

Aymen's plurilingual pedagogy in foundation English courses

Like Sara, I teach foundation English students at TAMUQ. My ideologies toward teaching English have also shifted over the past decade, and I have increasingly taken a more plurilingual approach. I believe that being a bilingual (Arabic and English) and sharing the students' first language (Arabic) can bridge the gap between transnational educators and their students. While the use of the first language is often discouraged at other institutions in the Gulf region and beyond, we are fortunate to have some agency in terms of how we teach our foundation English courses at TAMUQ.

So that my language ideologies and teaching approaches are not alien to my students, I usually introduce them to concepts such as translanguaging (García et al., 2017) and demonstrate how it can be used for language learning and identity development purposes. One of the focused activities I do with my foundation students is to ask them to read part of a story and then complete it, using background knowledge and their own creativity, in both English and Arabic. Below is an example of a text I use from a popular Qatari folktale (Fakhro, 2017, para. 4).

> Out in the open waters of the Arabian Gulf, the seafarers are fast asleep after a long day of diving for pearls. These precious hours are key to recuperate before dawn arrives and they have to start all over again, a grueling cycle that keeps going for months on end. But in the pitch darkness of the night, a loud scream is heard, waking up one of the divers on board. He understands it to be an urgent cry for help by a drowning crew member, and he quickly jumps towards the direction of the voice. Diving deeper into the darkness, he meets his fate at the hands of Bu Draeyah, the monster behind the feigned cries....

In my instructions, I ask them to be creative but also ensure continuity and coherence as they construct the text both in Arabic and in English. I ask for two paragraphs in English followed by two paragraphs in Arabic and that the Arabic paragraphs should be a continuation rather than a translation of the English paragraphs. I model the activity by producing and displaying my own responses/continuation to the text in both languages. Then I divide the students into groups and have them work on text continuation together before the activity is assigned as an individual task (see Figures 7.3 and 7.4 for examples of a student's text continuation in English and then Arabic). One of the positive outcomes of this translanguaging exercise is how students express that they feel at ease when they construct the Arabic text, and they claim more ownership over it.

One of the interesting responses I receive from some students is that their writing in English is better than Arabic, especially Arab students who have grown up in the diaspora. This is partly because they feel the pressure to write in the more formal register of Arabic (Modern Standard Arabic), but they are usually relieved when I tell them that they can use their dialect. Informal conversations with the students also revealed that they value this activity because

In the Arabian Gulf, the monster faked a cry to hunt for food every day. He eventually discovers a huge boat sailing in the middle of the cruel waters of the Gulf wherever the father of the sea (Bu Draeyah) finds it. The monster came so close to the boat, and he even cried feigned cries to deceive the crew members, and one of the crew members responded to the cries that the monster fabricated, although the voice was not normal, it was the loudest and the scariest voice he had ever heard. The seafarer (Saad) decided to jump into the deep, dark gulf to help the person who had fallen in. As he jumped, he saw a large black monster with red eyes. He was not sure whether the creature was a fish or a human.

He was faced with an unfamiliar and terrifying figure, his eyes red, his head the size of Saad's boat he was sailing on. He felt unbalanced, did he see a marine animal or a human being? The strange thing is that Saad went into a dazed state, and remembered his deceased father. His late father (Jassem) used to say: "You have to be careful on land once and at sea a thousand times," and Saad replies, "The land is my land and the sea is my sea." Uncle Jassem warns Saad whether he likes it or not. He says to him: "The sea has secrets that only God knows. if You sailed for centuries you cannot know everything about the depths of the seas."

FIGURE 7.3 Student's text continuation in English

لذلك يجب عليك ان تتبع نصيحتي يا أبني العزيز لتصبح بحار قوي كوالدك.فعلا أصبح سعد بحار كوالده واجداده على الرغم من إنه كان دائما
يضحك على حكايات والده فلم يؤمن بها منذ صغره. حتى شاء القدر أن يجمعه بالوحش في وسط بحار مياه الخليج العربي العميقة والمظلمة.
الوحش أبو دريعة تأمل بسعادة وفرح ضحيته وجعل ضحيته(سعد) يعيش اخر لحظاته بقلق وخوف شديد بعدها أقترب أبو دريعة من ضحيته، وهجم
الوحش الخبيث على سعد وبدأ ينهش لحمه وعظمه إلى أن أشبع الوحش رغبته في الافتراس فترك سعد ليبحث عن طعم اخر في مكان اخر. الوحش
ليس هدفه أكل الضحية وإنما تعذيبها بطريقة دموية ثم يرميها ليرمي الخوف في قلوب البشر. للأسف مات سعد موتة بشعة

الصباح استيقظوا البحارة ليكملوا رحلتهم، وكالعادة ذهب الطباخ ليجهز وجبة الإفطار للبحارة، وإذ به يتفاجأ بمنظر الجثة المشوهة التي تطفو .
بجانب القارب، ليهرع الطباخ نحو البحارة وأخبرهم أنه توجد جثة بنصف جسد وغير واضحة الملامح. البحارة علموا ان الجثة هي جثة سعد فقط
عن طريق شيء واحد وهو أنه لم يكن موجود في غرفته عندما استيقظوا، فقاموا البحارة بإيصال جثة سعد إلى أهله ولم يستطيع أي فرد من طاقم
البحارة أن يبرر أو يعتذر لأهل سعد عن ما حدث لأن وفاته كانت غامضة وحزينة. لتتم مراسم دفنه ودفن المأساة التي عاشها لوحده إلى الأبد.
البحار تبدو جميلة وهادئة من ظاهرها، ولكن في باطنها اسرار وعجائب

FIGURE 7.4 Student's text continuation in Arabic

it affords them the opportunity to use their native language. Some students are critical of educational policies that mandate the use of English while the official language of the country is Arabic, and this has been documented in empirical studies from our context too (Graham et al., 2021). Once the students submit their texts and have a grasp of the activity and the rationale behind it, I divulge to them that this activity stems from two main educational concepts which are translanguaging and intertextuality (Allen, 2000) and then I explain each one of them in lay terms.

My explanation of the concept of intertextuality revolves around the idea of text co-authorship. I simply inform the students that they are going to co-author the text by completing it using their understanding of the text as well as their schematic knowledge. Using other precepts from literacy education (Street, 1997), I introduce the students to the idea that a text can take multiple forms and may not be limited to a written text only. In this spirit, I use images and films to aid the students in the process of deriving meaning from multiple semiotic and multimodal resources.

An example of a regular image I use is the reproduction of the Monalisa by Duchamp. In this painting, Marcel Duchamp drew a mustache and a beard on Monalisa's original painting. I present this to the students as an example of a text co-authorship and ask them the following questions:

a. What do you know about the painting/image?
b. If you were the painter/artist, what message would you want to relay and why?
c. If you were to add/change anything, what would it be and why?

I give the students the option of discussing the questions in pairs or groups using the language of their choice (usually English or Arabic). As they commence the discussion, they often shuttle between the two languages and this pattern is also repeated when they present their answers to the whole class. As most students would identify the painting to be Monalisa's, they are surprised that someone would tamper with it and give it male characteristics (a mustache and a beard). Other students examine it more critically. One group of students explained that the author wanted to show that women, too, can grow mustaches and beards.

The discussion then veered into issues of gender, masculinity, femininity, and how gender roles and characteristics can be socially constructed.

An example of a multimodal and translingual film I often use is *City of Life* (2009) directed by Ali F. Mostafa. It is a multilingual Emirati film about life in Dubai, and the movie includes a multi-ethnic cast who speak Arabic, English, Hindi, and other languages, with English subtitles. We analyze the ways that the characters use various linguistic and semiotic resources to communicate in a multilingual setting. As it is about a city in the region and reflects a familiar cultural and linguistic landscape, my students find it interesting. Overall, my students show more motivation to engage when I bring a plurilingual approach to my foundation English classrooms.

Discussion and conclusion

Losey and Shuck (2022) in describing U.S. college and secondary classrooms and programs state that

> the dominance of English is so strong in educational policy and practice at those levels that it can lead some of us not only to wonder *how* to invoke the full range of our students' language skills and experiences in our teaching, but also to question if we even *should* invoke them.
>
> *(p. 3)*

As can be seen from each of our reflections on our shifting ideologies about teaching English or EMI content courses and descriptions of plurilingual writing assignments, we still teach through the medium of English, fulfilling our contractual agreements to QF and our home campuses, and still certainly teach features of English. In Foundation English, for example, we still help students to develop their English vocabulary and their English grammar and mechanics in writing and so forth, but we have transformed our assignments over time to better utilize the knowledge and multilingual resources that our students bring into our classrooms and help students to engage in reflective practices about the various languages they know (Raza et al., 2021). Rather than an English-only approach, we recognize that "languages are always in contact and complement each other in communication" (Canagarajah, 2013a, p. 4). We also try to draw students' attention to the totality of ways that we communicate and make meaning. That is a brief explanation of *how* we do it.

As to whether we *should* do it, we acknowledge that many of our students are at IBCs because they want a U.S.-based English-medium degree even if they do have concerns about its impact on their linguistic and cultural identities and want to be able to enhance their professional skills in Arabic too (Graham et al., 2021; Kane, 2014). The benefits of plurilingual pedagogy are that we can support students' writing development and professional skills in English, while also helping them to develop multilingual and multimodal skills (Tian et al., 2021). We can draw on a broader range of students' knowledge and experiences when we teach writing or other content classes. Importantly, we can help students see themselves as having a single communicative repertoire instead of a bifurcated linguistic identity, and we can help students feel comfortable bringing that entire repertoire to our classrooms.

We hope this chapter will inspire other EMI and IBC instructors within the Gulf region and beyond to critically reflect on their own teaching practices and think about how they might adapt a more plurilingual approach, even if it is just a small tweak, in order to help expand their students' full communicative repertoires.

References

Allen, G. (2000). *Intertextuality*. Routledge.

Barnawi, O. Z. (2018). *Neoliberalism and English language education policies in the Arabian Gulf*. Routledge.

Blommaert, J., & Rampton, B. (2012). Language and superdiversity. *MMG Working Papers, 12*(9), 7–36. Retrieved from www.mmg.mpg.de/workingpapers

Canagarajah, S. (2013a). Introduction. In S. Canagarajah (Ed.), *Literacy as translingual practice: Between communities and classrooms* (pp. 1–10). Routledge.

Canagarajah, S. A. (2013b). Negotiating translingual literacy: An enactment. *Research in the Teaching of English, 48*(1), 40–67.

Canagarajah, S. (2020). *Transnational literacy autobiographies as translingual writing*. Routledge.

Carnegie Mellon University (2021, July 7). *International Applicants—Undergraduate Admission*. Retrieved from https://www.cmu.edu/admission/admission/international-applicants

Conteh, J., & Meier, G. (2014). *The multilingual turn in languages education: Opportunities and challenges*. Multilingual Matters.

Cenoz, J., & Gorter, D. (2013). Towards a plurilingual approach in English language teaching: Softening the boundaries between languages. *TESOL Quarterly, 47*(3), 591–599.

CMU-Q Class of 2021: Largest percentage of Qataris in more than a decade. (2021, April 22). Carnegie Mellon University in Qatar. Retrieved from https://www.qatar.cmu.edu/news/cmu-q-class-of-2021/

Cross-Border Education Research Team (2020). *International campuses*. Retrieved from http://cbert.org/resources-data/intl-campus/

De Costa, P. I., Green-Eneix, C., & Li, W. (2021). Problematizing language policy and practice in EMI and transnational higher education: Challenges and possibilities. *Australian Review of Applied Linguistics, 44*(2), 115–128. https://doi.org/10.1075/aral.00036.edi

Fakhro, M. D. (2017, May 25). Stories from the Arabian Gulf: Bu Draeyah, Um Homar and the survival of Qatari folktales. Folklore Thursday. Retrieved from https://folklorethursday.com/folktales/stories-from-the-arabian-gulf-bu-draeyah-um-homar-and-the-survival-of-qatari-folktales/

Ferré, R. (2003). Bilingual in Puerto Rico. In S. G. Kellman (Ed.), *Switching languages: Translingual writers reflect on their craft* (pp. 137–138). University of Nebraska Press.

García, O., Johnson, S., & Seltzer, K. (2017). *The Translanguaging Classroom. Leveraging student bilingualism for learning*. Caslon.

Gogolin, I. (1997). The "monolingual habitus" as the common feature in teaching in the language of the majority in different countries. *Per Linguam, 13*(2). https://doi.org/10.5785/13-2-187

Graham, K. M., Elsheikh, A., & Eslami, Z. R. (2020). Reflection on the mobilities, immobilities, inequalities, and traveling ideas in Qatar. *The Journal of AsiaTEFL, 17*(2), 626–634. https://doi.org/10.18823/asiatefl.2020.17.2.20.626

Graham, K. M., & Eslami, Z. (2020). Translanguaging as an act of ethical caring in the US International branch campus. In C. C. Lin, & C. Zaccarini (Eds.), *Internationalization in action: Leveraging diversity and inclusion in globalized classrooms* (pp. 9–26). Peter Lang Publishing.

Graham, K. M., Eslami, Z. R., & Hillman., S. (2021). From English as *the* medium to English as *a* medium: Perspectives of EMI students in Qatar. *System, 99*, 1–13. https://doi.org/10.1016/j.system.2021.102508

Hesson, S., Seltzer, K., & Woodley, H. H. (2014). *Translanguaging in curriculum and instruction: A CUNY-NYSIEB guide for educators.* CUNY-NYSIEB, The Graduate Center, The City University of New York. Retrieved from https://www.cuny-nysieb.org/wp-content/uploads/2016/05/Translanguaging-Guide-Curr-Inst-Final-December-2014.pdf

Hillman, S. (2022). Navigating identity and belonging as international branch campus students: The role of linguistic shame. In S. Hopkyns, & W. Zoghbor (Eds.), *Linguistic identities in the Gulf: Waves of change* (pp. 215–230). Routledge.

Hillman, S., Graham, K. M., & Eslami, Z. R. (2019). Teachers' translanguaging ideologies and practices at an international branch campus in Qatar. *English Teaching & Learning, 43*(1), 41–63. https://doi.org/10.1007/s42321-018-0015-3

Hillman, S., Graham, K. M., & Eslami, Z. R. (2021). EMI and the international branch campus: Examining language ideologies, policies, and practices. *Australian Review of Applied Linguistics, 44*(2), 229–252. https://doi.org/10.1075/aral.20093.hil

Hillman, S., & Ocampo Eibenschutz, E. (2018). English, Super-diversity, and identity in the state of Qatar. *World Englishes, 37*(2), 228–247. https://doi.org/10.1111/weng.12312

Horner, B., Lu, M.-Z., Royster, J. J., & Trimbur, J. (2011). Language difference in writing: Toward a translingual approach. *College English, 73*(3), 303–321.

Horner, B., NeCamp, S., & Donahue, C. (2011). Toward a multilingual composition scholarship: From English only to a translingual norm. *College Composition and Communication, 63*(2), 269–300.

Jenkins, J. (2014). *English as lingua Franca in the international university: The politics of academic English language policy.* Routledge.

Jenkins, J., & Mauranen, A. (2019). *Linguistic diversity on the EMI campus.* Routledge. https://doi.org/10.4324/9780429020865

Kane, T. (2014). Whose lingua franca? The politics of language in transnational medical education. *The Journal of General Education, 63*(2–3), 94–112.

Kellman, S. G. (2003). *Switching languages: Translingual writers reflect on their craft.* University of Nebraska Press.

Kubota, R. (2016). The multi/plural turn, postcolonial theory, and neoliberal multiculturalism: Complicities and implications for applied linguistics. *Applied Linguistics, 37*(4), 474–494. https://doi.org/10.1093/applin/amu045

Kusters, A. (2021). Introduction: The semiotic repertoire: Assemblages and evaluations of resources. *International Journal of Multilingualism, 2.* https://doi.org/10.1080/14790718.2021.1898616

Losey, K. M., & Shuck, G. (2022). Plurilingualism for US writing classrooms. In K. M. Losey, & G. Shuck (Eds.), *Plurilingual pedagogies for multilingual writing classrooms: Engaging the rich communicative repertoires of US students* (pp. 1–11). Routledge.

Macaro, E., Curle, S., Pun, J., An, J., & Dearden, J. (2018). A systematic review of English medium instruction in higher education. *Language Teaching, 51*(1), 36–76. https://doi.org/10.1017/S0261444817000350

Machado, E., & Flores, T. T. (2021). Picturebook creators as translingual writing mentors. *Language Arts, 98*(5), 235–244.

Nebel, A. (2017). Linguistic superdiversity and English-medium higher education in Qatar. In L. Arnold, A. Nebel, & L. Ronesi (Eds.), *Emerging writing research from the middle East-North Africa region* (pp. 27–40). The WAC Clearinghouse and University Press of Colorado.

Okara, G. (2003). African Speech...English words. In S. G. Kellman (Ed.), *Switching languages: Translingual writers reflect on their craft* (pp. 185–187). University of Nebraska Press.

Ollerhead, S., Choi, J., & French, M. (2018). Introduction. In J. Choi, & S. Ollerhead (Eds.), *Plurilingualism in teaching and learning: Complexities across contexts* (pp. 1–17). Routledge.

Pessoa, S., & Rajakumar, M. (2011). The impact of English-medium higher education: The case of Qatar. In A. Al-Issa, & L. S. Dahan (Eds.), *Global English and Arabic: Issues of language, culture, and identity* (pp. 153–178). Peter Lang.

Phan, L. H. (2017). *Transnational education crossing 'Asia' and 'the West': Adjusted desire, transformative mediocrity, neo-colonial disguise.* Routledge.

Phan, L. H., & Barnawi, O. Z. (2015). Where English, neoliberalism, desire and internationalization are alive and kicking: Higher education in Saudi Arabia today. *Language & Education: An International Journal, 29*(6), 545–565. https://doi.org/10.1080/09500782.2015.1059436

Piccardo, E. (2013). Plurilingualism and curriculum design: Toward a synergic vision. *TESOL Quarterly, 47*(3), 600–614. https://doi.org/10.1002/tesq.110

Qatar Foundation. (2020). QF and TED launch TEDinArabic—a global platform for showcasing ideas in the Arabic language. Retrieved from https://www.qf.org.qa/stories/qf-and-ted-launch-tedinarabic-a-global-platform-for-showcasing-ideas

Qatar Foundation. (2022). Universities and higher education programs. https://www.qf.org.qa/education/higher-education

Raza, K., Coombe, C., & Reynolds, D. (2021). Past, present, and ways forward: Toward inclusive policies for TESOL and multilingualism. In K. Raza, C. Coombe, & D. Reynolds (Eds.), *Policy development in TESL and multilingualism: Past, present and the way forward* (pp. 1–13). Springer.

Reynolds, D. (2019). June 25. Language policy in globalized contexts. *WISE*, Qatar Foundation. Retrieved from https://www.wise-qatar.org/app/uploads/2019/08/language-policy-in-globalized-contexts.pdf

Reynolds, D. (2021a). Reflections of (Dis)location: What is "Intercultural Communication" in transnational higher education English-medium instruction? *RELC Journal, 52*(2), 253–269. https://doi.org/10.1177/00336882211017554

Reynolds, D. (2021b). The E's of TNHE and EMI: A phenomenographic lens. *Australian Review of Applied Linguistics, 44*(2), 253–259. https://doi.org/10.1075/aral.20111.rey

Rymes, B. (2010). Communicative repertoire. In C. Leung & B. Street (Eds.), *The Routledge companion to English studies* (Chapter 19). Routledge.

Sahan, K., Galloway, N., & Mckinley, J. (2022). 'English-only' English medium instruction: Mixed views in Thai and Vietnamese higher education. *Language Teaching Research.* https://doi.org/10.1177/13621688211072632

Sahan, K., & Rose, H. (2021). Problematising the E in EMI: Translanguaging as a pedagogic alternative to English-only hegemony in university contexts. In B. Paulsrud, Z. Tian, &

J. Toth (Eds.), *English-medium instruction and translanguaging* (pp. 1–14). Multilingual Matters. https://doi.org/10.21832/9781788927338-005

Shikaki, L. (Fall 2013). Laila Shikaki, bilingual. *Mixtini Matrix*.

Street, B. (1997). The implications of the 'New Literacy Studies' for literacy education. *English in Education*, *31*(3), 45–59.

Tian, Z., Aghai, L., Sayer, P., & Schissel, J. L. (2021). Envisioning TESOL through a translanguaging lens in the era of post-multilingualism. In Z. Tian, L. Aghai, P. Sayer, & J. L. Schissel (Eds.), *Envisioning TESOL through a translanguaging lens: Global perspectives* (pp. 1–20). Springer.

PART 3

Implications and applications of plurilingual pedagogy in teaching and learning

8

RETHINKING LEARNING AND TEACHING USING PLURILINGUAL PEDAGOGY IN THE UAE

Challenges and success stories[1]

Telma Gharibian Steinhagen

Overview: Translanguaging pedagogy

Numerous researchers, such as Cook (2001), García (2009), Cummins (2011), García et al. (2016), and Lin and He (2017), have suggested the intentional use of the learners' first language in (second) language classes in order to facilitate learning and enhance the students' reflection on language in general. One of the ways to do it is to apply "translanguaging" approaches. The term was coined by Cen Williams in 1994 and became prominent during the "Multilingual Turn," after which monolingualism in language learning lost its power as the norm (Carroll & Hoven, 2016).

Translanguaging refers to the speaker's construction and use of original, complex, and interrelated discursive practices that cannot be easily assigned to a traditional definition of language as a system of signs and rules. Instead, this approach considers a speaker's complete language repertoire (García & Wei, 2014). Challenging the monolingual habitus (Gogolin, 1994), translanguaging is a flexible pedagogical tool of linguistic resources used by bilinguals that has the potential to liberate the voices of language-minoritized students by facilitating communication and a deeper understanding of words (García, 2014; García et al., 2016). In short, it is a tool that builds on the multiple, mobile communicative repertoires of learners and their families (Hornberger & Link, 2012).

Translanguaging has also been discussed widely by the international scientific community in relation to identity affirmation and its role in increasing students' empowerment and self-esteem (Cummins, 2000, 2009). According to Bourdieu (1991), language is not only a means of communication but also a tool to pursue interests and display competence. When employed as an educational practice in the classroom, translanguaging allows minority students to feel empowered by conceiving of their first language as a "symbolic capital" (Blackledge & Pavlenko, 2001).

DOI: 10.4324/9781003315971-12

In the European context, plurilingual pedagogy is the term used to represent practices such as translanguaging, which embrace the whole linguistic repertoire of the learner. Throughout this chapter, both terms will be used interchangeably to emphasize the empowering and liberating nature of translanguaging and plurilingual education (Blackledge & Pavlenko, 2001; Cummins, 2011). The empowering nature of translanguaging draws upon Freire's ideas of the participatory and liberating nature of education, whereby minority students are given the opportunity to develop their ideas and realize their abilities in their home language (Freire, 1972).

The social context and translanguaging pedagogy in the UAE

The present chapter focuses on translanguaging in the specific context of the United Arab Emirates (UAE), where the language of instruction and communication in higher education is mostly English, due to the goal to promote the modernization of the country (Burden-Leahy, 2009). English is seen as the language of modernity and progress, while Arabic plays a secondary role in society and educational systems.

In the seven Emirates, only about 18 percent of the population are Emirati (The Official Portal of the UAE Government, 2019). This oil-rich country has relied on a foreign workforce since the early 1970s, including in the education sector, and it provides free education at all levels to its citizens, except in private universities and in all postgraduate studies (Al-Khouri, 2012; Burden-Leahy, 2009). The residents of the UAE comprise more than 200 nationalities, and they use English as the main language of communication (The Official Portal of the UAE Government, 2019). According to the country's constitution, however, Arabic is the official language and there is, in fact, no official policy stating that English is the language of instruction at the tertiary level (Clarke, 2007; Gallagher, 2011).

This gap in the policy, combined with the country's extensive multicultural and multilingual communities, opens room for discussions on the potential of translanguaging pedagogy. While translanguaging refers to integrating minority students' native languages into mostly English-speaking classrooms, given the specific constellation of the linguistic landscape in the Arabian Peninsula, the term translanguaging cannot be used the same way as it is used outside this area since mostly expatriates teach in the country's educational institutions (Carrol & van den Hoven, 2016).

Because non-Arab expatriates constitute the majority of the UAE educators, they are not motivated to learn Arabic, the official language of their host country and the first language of their students, which triggers discussions on whether applying plurilingual approaches in the UAE educational settings would be acceptable to these teachers or even fruitful. The dominant role of English as the main language of communication and education and, therefore, as the language of social and economic advancement gives it a priority to the Emiratis. In its local dialect, *Khalīji*, Arabic remains the language of communication for Emiratis; however, as the language of identity, culture, and religion, Arabic has lost its social prestige due to the country's specific population demographics (Ayari, 1996; Taha, 2017; Taha-Thomure, 2019). In many institutions, curricula and textbooks are imported directly from the United States or the UK, without taking into consideration that Emirati students do not live in an English-speaking country, so the curricula are not adapted to their needs. A closer look at the textbooks and syllabi of any course at a university or college in the UAE reveals the Anglo-Saxon hegemony in education. As an expatriate educator in the UAE, the author has not come across any textbooks or syllabi that attempt to tailor their content to students' lived experiences and home language so far.

Another problem arises when we take a closer look at Arabic itself. In its variation of the *Khalīji* dialect, Arabic is the common language of communication among Emiratis. It is important to point out that Modern Standard Arabic (MSA), or Fusha, which is used in written communication, education, media, and during official occasions is not the spoken variety of any other Arab country. Rather, Fusha is another *lingua franca* used by the Arabic-speaking populations as a common language, being imbued with great value and prestige (Ayari, 1996; Taha, 2017; Taha-Thomure, 2019). Fusha is very much associated with an Arab identity as the language of the Holy *Qur'an*. The many Arabic dialects are considered as inferior and less prestigious among Arabs. Therefore, educational institutions in the UAE face challenges when promoting Arabic in education at all levels (Taha, 2017; Taha-Thomure, 2019). It is also important to know that the correct use of MSA is a marker of education and prestige. As a result, currently, there is a heated debate among Arab scholars concerning the role and status of MSA and the dialects that are spoken in each country where the official language is Arabic (Abu-Rabia, 2000; Ayari, 1996).

Due to the social and linguistic peculiarities of the UAE, three factors have become apparent that make the context of teaching and research different in this area. These factors are as follows:

1. the dominant role of English in tertiary education;
2. the significance of Arabic for identity and nation building;
3. the implicit exclusion of Arabic as the language of education.

The study: Students' perception of translanguaging

Considering the sociocultural contexts in which languages are used and taught and the educational challenges the UAE faces today, the author started her higher education teaching career in the UAE with the following question in mind: if translanguaging pedagogy were to be employed in her classes, how would her students perceive her teaching approach? The university students' perceptions on translanguaging and translanguaging pedagogy in the UAE are important because the subjects in most higher education institutions are taught in English. Translanguaging advocates that the existing linguistic repertoire of learners plays an important role in the learning process; therefore, the author of this chapter regularly applied translanguaging approaches in her classes in an effort to accommodate her students' plurilingual and pluricultural repertoires, namely their home language, Arabic. To answer the above question, she started a research project focused on the implementation of the translanguaging pedagogy in her classes. Some of the translanguaging approaches used were employing various methods of cooperative learning, offering students literature and resources in both Arabic and English, creating multilingual spaces where students can employ their languages during class activities, or encouraging students to create a glossary of technical terms in both languages. These approaches were employed in her courses every semester, followed by collecting the students' perceptions of translanguaging as answers to a set of focused questions (mentioned below). The goal of this exercise was to optimize teaching and learning in a plurilingual classroom.

The author has taught courses with the title *English in the Professions* where students enrolled in the College of Education and the College of Psychology learned how to use English in their future professions, as teachers or as psychologists. There are normally 24 to 26 Emirati female students in each class, and the average age is 21 years old. The author collected 230 student testimonials over a period of five years (2016 to 2022). The native language of the students is Arabic, Khalīji dialect, but they are fairly proficient in MSA due to their schooling (Dillon & Gallagher, 2022).

The author asked students at the end of each semester and after posting the grades to write feedback commenting on their translanguaging learning experience by answering the following questions:

1. What were your first thoughts when a non-Arab teacher tried to use Arabic in class?
2. How would you describe your feelings when you saw your English teacher trying to use Arabic in class?
3. Was it a new experience for you to see that your English teacher is trying to learn Arabic?
4. Do you think it is a good or a bad method to use Arabic in an English class? Please explain.
5. Were you given the opportunity to speak and share your opinion and point of view in this class?
6. What are the things you have done in this class that you have not encountered before?
7. How was the cooperation with your classmates?
8. Do you think that you developed new learning skills in this class?
9. Did the things that we did in this class make sense to you?
10. Do you think that you will apply the things you have learned in this class in other classes or in your profession?

The students were allowed to answer either in Arabic or in English and were asked to write a reflection on the instructor's teaching in which they gave a general evaluation of her teaching. The reflections collected in each class were mostly 500 words in length. The author asked her research assistant to translate the feedback written in Arabic, and a colleague from the Department of Arabic verified these translations.

The students' responses were then grouped into three main categories, all of which indicating the positive perceptions of these students toward pedagogical translanguaging:

a. the teacher as a translanguager;
b. translanguaging for empowerment and a positive learning atmosphere;
c. the translanguaging teacher as a role-model.

Collected data from student feedback has indicated that the instructor's positive attitude toward the Arabic language and her systematic endeavors to integrate it into her teaching are perceived positively by students. This has been made evident by the numerous comments in which the students emphasized how positively they perceived their learning experience in her class.

The teacher as a translanguager

The responses made it clear that the students valued the fact that the author had some Arabic knowledge and was eager to learn more. Although her knowledge of Arabic is very limited, students perceived her efforts in a positive way. As part of her undergraduate degree in English Linguistics and Literary Studies in Germany, the author had to demonstrate knowledge of a language from outside the Indo-European family. Given this requirement, she took Arabic classes, so she has knowledge of how to write in Arabic and some knowledge of Arabic grammar. Despite her limited proficiency in Arabic, her students were impressed by her efforts to use their first language. In their feedback, many students wrote that she speaks Arabic, which is not entirely true. However, throughout the semester, whenever the author encountered a specific term closely related to the content of the course she was teaching, such as "constructivism" or "thesis statement," she wrote it down and found its Arabic equivalent by asking her Arabic-speaking colleagues for help. In time, this glossary has grown to more than 300 words; it is what she called her "cheat sheet." Students appreciated her asking them to share terms in Arabic and then taking out her "cheat sheet" and writing them down. This approach was perceived by a student as follows:

> [I] Am not really that good at English. Sometimes I don't understand the word you saying but it seem that everyone on the class get it. And at that time you take your paper and give us the Arabic word of it. That was helpful. A lot, thank you. (original in English)

Translanguaging for empowerment and positive learning atmosphere

Throughout the learning process, students have described their experiences by using words such as "proud," "connected," "happy," "comfortable," and "beautiful feeling." They have indicated that translanguaging allows Emirati students to use their linguistic repertoire to better understand the content, which in turn motivated them to contribute to class discussions. More importantly, translanguaging puts them in a new state of mind on the use of EMI.

In several of their comments, students emphasized that the reason for their positive attitude toward the author's teaching was that they felt she valued their first language and recognized it as an asset in an English-speaking class. This mutual respect conveyed by translanguaging made them more attentive and active, as the following comments suggest:

> It's a beautiful feeling that our English language teacher knows how to speak in Arabic because that makes us care more about the subject and contribute in answering. (original in Arabic)
>
> Combining Arabic language in an English course is a wonderful and effective way to learn because it opens different ways to understand especially for the student who faces difficulties in understanding some vocabulary. (original in Arabic)
>
> From my experience I can say that the (persons) teachers who learn Arabic and are still learning are better in their relationship with the student. I can say that this is a good method to strengthen the relationship between the students and the teacher. (original in Arabic)
>
> I felt that the teacher like sciences and Arabic because she is trying to learn our language and that is a thing that I am proud of because I have a teacher who also can write and speak in Arabic (Fusha). The pros are that the teacher gives us enough information and presents in a nice way and she can attract us [...] (original in Arabic)
>
> I found it very sweet when the teacher used the Arabic language in the class for the first time because it showed me that the teacher cares about my mother tongue and I am proud of that. I find using Arabic language during the English language class is a great method because it creates an enjoyable environment. I don't know why but it motivates me to appreciate and learn the English language. (original in Arabic)
>
> I feel happy and proud of Arabic language when I see foreign teachers are learning Arabic language, and I feel proud of the teachers when they are trying to learn the Arabic language because they give us a good example for learning other languages. (original in Arabic)
>
> It was a first time to see a teacher try to learn Arabic, which makes me proud that you value it as we do. When I saw your motivation to discover new meanings and letters you gave me the incentive to learn English fluently and to discover new words. (original in Arabic)

These are only a few examples extracted from 230 testimonials. All of them highlight the positive feelings the students experienced in a class where the use of Arabic was not banned but encouraged.

In several other comments the students wrote that, although they were aware of the importance of English in the UAE and throughout the world, they felt a certain discomfort when there was no room for using their first language for learning purposes:

> I actually feel very comfortable with Arabic, so each English class is kind [of] torturing so when Arabic words are used, I can easily relate and imagine the meaning. (original in English)
>
> I felt comfortable because it helps student that are not good in English and they don't know how to say their questions. (original in English)

That the dogmatic monolingual teaching in a multilingual class is in many respects counterproductive and does not facilitate second language acquisition (SLA) has been known to the scientific community for more than two decades. Research by Butzkamm (1973), Cummins (1979), and Cook (2001), for example, has emphasized the role and effectiveness of using students' first language when teaching a foreign language or when teaching in a foreign language. As indicated by the Content and Language Integrated Learning (CLIL) methods, the first language is used as a scaffolding tool to convey definitions and meanings in a certain subject (Lin & He, 2017). Despite these findings, in the UAE there is a strong push for using only English as a language of instruction.

Given that at most higher education levels English is the medium of instruction in the UAE, the picture becomes even grimmer. Carroll and van den Hoven (2017) noted that the use of Arabic is considered as "taboo" in the English-medium content classes. This still happens in the UAE despite the consensus in the literature on SLA and EMI that the systematic use of the first language as a scaffolding tool promotes effective learning (Lin & He, 2017; Lorenzo & Rodríguez, 2014; Nikula & Moore, 2019). This restrictive approach also ignores the fact that recent literature on translanguaging emphasizes that using the students' entire linguistic repertoire in the classroom facilitates learning and contributes to sustainable cognitive growth (Creese & Blackledge, 2010; García & Li, 2014; Hornberger & Link, 2012).

By juxtaposing students' perspectives on translanguaging and the existing research in relevant disciplines, we can conclude that

1. students feel empowered when translanguaging is implemented by an expatriate teacher in the classroom;
2. students perceive a power shift when their home language gains academic value and prestige, which motivates them to participate more in class activities;
3. students feel that the expatriate teacher appreciates their home language and considers it as a valuable asset for further academic advancement.

Since the focus of this chapter is exclusively on the experiences of students in a translanguaging class and their perceptions of this teaching approach in the UAE context, students' feedback that underlines the effectiveness of translanguaging as a learning facilitator in the classroom will not be discussed. However, it should be noted that every student claimed in their reflections that, in their view, the use of Arabic in the classroom enabled them to understand and remember the subject matter better.

The translanguaging teacher as a role-model

A novel tendency that emerged from the students' feedback was that translanguaging changes their perception on teaching and learning. In some of their feedback, students stated that the expatriate faculty's teaching would have better results if they integrated Arabic into their instruction:

> I encourage the teachers to go in deep with Arabic language and I may start also to learn other language. (original in Arabic)
>
> I also, believe that using the mother tongue in explaining something will make the information easier to learn. So, I encourage every teacher to use the mother tongue when teaching so the results will be better. (original in Arabic)
>
> All of us know that English is the global language nowadays and it's the language of work and education but we should not "bury" our language by our hands because we are Arabs. With Arabic we are a "family" and we have to use the Arabic language in classes, meetings, and work. This could be done by teachers and students when they start talking Arabic. (original in Arabic)

As the testimonies above indicate, students clearly see a teacher who tries to integrate their first language in the classroom as a role-model. They convey that even limited knowledge of their home language by the instructor can positively impact the learning atmosphere in the classroom and the connection between learners and teachers.

> I encourage everyone not just the teachers to learn more than a language because that allow them to communicate with many nationalities and to build more relationships. (original in English)
>
> I feel happy and proud of Arabic language when I see foreign teachers are learning Arabic language, and I feel proud of the teachers when they are trying to learn the Arabic language because they give us a good example for learning other languages. Also learning other languages than our mother tongue is useful for the person in his social, scientific, and practical life. Also, when the teacher uses some terminologies from the Arabic language in the class, that help the students to understand. (original in English)

> I wish that all the teachers commit to mention important Arabic terminology in the class. (original in Arabic)

Interestingly, many students in the author's courses are prospective teachers. So, they also consider implementing translanguaging pedagogy as future educators, as indicated by their answers below:

> I think that this method is very useful, effective, stimulating and makes the information easy. (original in English)
>
> The strategies that the teacher Telma uses are great strategies and they have effectiveness. And honestly, I think of using them when I become a teacher. (original in Arabic)

In addition to considering the author as a role-model for teaching in her institution because of her translanguaging approaches among a few educators, some students feel that when instructors in general try to learn and use Arabic, they get to experience firsthand the difficulties and challenges of learning and using a foreign language, so they will be more tolerant when students do not achieve the standard levels of monolingual language proficiency. In the following reflection, a student explains this perception:

> She understands that this is not ... like, we can sometimes make mistakes, and this is okay, because it is your second language. [...] (original in English)

The student comments presented here suggest that translanguaging creates a new power relationship between teachers and learners. It can be argued, therefore, that the UAE expatriate teacher is not necessarily the one with "symbolic capital" (Bourdieu et al., 1991) because of using the English language, but the learners themselves who try to navigate their way in a new society, culture, and language and appreciate its value as a learning facilitator.

These perceptions can be summed up as follows:

1. Students perceive the use of their home language in the classroom as inspiring and state that the strategic use of their first language facilitates a better understanding of the learning material.
2. An expatriate teacher who tries to learn their home language is perceived by the students as a role-model for learning. It is reassuring for students to see their teacher is also a learner who can relate to their experience of learning a new language. In addition, when the expatriate teacher learns their home language, he or she is perceived as a person who is aware of the pitfalls and challenges of learning and therefore values them differently than an expatriate teacher whose learning experience of Arabic is limited or non-existent and who might not be as tolerant of deviations from standard language norms as the former one.

3. In higher education contexts where expatriates teach future Emirati teachers, such instructors who apply translanguaging strategies are perceived as role-models of teaching. Students who experience translanguaging pedagogy in class appreciate its benefits and express interest in adopting this strategy in their own teaching practice.

Final considerations

These sample responses open up a new perspective on the translanguaging pedagogy and its effect in the UAE context. Further research needs to be conducted, and a larger data set is needed to ascertain the claim that translanguaging pedagogy has the potential to empower the teacher in the classroom and establish a more dialogical learning environment. Notably, the liberating and empowering effect of using the first language in the learning process has been emphasized in various educational contexts other than that of the Arabian Peninsula as well (Pütz et al, 2001; Phipps & Gonzalez, 2004; Taylor et al., 2008; West et al., 2017).

In this chapter, the reader was guided through the journey of an expatriate teacher who employed translanguaging pedagogy in a unique social, cultural, linguistic, and economic context. The reader was also given insight into students' perceptions on translanguaging in the UAE. The students' feedback alone, which was considered to be a teaching evaluation for the author, has revealed new views on translanguaging and shed new light on notions of "linguistic hegemony" (Flores, 2016) and "linguistic imperialism" (Phillipson, 1992) previously discussed by researchers from Europe and the United States. Yet, in the UAE context, it is not the minority or migrant students in mainstream educational institutions who experience the challenging "monolingual habitus" in all its aspects, but the Emirati students. The dramatic consequences of this "linguistic imperialism" (Phillipson, 2001, 2017) have been discussed in many contexts where a language becomes dominant. Scholars such as Phillipson (1992), Pakir (1999), and Skutnabb-Kangas (2000) use rather harsh depictors for the dominant language, ranging from "killer language" to "linguistic genocide." However, it is counterproductive to start a discussion on the role of English in the region and the extinction of other languages due to its assimilation. English is and will remain the *lingua franca* in economic and political sectors, as well as in education. It is and will remain the "symbolic capital" needed to access the job market and acquire wealth for future generations of Emiratis. In other words, no other language can replace English as a *lingua franca* in the UAE. Therefore, a more conciliatory view of English as an auxiliary language will be more productive when discussing education in plurilingual societies, such as the UAE (House, 2003). In this context, translanguaging as a pedagogical tool can be a solution to overcome the challenge of silenced identities in the UAE. The implications for teaching following this "journey" of an expatriate teacher suggest that there is a dire need for a change in the teaching paradigm in the UAE. Plurilingual pedagogy can open new possibilities and could be an integral part for curricular development across disciplines. For the economic and educational advancement of the UAE, future generation of students and teachers should be aware of the value of their home and national language. For now, it would be beneficial for learners to consider cross-curricular integration and promotion of both English and Arabic at all educational levels. Unfortunately, Arabic language education plays only an exotic role in the linguistic landscape of the UAE as of now, being suggestively described by some researchers as a "deserted island" (Taha-Thomure, 2019). Only by giving Arabic the status it deserves will the sustainable intellectual growth that is desired for future generations be effectively promoted.

The key to an education that leads to the transformation and empowerment of the Emirati society as a whole is its reliance on its local language and culture. Unfortunately, the current trend is to allow Western, profit-driven corporations to take over Emirati educational institutions instead of giving the national language the prestige it deserves. We should consider, instead, the Arabic language as an integral part of the national education and curricular development so that Emirati students will acquire essential skills for the professional challenges ahead. So far, divergences in theory and practice in higher education are real due to the way educational institutions are formed and reformed (Matsumoto, 2019).

Although the results presented in this chapter have their limitations due to the small amount of data collected so far, the author could confidently conclude that the use of translanguaging in her classes is a process that can lead to identity affirmation, better self-conceptualization, and linguistic empowerment. These conclusions confirm the results of previous studies conducted by Cummins et al. (2005, 2015) and Lin and He (2007). Encountering in her students' feedback words such as "proud," "comfortable," "happy," and "secure" prompted the author to read them as "invivo codes" based on the coding process suggested by grounded theory (Strauss & Corbin, 1998). By expanding the questions posed in this chapter to a larger-scale study that will include quantifying research methods, the author hopes to acquire more reliable results about the benefits of translanguaging in a plurilingual classroom.

Note

1 The author would like to thank her colleague and friend Dr. Ileana Baird for her attentive reading and commenting on drafts of this volume and her chapter. Thanks are also due to her Arabic-speaking colleagues, especially to her friend, her Arabic professor and colleague Dr. Ahmad Aljanadbah, Arabic-speaking librarian, Ms. Hanin Abueida, as well as her student research assistants who have assisted her by translating from Arabic into English the student testimonies included in this chapter.

References

Abu-Rabia, S. (2000). Effects of exposure to literary Arabic on reading comprehension in a diglossic situation. *Reading & Writing*, *13*(1), 147–157. https://doi.org/10.1023/A:1008133701024

Abu-Rabia, S. (2000). Effects of exposure to literary Arabic on reading comprehension in a diglossic situation. *Reading and writing. An Interdisciplinary Journal, 13*(1-2), 147–157. https://doi.org/10.1023/A:1008133701024

Al-Khouri, A. M. (2012). Corporate government a trategy development: A case study. *Business Management Dynamics, 2*(1), 5–24. chrome-extension://efaidnbmnnnibpcajpcglclefindmkaj/http://bmdynamics.com/issue_pdf/bmd1102460524.pdf

Ayari, S. (1996). Diglossia and illiteracy in the Arab world. *Language, Culture and Curriculum, 9*(3), 243–253. https://doi.org/10.1080/07908319609525233

Babson, A. (2012). Bilingual education in the 21st century: A global perspective by Ofelia García. *Journal of Linguistic Anthropology, 22*(3), 254–256. https://doi.org/10.1111/j.1548-1395.2012.01130.x

Blackledge, A., & Pavlenko, A. (2001). Negotiation of identities in multilingual contexts. *International Journal of Bilingualism, 5*(3), 243–257. https://doi.org/10.1177/13670069010050030101

Bourdieu, P. (1977). *Outline of a theory of practice* (R. Nice, Trans: Cambridge University Press.

Bourdieu, P. (1991). *Language and symbolic power* (G. Raymond & M. Adamson, Trans.). Polity Press.

Burden-Leahy, S. M. (2009). Globalisation and education in the postcolonial world: The conundrum of the higher education system of the United Arab Emirates. Comparative Education, 45(4), 525–544.

Butzkamm, W. (1973). *Aufgeklärte einsprachigkeit. Zur entdogmatisierung der methode im fremdsprachenunterricht* [Enlightened monolingualism. Taking the dogma out of foreign language methodology]. Quelle & Meyer.

Carroll, K., & Hoven, M. (2016). Translanguaging within higher education in the United Arab Emirates. In C. Mazak & K. Carroll (Eds.), *Translanguaging in higher education: Beyond monolingual ideologies* (pp. 141–156). Multilingual Matters. https://doi.org/10.21832/9781783096657-010

Clarke, M. (2007). Language policy and language teacher education in the United Arab Emirates. *TESOL Quarterly, 41*(3), 583–591. https://doi.org/10.1002/j.1545-7249.2007.tb00090.x

Cook, V. (2001). Using the first language in the classroom. *Canadian Modern Language Review, 57*(3), 399–423. https://doi.org/10.3138/cmlr.57.3.402

Corbin, J. M., & Strauss, A. L. (1998). *Basics of qualitative research: Techniques and procedures for developing grounded theory.* Sage.

Council of Europe. (n.d.). *Language policy documents.* https://www.coe.int/en/web/common-european-framework-reference-languages/documents

Creese, A., & Blackledge, A. (2010). Translanguaging in the bilingual classroom: A pedagogy for learning and teaching? *The Modern Language Journal, 94*(1), 103–115. https://doi.org/10.1111/j.1540-4781.2009.00986.x

Cummins, J. (1979). Linguistic interdependence and the educational development of bilingual children. *Review of Educational Research, 49*(2), 222–251. https://doi.org/10.3102/00346543049002222

Cummins, J. (2000). *Language, power and pedagogy: Bilingual children in the crossfire.* Multilingual Matters.

Cummins, J. (2005). A proposal for action: Strategies for recognizing heritage language competence as a learning resource within the mainstream classroom. *The Modern Language Journal, 89*(4), 585–592. https://www.jstor.org/stable/3588628

Cummins, J. (2009). Pedagogies of choice: Challenging coercive relations of power in classrooms and communities. *International Journal of Bilingual Education and Bilingualism, 12*(3), 261–271. https://doi.org/10.1080/13670050903003751

Cummins, J. (2011). Literacy engagement: Fueling academic growth for English learners. *The Reading Teacher, 65*(2), 142–146. https://doi.org/10.1002/TRTR.01022

Cummins, J., Bismilla, V., Chow, P., Giampapa, F., Cohen, S., Leoni, L., Sandhu, P., & Sastri, P. (2005). Affirming identity in multilingual classrooms. *Educational Leadership, 63*(1), 38–43. chrome-extension://efaidnbmnnnibpcajpcglclefindmkaj/https://ritell.org/resources/Pictures/Fall%202016%20Conference%20Resources/Identity%20 Texts.pdf

Cummins, J., Hu, S., Marcus, P., & Montreo, M. K. (2015). Identity texts and academic achievement: Connecting the dots in multilingual school contexts. *TESOL Quarterly, 49*(3), 555–581. https://doi.org/10.1002/tesq.241

Flores, N. (2016). A tale of two visions: Hegemonic whiteness and bilingual education. *Educational Policy, 30*(1), 13–38. https://doi.org/10.1177/0895904815616482

Freire, P. (1972). *Pedagogy of the oppressed* (M. B. Ramos, Trans.). Herder and Herder.

Gallagher, K. (2011). Bilingual education in the UAE: Factors, variables and critical questions. *Education, Business and Society: Contemporary Middle Eastern Issues, 4*(1), 62–79. https://doi.org/10.1108/17537981111111274

García, O., Skutnabb-Kangas, T., & Torres-Guzman, M. E. (Eds.). (2006). *Imagining multilingual schools: Languages in education and glocalization.* DeGruyter.

García, O. (2009). *Bilingual education in the 21st century: A global perspective.* Wiley-Blackwell.

García, O., & Beardsmore, H. B. (2009). *Bilingual education in the 21st century: A global perspective.* Wiley-Blackwell.

García, O., & Li, W. (Eds.). (2014). *Translanguaging: Language, bilingualism and education.* Palgrave Macmillan.

García, O., Johnson, S., & Seltzer, K. (2016). *The translanguaging classroom. Leveraging student bilingualism for learning.* Caslon.

García, O., Skutnabb-Kangas, T., Torres-Guzmán, M. E., & ebrary, I. (2006). *Imagining multilingual schools: Language in education and glocalization.* Multilingual Matters.

Gogolin, I. (1994). *Der monolinguale habitus der multilingualen schule* [The monolingual habitus of the multilingual school]. Waxmann.

Hornberger, N. H., & Link, H. (2012). Translanguaging in today's classrooms: A biliteracy lens. *Theory into Practice, 51*(4), 239–247. https://doi.org/10.1080/00405841.2012.726051

House, J. (2003). English as a lingua Franca: A threat to multilingualism? *Journal of Sociolinguistics*, 7(4), 556–578. https://doi.org/10.1111/j.1467-9841.2003.00242.x

Lin, A. M. Y., & He, P. (2017). Translanguaging as dynamic activity flows in CLIL classrooms. *Journal of Language, Identity & Education, 16*(4), 228–244. https://doi.org/10.1080/15348458.2017.1328283

Lorenzo, F., & Rodríguez, L. (2014). Onset and expansion of L2 cognitive academic language proficiency in bilingual settings: CALP in CLIL. *System*, 47, 64–72. https://doi.org/10.1016/j.system.2014.09.016

Matsumoto, A. (2019). Literature review on education reform in the UAE. *International Journal of Educational Reform, 28*(1), 4–23. https://doi.org/10.1177/1056787918824188

Nikula, T., & Moore, P. (2019). Exploring translanguaging in CLIL. *International Journal of Bilingual Education and Bilingualism, 22*(2), 237–249. https://doi.org/10.1080/13670050.2016.1254151.

Pakir, A. (1999). Connecting with English in the context of internationalisation. *TESOL Quarterly, 33*(1), 103–114. https://doi.org/10.2307/3588193

Pavlenko, D. A., & Blackledge, D. A. (2004). *Negotiation of identities in multilingual contexts.* Channel View.

Phillipson, R. (1992). *Linguistic imperialism.* Oxford University Press.

Phillipson, R. (2001, April 18). Comment & analysis: English is taking over in Europe: In Brussels some languages are more equal than others. *The Guardian*. https://www.theguardian.com/world/2001/apr/18/eu.languages

Phillipson, R. (2017). Myths and realities of 'global' English. *Language Policy*, *16*(3), 313–331. https://doi.org/10.1007/s10993-016-9409-z

Phipps, A. M., & Gonzalez, M. (2004). *Modern languages: Learning and teaching in an intercultural field*. Sage. https://doi.org/10.4135/9781446221419

Pütz, M., Fishman, J. A., & Neff-van Aertselaer, J. (2006). Introduction: Along the routes to power. In M. Pütz, J. A. Fishman, J. Neff-van Aertselaer, & C. Baker (Eds.), *'along the routes to power': explorations of empowerment through language* (pp. xiii–xxii). De Gruyter.

Saiegh-Haddad, E. (2003). Linguistic distance and initial reading acquisition: The case of arabic diglossia. *Applied Psycholinguistics*, *24*(3), 431–451. https://doi.org/10.1017/S0142716403000225

Skutnabb-Kangas, T. (2000). *Linguistic genocide in education—Or worldwide diversity and human rights?* Lawrence Erlbaum.

Skutnabb-Kangas, T. (2009). *Social justice through multilingual education*. Multilingual Matters.

Strauss, A. L., & Corbin, J. M. (1998). *Basics of qualitative research: Techniques and procedures for developing grounded theory* (2nd ed.). Sage.

Taha, H. (2017). Arabic language teacher education. In A. Gebril (Ed.), *Applied linguistics in the middle East and North Africa* (pp. 267–287). John Benjamins.

Taha-Thomure, H. (2008). The status of Arabic language teaching today. *Education, Business and Society: Contemporary Middle Eastern Issues*, *1*(3), 186–192. https://doi.org/10.1108/17537980810909805

Taha-Thomure, H. (2019). Arabic language education in the UAE: Choosing the right drivers. In: K. Gallagher (Ed.), *Education in the UAE: Innovation and transformation* (pp. 161–179). Springer. https://doi.org/10.1007/978-981-13-7736-5_5

Taylor, L. K., Bernhard, J. K., Garg, S., & Cummins, J. (2008). Affirming plural belonging: Building on students' family-based cultural and linguistic capital through multiliteracies pedagogy. *Journal of Early Childhood Literacy*, *8*(3), 269–294. https://doi.org/10.1177/1468798408096481

Taylor, S. K., & Snoddon, K. (2013). Plurilingualism in TESOL: Promising controversies. *TESOL Quarterly*, *47*(3), 439–445. https://doi.org/10.1002/tesq.127

Thomure, H. T., & Speaker, R. B. (2018). Arabic language arts standards: Revolution or disruption? *Research in Comparative and International Education*, *13*(4), 551–569. https://doi.org/10.1177/1745499918807032

West, A. L., Zhang, R., Yampolsky, M., & Sasaki, J. Y. (2017). More than the sum of its parts: A transformative theory of biculturalism. *Journal of Cross-Cultural Psychology*, *48*(7), 963–990. https://doi.org/10.1177/0022022117709533

Williams, C. (1994). Arfarniad o ddulliau dysgu ac addysgu yng nghyd-destun addysg uwchradd ddwyieithog, [An evaluation of teaching and learning methods in the context of bilingual secondary education]. [Unpublished doctoral dissertation]. University of Wales, Bangor.

9

FROM THEORY TO PRACTICE

Ways to implement plurilingual pedagogy in educational institutions in the Arabian Peninsula

Daniela Coelho and Telma Gharibian Steinhagen

Introduction

As explained in the introduction to this volume and extensively discussed in many of its previous chapters, plurilingual pedagogy is an approach to teaching and learning that capitalizes on the learners' linguistic and cultural backgrounds to support learning. As expressed by Piccardo et al. (2022), "a plurilingual approach encourages learners to look for the links between languages, and between language and culture, as well as increasing their awareness of how languages – including their mother tongue(s) – operate, so that they acquire a new feeling for the place and role of different registers and varieties" (p. 10). Given its fluid and flexible nature, this approach has potential in multilingual and multicultural contexts, presenting itself as a powerful pedagogy that empowers students and transforms the way they embrace learning and language learning in particular (see, e.g., the introduction to this volume, Coelho & Steinhagen (this volume)).

However, in this field, one of the main concerns expressed by researchers and teachers is that bridging the gap between theory and practice may present some obstacles (Galante et al., 2020). Despite the acknowledgment of plurilingual pedagogy as a powerful strategy in teaching and learning reported by teachers in recent studies (Davy & French, 2018; Ellis, 2016; French, 2015 as cited in Ollerhead et al., 2018 McMillan & Rivers, 2011; Nambisan, 2014;), unpreparedness and scarcity of resources emerge as some of the main reasons why a plurilingual approach is hardly implemented at schools and universities (Galante et al., 2019, 2020). This could be attributed to the fact that the literature available often explores affordances and challenges in plurilingual teaching, but "very few (if any) articles (…) instruct educators on how they can begin to implement this

DOI: 10.4324/9781003315971-13

practice [in specific, translanguaging within the plurilingual approaches] into their teaching" (Nambisan, 2014, p. 32). The goal of this chapter is precisely to serve this purpose. We debate misconceptions, discuss prerequisites, and provide suggestions, ideas, and examples on how plurilingual pedagogy could be applied, mainly based on the personal experiences of the authors. Therefore, this chapter will present an unconventional format where practicality, hopefully, will prevail. Its primary aim is to support teachers willing to become more acquainted with how to implement plurilingual pedagogy even if they are not proficient in the home language(s) of their students.

The suggestions made in this chapter are based on results of other studies or on experiences reported by other teachers in scientific articles, but they are also heavily based on the authors' own experiences as teachers who often apply the plurilingual approach in their classes and on their informal observations of their students' reactions to such approaches. Further empirical research could be required to provide further evidence of the effectiveness of this approach in other contexts.

Implementing plurilingual pedagogy: Prerequisites, contexts, steps, and strategies

Prerequisites

Plurilingual pedagogical practices may sometimes be associated with some misconceptions. For example, some claim that a monolingual approach is more conducive to actual learning because including other languages in the learning process delays the development of the target language or the language of instruction or the content being covered (as discussed in Cummins, 2007; see more examples in the table below). The authors themselves encounter the above-mentioned attitude toward plurilingual pedagogy in their daily teaching practice coming from both teachers and students at times (see Coelho (this volume) for an example). Misconceptions like these may hinder the change of mindset required for a successful application of plurilingual pedagogy. According to Galante et al.'s (2019) *Collaborative Framework for Implementation of Plurilingual Pedagogy*, there are four main prerequisites for a smooth transition from a monolingual approach to a plurilingual one: learner-centered plurilingual pedagogy, openness to all languages, administrative support, and collaborative weekly checks. Drawing on these, a table is presented below which puts prerequisites and misconceptions side by side in an effort to provide evidence on how capitalizing on the prerequisites may help dismiss some of these misconceptions and may contribute to the mindset shift necessary for plurilingual pedagogy implementation. As in any other context, anything that is considered new and potentially disrupts the believed or prescribed "normalcy" of a habitual procedure needs time to be acknowledged, understood, familiarized with, and, likely, implemented. Therefore, Table 9.1 can also be seen as a checkpoint for

TABLE 9.1 Misconceptions associated with plurilingualism and prerequisites for the transition from monolingual to plurilingual approach

Misconception	*Prerequisites with rationale*
The monolingual approach is the better option and, therefore, should be the norm.	*Openness to all languages* (Galante et al., 2019) Given the traditional, prevailing presence of the monolingual stance in the language education discourse, literature, and even teacher training (Cummins, 2007; McMillan & Rivers, 2011), it is only natural to expect that current day teachers will favor it. Nevertheless, there is "no empirical justification for any absolute exclusion of a students' L1 from TL instruction" (Cummins, 2007, p. 227). Therefore, as a teacher or even teacher trainer, the major step toward a mindset shift is to acknowledge that the monolingual principle is not *the* one axiomatic truth. Other methods and strategies should be considered. In fact, eventually it does not matter whether the teaching setting embraces or bans plurilingual pedagogy. The multilingual learner will naturally employ their entire linguistic repertoire while learning (Cenoz et al., 2001)
"I don't speak the first (L1)/ home language(s) of my students, so I cannot apply this pedagogy."	*Openness to all languages* (Galante et al., 2019) The adoption of a plurilingual pedagogy is sometimes mistaken by an approach that allows L1 use in class or in which teachers utilize their students' L1s to support learning; hence this claim is often present in studies that collect teachers' opinions (e.g., Nambisan, 2014). Many educators even believe that employing a plurilingual pedagogy *is* the use of L1 entirely and allowing students to, for example, write papers in L1. The idea is, though, that L1 should be employed as a scaffolding tool and a facilitator. This has been researched and proposed by CLIL (Content and Language Integrating Learning) literature, such as Martínez-Adrián et al. (2019) or Lin et al. (2017), just to mention a few. The authors are not denying that teachers' proficiency in the languages of their students may contribute to a more solid plurilingual approach application, but it is not invariably essential. Teachers can teach a multilingual class using a plurilingual stance without speaking any of their students' languages or having very limited knowledge of some of their languages (see examples in Coelho (this volume) or Gharibian & Said (2021)). Other languages can, thus, be seen as not only linguistic resources but also as cognitive ones (Cummins, 2007). Furthermore, plurilingual pedagogy considers elements other than the known languages as equally fundamental in the learning process, such as their prior experience in learning, their cultural repertoires, and their metalinguistic and metacognitive skills (Piccardo, 2013). Having said this, perhaps a more appropriate prerequisite in this case would be *openness to all languages, cultures, and learning strategies.*

(*Continued*)

TABLE 9.1 Misconceptions associated with plurilingualism and prerequisites for the transition from monolingual to plurilingual approach (*Continued*)

Misconception	*Prerequisites with rationale*
Educational policy widely stands for language-of-instruction-only or target-language-only methods.	*Administrative support* (Galante et al., 2019) In the first author's experience as a teacher educator, she often emphasizes that adhering to the local educational vision or school educational philosophy is essential; however, she also naturally adds that the existence of a specific vision or philosophy does not necessarily mean non-recognition of other complementary philosophies. Besides the previously mentioned tendency to stand for the traditional monolingual approach on the part of educational entities (Cummins, 2007; McMillan & Rivers, 2011), it is also often stated in literature on the topic that lack of support hinders the adoption of a plurilingual approach (Piccardo & Galante, 2018). We believe in open dialogues with administration boards that may trigger interesting discussions about the value of plurilinguality. The authors, personally, have been surprised by the open receptivity of the EMI educational institution where they worked and which supported their implementation of the plurilingual approach in all classes for research purposes. From their own experience, they can claim that the monolingual habitus (Gogolin, 1994) is fading even at the senior management level.
The implementation of plurilingual pedagogy is to be decided by the teacher.	*Learner-centered plurilingual pedagogy* (Galante et al., 2019) Conceivably one of the most important prerequisites for a shift from a monolingual lens to a plurilingual one is the understanding that students are at the heart of the decision to adopt a plurilingual stance in their learning. Similarly to most language teachers around the world who have traditionally been educated that the monolingual approach works best (Cummins, 2007), so have students many a time. Therefore, it is crucial to feel their pulse in this matter to develop awareness on how their plurilingual repertoires work and can help. Plurilingual instruction takes this into account because, as Galante et al. (2020) stated, it "requires that learners examine their linguistic and cultural experiences from their own perspectives, without the imposition of dictation of norms, which affords instruction that is learner-centered" (p. 982). See the next pages for ideas on how to do this.

(*Continued*)

TABLE 9.1 Misconceptions associated with plurilingualism and prerequisites for the transition from monolingual to plurilingual approach (*Continued*)

Misconception	*Prerequisites with rationale*
"If I allow the use of certain languages in the classroom, I may be excluding students who do not understand them."	*Learner-centered plurilingual pedagogy* (Galante et al., 2019) Some research studies have reported concerns coming from teachers and students alike regarding the exclusion of students from the learning process if a plurilingual pedagogy is applied, particularly in multilingual and multicultural classes (Coelho (this volume); Ellis, 2016). "[I]t is imperative to implement it without compromising inclusivity, as this may contribute to disengagement instead of working as a catalyst of learning." (Coelho, this volume, p. 110). If implemented after an investigation of student preferences and if its goals are clearly explained, this can be avoided. Plurilingual pedagogy implies strategies that encourage student agency and role reversal, i.e., students becoming teachers (Galante et al., 2020); thus, exclusion would only happen if there is a misunderstanding of the goals of the approach or if it is imposed on instead of welcomed by students.
"There is no point in applying plurilingual pedagogy if I am the only one. It will be confusing for the students."	*Weekly collaborative checks* (Galante et al., 2019) In a study that surveyed higher education students on their openness to plurilingual strategies applied in a course of English academic writing (Coelho, this volume), "around 90% of students surveyed confirmed enjoyment and openness to the plurilingual practices fostered in classes" (p. 108). Confusion or uneasiness due to only one teacher openly using them was not reported by the surveyed students. In fact, Gharibian and Said (2021) emphasized that in a variety of student feedback and evaluations, the authors encountered joyous student voices wishing that all educators would apply the plurilingual approach. Even though the danger of causing confusion does not seem, personally, realistic based on the above studies, there are ways to support consistency. Informal talks with colleagues, discussions at professional development days, participation in joint school projects, or active involvement in school communities of practice could all be valuable ways to keep a plurilingual pedagogy running steadily if welcomed by students.

teachers to utilize in order to verify if they are ready to embrace plurilingualism in their educational settings.

Contexts

A plurilingual pedagogy may be applied in any context as long as teachers and students are receptive. Below is a list of a variety of educational contexts where plurilinguality may be taken into consideration:

- language learning settings OR content learning settings (including CLIL or EMI contexts);
- contexts in which the teachers speak the language(s) of their students OR in which the teachers do not speak the language(s) of their students;
- environments where the students speak other languages that the teacher may know OR where the students do not speak other languages the teacher may know;
- homogeneous (monolingual, monocultural, and same ability cohorts) OR heterogeneous (plurilingual, pluricultural, and mixed-ability cohorts);
- settings where the students have an elementary knowledge of the language of instruction/target language OR where the students have an advanced knowledge of the language of instruction/target language.

Steps

Even though a step-wise approach to implementing a plurilingual pedagogy might not be recommendable given that teaching and learning are, by no means, a linear process and represent a setting where human and contextual factors play a vital role, for the *novice* plurilingualism supporter, a general overview on how to enable plurilingual practices in a gradual and successive manner may be the most advantageous. Below, there is a list of steps that can be taken toward plurilingualism operationalization. The steps are cyclical, they contemplate evaluation and re-evaluation of practices, and teachers can decide which step to take first depending on their contexts. For example, if teachers already know themselves in regard to plurilingualism (Step 0) and they know their students as well (Step 1), they can choose to initiate the process in Step 2 (Table 9.2).

The scheme below summarizes the steps toward the implementation of plurilingual pedagogy.

TABLE 9.2 Steps toward the implementation of plurilingual pedagogy with explanations

Step 0 Embody	**Understand yourself as a teacher** It has been reported in some studies that sometimes teachers show general appreciation of the linguistic resources their students have, but do not see a role for those resources in their classes (Ollerhead et al., 2018b). Thus, it is important to see if you fall under this category. You will need to move from showing interest in the topic, reading about it, and accepting its potential to truly understanding if you would like to engage in it and to apply it in day-to-day teaching. Your intrinsic motivation will make you feel more confident and credible while applying it. Find out if you are ready to embody it! **How can you find out?** • Read articles describing studies where this approach has been used. • Watch videos of classes where plurilingual pedagogy is being applied (e.g., Dela Cruz and Nguyen (2019) – Plurilingual Approach to Teaching Second Language Vocabulary – https://youtu.be/v9L2b6bbrEw). • Explore websites and blogs that report on uses of the plurilingual stance or provide ideas and resources (e.g., Galante (2017) – Plurilingual and Pluricultural tasks – https://www.breakingtheinvisiblewall.com/tasks). • Design a lesson plan of your own in which you believe you could encourage plurilingualism and see how you would feel applying it.
Step 1 Evaluate	**Feel the pulse of your students** As mentioned before in this chapter, students are at the center of any learning moment and even more when it comes to inviting them to embrace "new" teaching and learning methods. You can prepare one or more activities to assess their predisposition to engage in plurilingualism. Some examples of these activities can be the following: • Ask them to introduce themselves by explaining what their names mean in Arabic (or their other languages/origins). Arabic (and other language) names often have a meaning. This approach opens the room for further discussions about the origin and history behind each name and shows your openness as an educator to explore your students' world. You can also ask them to write a short text on the origins of their names. Assess how detailed and engaged they seemed in the task based on their written output. • Ask them to introduce themselves while also mentioning certain topics in a list prepared by you and which should include languages that they speak or are surrounded by. Observe their satisfaction/dissatisfaction while mentioning these. • Ask them to do a short presentation on (other) cultures that influenced their own culture. Observe their satisfaction/dissatisfaction while doing so. • Depending on the maturity of your students, you may want to directly ask them if they want to use other known languages in the learning process, via either a survey or a whole-class question/discussion. These activities can be adapted depending on the subject you teach. If you teach math, for instance, you may want to turn the second activity into a statistical task, i.e., collecting answers for a table or a graph on the number of languages spoken by class students.

(*Continued*)

TABLE 9.2 Steps toward the implementation of plurilingual pedagogy with explanations (*Continued*)

<table>
<tr><td colspan="2">If the general feeling is that the students are open to plurilingual pedagogy, you may proceed to Step 2.
If the general feeling is that the students are not open to plurilingual practices, your best option is not to apply it.</td></tr>
<tr><td>Step 2
<u>Empathize</u></td><td>Talk to your supervisors
After assessing your students' and your own predisposition to embrace plurilingualism, it is time to convey this to your supervisor, head of the department, or principal/dean, depending on the culture of the institution you work for. This step could also be done before Step 1. As per Galante et al.'s (2019) Collaborative Framework for Implementation of Plurilingual Pedagogy, administrative support is a fundamental element. Open discussions with your schools' administrative team may lead to interesting curriculum development and enhancement endeavors. If you are sure you are ready and believe your students are interested based on your analysis of Steps 0 and 1, show evidence of this to your supervisors, for instance, by sharing the activities developed with your students in Step 1.</td></tr>
<tr><td>Step 3
<u>Encourage</u></td><td>Create a learning environment where plurilingualism flows naturally
Drawing from the results of your analysis/observation in Step 1, you can now start encouraging them to embrace plurilingual practices at their own will. Capture specific class moments that are favorable to capitalize on their linguistic and cultural repertoires for learning purposes.
For instance,
• If you see that a student did not understand a term/concept, encourage him/her to look it up in other known languages.
• If you see that a student is having trouble grasping a certain topic, encourage other students who speak his/her language(s) to explain it using that language.
• If you see that a student may need a word or two in their languages to understand a topic, use a "cheat sheet" (a glossary of English–Arabic terminologies) to provide your students with suitable terminology and to challenge them to make use of their entire linguistic repertoire (see example in Gharibian (this volume)).

Help them to consider their first/home language(s) as a "symbolic capital" (Bourdieu, 1991). Here, you as an educator have to display a profound acknowledgment that the first/home language(s) is a part of curricular action and should be an integral part of learning in your classroom. With this approach, you signal to your students that their first/home language(s) has a prestigious role in education and is not only a "home language." This encouragement may contribute to students feeling comfortable and relaxed whenever they need to utilize other languages.</td></tr>
</table>

(*Continued*)

TABLE 9.2 Steps toward the implementation of plurilingual pedagogy with explanations (*Continued*)

Step 4 Engage	**Explore different plurilingual possibilities** Depending on how your students responded to your initial encouragement in Step 3, start exploring other possibilities by making suggestions of other plurilingual practices and assessing their openness. See suggestions of strategies in the heading Strategies.
Step 5 Evaluate	**Evaluate again!** After some time of applying plurilingual pedagogy, feel the pulse of your students again (Step 1). Look for indicators that the plurilingual stance utilized during your teaching is welcome and fruitful. Check for these: • Did the utilization of plurilingual practices become a habit in your classes? • Do your students draw on plurilingual practices naturally without your encouragement? • Do your students suggest/request more/other plurilingual practices that you had not thought of? • Do you recognize signs of a general improved understanding of topics since the plurilingual pedagogy started being implemented? If you answered "yes" to the majority of the questions, it may be a sign that the plurilingual stance is effective (See Figure 9.1 for a summary of all the steps).

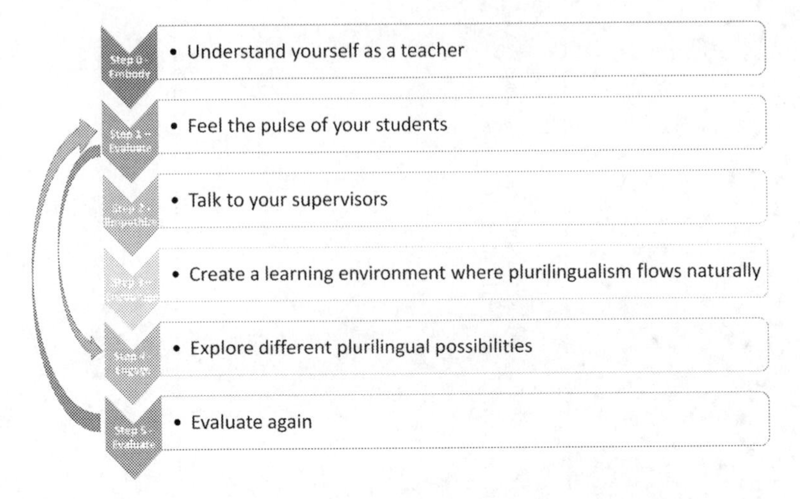

FIGURE 9.1 Steps toward the implementation of plurilingual pedagogy

Strategies

This section intends to suggest pedagogical strategies and activities that foster plurilingualism as a learning resource. Table 9.3 presents the strategies, resources, and, in some cases, examples of these strategies used in real classrooms.

Final note

While the authors understand that a model of prerequisites, steps, and strategies, as the one presented here, may not suit every teaching and learning setting within the Arabian Peninsula or the world, they truly hope that it has created a space for a better understanding of the requirements and possibilities of the plurilingual pedagogy. Even if some teachers may still feel uncertain about applying plurilingualism in the classroom, becoming plurilingual pedagogically literate will, at least, serve as an acknowledgment of students' diverse cultural and linguistic backgrounds and, perhaps, gradually contribute to the recognition of the plurilingual stance, or others that honor students' diverse linguistic and cultural repertoires, as an approach that may walk hand in hand with the monolingual perspective. Most importantly, we hope teachers who have always been interested in the topic will be able to see in this chapter the user-friendly, accessible guidance and support they needed to finally apply it, becoming agents of change and appreciating the importance of flexibility and fluidity in language education.

TABLE 9.3 Plurilingual strategies

Strategies	*Examples*
Translating (Duarte & van der Ploeg, 2019) Encourage your students to look for translations of certain terms and concepts that may cause difficulty. Sometimes, seeing the term or concept written in another language that the students know may improve their understanding of the topic. According to Coelho (this volume), the students surveyed in her study claimed that "the possibility of translating fostered understanding, thus opening room for more academic success." (p. 109)	Students in one of the first author's courses who are teachers of French know that the first author speaks French as well; therefore, sometimes they ask her to translate the names of certain learning theories or pedagogical methods into French so that they understand better even though English is the language of instruction. The same can be done by the students themselves. **Resources required** Reputable online dictionaries.
Interaction in other languages (Duarte & van der Ploeg, 2019; Henderson & Ingram, 2018) Promote interactions and discussions among students in other languages that they would like to use. Even though you may want your students to share their final product in the target language or language of instruction, allowing for discussions in other languages may help them engage in more fruitful interactions in which their ideas flow more naturally. This may contribute to an enriched final product.	The second author often asks her students to write short reflections about their experiences in her classes while embedding and integrating Arabic. She encourages and invites the students to discuss and employ L1 in their literature reviews and discussions. Most of the times, they will be surprised since they are used to being in classes where the use of Arabic was considered as taboo (Carroll & Hoven, 2016). While teaching on online mode, when students were invited to go to break-out rooms for class discussions, it was natural to hear them discuss in Arabic if all members spoke Arabic. When the first author popped in to monitor and guide discussions, she remained silent while listening to them discussing in Arabic and would then eventually request a summary of what they had discussed so far in English. **Resources required** N/A

(*Continued*)

TABLE 9.3 Plurilingual strategies (*Continued*)

Strategies	*Examples*
Language comparisons (Duarte & van der Ploeg, 2019) In language learning contexts, this strategy can have a huge impact. Students can capitalize on their prior linguistic knowledge to make comparisons that lead to a better understanding on how the language they are learning works. Encourage your students to draw such comparisons, for example, focusing on common mistakes made because of the influence of L1.	In the first author's academic writing in English course, she noticed that Arabic-speaking students tend to make the same mistake in sentences where the conjunction *although* is used. They write "Although it was raining, *but* we went to play outside." So, she asked them if that was the structure in Arabic. After confirmation, she drew their attention to the fact that "but" is not necessary in the English structure as it is in Arabic. The same applied to a tendency to double subjects in English sentences (e.g., My mother she loves cooking.). After realizing that that was common in Arabic, she called their attention to the fact that this should not be done in English. Comparisons and drawing attention to differences may help avoid mistakes. **Resources required** N/A
Use of other languages in research projects (Duarte & van der Ploeg, 2019; Hillman et al., this volume) Despite the overwhelming presence and value of English as the language of research, investigation and knowledge dissemination can be done in any language. Building on your students' linguistic backgrounds, encourage them to search for sources in all languages they know and to incorporate them into their projects.	**References:** - NAZIR, F. (2018), «Stimulus-Response Theory: A case study in the Teaching and Learning of Malay language among year 1 pupils », *The Journal of Social Sciences Research*, 10(4), pp.153-157. - THOMSON, F & P. WOLSTENCROFT (2021), *The Trainee Teacher's Handbook, A Companion for initial teacher training*, SAGE Publications. *-ROGERS, R. Carl. [1961]. The development of the person, Paris: Interéditions, 2005.* *-Fondements linguistiques et psychologiques de la méthode des séries de François Gouin (1880)* **FIGURE 9.2** Example of bibliographic references in English and French used in a student project **Resources required** Library with extensive multilingual resources.

(*Continued*)

TABLE 9.3 Plurilingual strategies (*Continued*)

Strategies	*Examples*
Peer-to-peer instruction (Abiria et al., 2013) Especially in settings where you do not speak the language of your students, their language(s) can still be welcomed. One way to do so is to encourage peer-to-peer teaching with students who share the same language. This can be done either at a specific moment when you realize a student (or more) is not following you due to language issues or you can turn it into a routine, for example, you can end your classes with a group review session in which same language students sit together and summarize to each other the topics learned.	In the first author's classes, she often asks the same language students to support another student who is struggling to understand a topic/term/concept even after she tried to simplify it or used gestures. **Resources required** N/A
Dual language projects (Cummins, 2007) OR **another language projects** In contexts where understanding the content is more important than developing linguistic skills, teachers may be open to submission of projects in other languages, as long as they can read/understand those languages or can resort to a co-teacher who does.	Even though the first author teaches in an EMI model, having teachers and future teachers in her education courses who are better speakers of/writers in French, she has allowed them to submit some projects or even test answers in French. 5- You are preparing a reading comprehension lesson on the topic of Expo 2020 for your grade 10. Describe ONE **post-reading activity** that you could include and **justify** your choice. (4) Please, do not write more than **70** words. Make sure your description is brief and straight to the point. Post-reading activity: Utiliser un tableau, avec questions clés: Où / Quand / Quoi / Pourquoi ? Cette méthode permettera aux élèves de structurer les points importants, et ainsi rendre l'activité plus accessible et motivante. 4 **FIGURE 9.3** Example of test answer in another language other than the one in the question (produced by Samia Debbi, 2021)

(*Continued*)

TABLE 9.3 Plurilingual strategies (*Continued*)

Strategies	*Examples*
	In a professional development certificate offered in English in the first author's workplace, trainers have allowed final modular assignments to be submitted either in English or in Arabic. For the Arabic ones, the first author's Arabic-speaking colleagues assisted. Coelho, Khalil, and Shankar (2022) found out in a study that surveyed UAE school teachers on their views and uses of plurilingual pedagogy that 5.5% of teachers said they accept assignments and projects in other languages. **Resources required** A co-teacher may be required.
Pre-tasking in other languages (Van Viegen, 2020) As mentioned before, sometimes ideas flow more naturally in the students' first/home language(s); therefore, planning or brainstorming tasks may become more prolific if other languages are used (see also Gharibian & Said (2021)). This practice may also contribute to a more confident and rich planning task that will result in a better quality final product in the target language or language of instruction (see also Chen et al. (2019))	In both authors' teaching contexts, students may plan their writing activities using whichever language they prefer. They can do research in the language of their choice as long as they present the final product in English. The second author creates spaces where using materials and resources in both languages is possible. She works in close cooperation with an Arabic-speaking librarian and an Arabic-speaking colleague. For instance, if the topic of the class is bilingualism in education, she asks the librarian to provide her with articles, book chapters, and other resources in Arabic in addition to English materials. While students are doing their literature review in class, an Arabic-speaking colleague joins her to discuss the academic articles with students in Arabic. The effect in this type of class is twofold: students feel that their first language has gained value as a language that can be employed in academic settings and it empowers them in terms of identity affirmation as described by Cummins et al. (2005). In addition, resorting to both languages in academic settings is used in her class as a differentiation tool. Students with a lower performance in English embrace the use of Arabic and can participate in the class discussion after reading the materials in Arabic. This knowledge later improves their understanding of English materials for their literature review. **Resources required** N/A

(*Continued*)

TABLE 9.3 Plurilingual strategies (*Continued*)

Strategies	*Examples*
Grouping students based on language(s) (Tian, 2020) There are moments when having a partner that speaks the same language may contribute to a more confident attitude toward learning. This may work as the More Knowledgeable Other concept (Vygostky, 1991) where students who are one step ahead may support other students that speak the same language (other than the instruction one). While it might spark some controversy since it may be understood as a discriminatory organization of class (per language), this is a method that can be used only occasionally, for example, in group activities, brainstorming tasks, discussion activities, and research projects.	Even though this is not a practice in the authors' classes, they have noticed that students naturally organize themselves in same-language groups for group projects whenever possible. **Resources required** N/A
Collaborative learning (Bossche et al., 2006; Hmelo-Silver, 2013; Rajendram, 2019; Trentin, 2010) Make collaborative learning the integral part of your teaching practice. Collaborative learning can help you as a differentiation tool as well as a learning arrangement where students discuss their topics and their assignments in both languages. In addition, exchanging ideas and discussing topics and research findings raise their metalinguistic awareness.	The second author employed a range of cooperative teaching methods in her classes as described in the pre-tasking section. The vast majority of cooperative learning methods can be used for integrating Arabic in class. Due to their nature, they can be used as differentiation tools. Students with lower performance levels in English prefer to contribute in Arabic and bring a different perspective to the group work. In EMI contexts, the monolingual approach, on the other hand, may marginalize students whose English is not at the same level as their Arabic. **Resources required** N/A

(*Continued*)

TABLE 9.3 Plurilingual strategies (*Continued*)

Strategies	*Examples*
Utilizing multimodality (Lin, 2010 in Lin et al., 2020) In our superdiverse multilingual and multicultural classes, we will most certainly encounter superdiverse ways of learning too. The way we see teaching and learning is often culturally rooted, meaning that certain teaching and learning strategies work better with some students but may not appeal to others. Applying multimodality can represent a way to incorporate inclusive learning in your teaching since you will be catering to a variety of cultural ways of learning. Some examples of multimodal resources can be diagrams, videos, pictures, demonstrations, actions, or experiments (Lin et al., 2020).	In the first author's experience teaching in five different countries, it has become clear that there is no one-size-fits-all strategy to teach the exact same topic. It has been noticed that, culturally, some students prefer to simply be lectured, while others see active participation in learning as key to success. She has learned to adapt and update her resources accordingly after "feeling the pulse" of her students. When in doubt, the best approach is to always incorporate variety. One example of an update the first author felt compelled to make in her teaching materials had to do with contemplating cultural aspects. For example, while asking her UAE students to combine two sentences using the appropriate conjunction (*It is raining. We will not play outside.* Expected answer: *It is raining, so we will not play outside.*), she realized they struggled with finding the right conjunction because for them playing outside when it rains is a must! In a country where it rarely rains, when it does, everyone goes out to enjoy the rain and drive in the desert. This generated an interesting class discussion and triggered a change in her as a teacher and creator of some of her class materials. Class activities, materials, and topics need to be meaningful and relatable to our students, and not solely "measured" by the target language standards. **Resources required** A range of non-copyrighted pictures, videos, and infographics. A bank of participatory, experiential activities that require the students to learn by doing (e.g., role plays, demonstrations, presentations, case studies, scenario analysis, problem-solving, etc.).

Bibliographic references

Abiria, D. M., Early, M., & Kendrick, M. (2013). Plurilingual pedagogical practices in a policy-constrained context: A northern Uganda case study. *TESOL Quarterly, 47*(3), 567–590.

Bossche, P., Segers, M., & Kirschner, P. A. (2006). Social and cognitive factors driving teamwork in collaborative learning environments: Team learning beliefs and behaviors. *Small Group Research, 37*(5), 490–521. https://doi.org/10.1177/1046496406292938

Bourdieu, P., & Thompson, J. B. (1991). *Language and symbolic power.* Harvard University Press.

Carroll, K., & Hoven, M. (2016). 8. Translanguaging within higher education in the United Arab Emirates. In C. Mazak & K. Carroll (Ed.), *Translanguaging in higher education: Beyond monolingual ideologies* (pp. 141–156). Multilingual Matters. https://doi.org/10.21832/9781783096657-010

Cenoz, P. J., Hufeisen, D. B., & Jessner, D. U. (2001). *Cross-linguistic influence in third language acquisition: Psycholinguistic perspectives.* Channel View Publications. Retrieved from https://go.exlibris.link/gBmYv2Jv

Chen, F., Tsai, S., & Tsou, W. (2019). The application of translanguaging in English for specific purposes writing course. *English Teaching & Learning, 43*(1), 65–83.

Coelho, D. (2023). Plurilingual pedagogy in higher education in the UAE: Student voices in an academic writing course. In D. Coelho & T. Steinhagen (Eds.), *Plurilingual pedagogy in the Arabian Peninsula: Transforming and empowering students and teachers* (pp. 95–113). Routledge.

Coelho, D., Khalil, N., & Shankar, D. D. (2022). Teachers' perspectives and 'invisible' uses of plurilingual pedagogies in UAE K-12 schools. *International Journal of Multilingualism.* https://www.tandfonline.com/doi/abs/10.1080/14790718.2022.2099400

Cummins, J. (2007). Rethinking monolingual instructional strategies in multilingual classrooms. *Canadian Journal of Applied Linguistics (CJAL)/Revue canadienne de linguistique appliquée (RCLA, 10*(2), 221–240.

Cummins, J., Bismilla, V., Chow, P., Giampapa, F., Cohen, S., Leoni, L., Sandhu, P., & Sastri, P. (2005). Affirming identity in multilingual classrooms. *Educational Leadership, 63*(1), 38.

Davy, B., & French, M. (2018). The plurilingual life. A tale of highs school students in two cities. In J. Choi, & S. Ollerhead (Eds.), *Plurilingualism in teaching and learning. Complexities across contexts* (pp. 165–181). Routledge.

Dela Cruz, J. W., & Nguyen, T. M. C. [John Wayne Dela Cruz]. (2019, 21 March). *Plurilingual Approach to Teaching Second Language Vocabulary* [Video]. YouTube. https://youtu.be/v9L2b6bbrEw

Duarte, J., & van der Ploeg, M. (2019). Plurilingual lecturers in English medium instruction in The Netherlands: The key to plurilingual approaches in higher education? *European Journal of Higher Education, 9*(3), 268–284.

Ellis, E. (2016). *The plurilingual TESOL teacher. The hidden languaged lives of TESOL teachers and why they matter.* De Gruyter Mouton.

Galante, A. (2017). *Plurilingual and Pluricultural Tasks.* Breaking the Invisible Walls. https://www.breakingtheinvisiblewall.com/tasks

Galante, A., Okubo, K., Cole, C., Abd Elkader, N., Wilkinson, C., Carozza, N., Wotton, C., & Vasic, J. (2020). "English-only is not the way to go:" Teachers' perceptions of plurilingual instruction in an English program at a Canadian university. *TESOL Quarterly Journal, 54*(4), 980–1009.

Galante, A., Okubo, K., Cole, C., Elkader, N., Carozza, N., Wilkinson, C., Wotton, C., & Vasic, J. (2019). Plurilingual in higher education: A collaborative initiative for the implementation of plurilingual pedagogy in an English for academic purposes program at a Canadian University. *TESL Canada Journal, 36*(1), 121–133.

Gharibian S, T., & Said, F. (2021). "We should not bury our language by our hands": Crafting creative translanguaging spaces in higher education in the UAE. Papadopoulos, I. (Ed.). *Applied linguistics research and good practices for multicultural and multilingual classrooms.* Nova Science.

Gogolin, I. (1994). *Der monolinguale Habitus der multilingualen Schule.* [The monolingual habitus of the multiligual school]. Waxmann, Münster.

Henderson, K., & Ingram, M. (2018). "Mister, you're writing in Spanglish": Fostering spaces for meaning making and metalinguistic connections through teacher translanguaging shifts in the bilingual classroom. *Bilingual Research Journal, 41*(3), 253–271.

Hillman, S., Reynolds, D. & Elsheikh, A. (2023). Expanding communicative repertoires through plurilingual pedagogies in international branch campus classrooms in Qatar. In D. Coelho & T. Steinhagen (Eds), *Plurilingual Pedagogy in the Arabian Peninsula: Transforming and Empowering Students and Teachers* (pp. 114–130). Routledge.

Hmelo-Silver, C. E. (2013). *The international handbook of collaborative learning.* Routledge, Taylor & Francis Group.

Lin, A. M. Y., & He, P. (2017). Translanguaging as dynamic activity flows in CLIL classrooms. *Journal of Language, Identity & Education, 16*(4), 228–244. https://doi.org/10.1080/15348458.2017.1328283

Lin, A., Wu, Y., & Lemcke, J. (2020). It takes a village to research a village'. Conversations between Angel Lin and Jay Lemcke on contemporary issues in translanguaging. In S. Lau, & S. Van Viegen (Eds.), *Plurilingual pedagogies: Critical and creative endeavors for equitable language (in) education* (pp. 47–74). Springer.

Martínez-Adrián, M., Martínez-Adrián, M., Gutiérrez-Mangado, M. J., & Gallardo-del-Puerto, F. (2019). Introduction: L1 use in content-based and CLIL settings. *International Journal of Bilingual Education and Bilingualism, 22*(1), 1–4. https://doi.org/10.1080/13670050.2018.1508279

McMillan, B. A., & Rivers, D. J. (2011). The practice of policy: Teacher attitudes toward "English only". *System, 39*, 251–263.

Nambisan, K. A. (2014). *Teachers' attitudes towards and uses of translanguaging in English language classrooms in Iowa* [unpublished master's thesis]. Iowa State University.

Ollerhead, S., Choi, J., & French, M. (2018). Introduction. In J. Choi, & S. Ollerhead (Eds.), *Plurilingualism in teaching and learning. Complexities across contexts* (pp. 1–17). Routledge.

Ollerhead, S., Prinsloo, M., & Krause, L.-S. (2018b). Translingual innovation within contact zones. Lessons from Australian and South African schools. In J. Choi, & S. Ollerhead (Eds.), *Plurilingualism in teaching and learning. Complexities across contexts* (pp. 147–164). Routledge.

Piccardo, E. (2013). Plurilingualism and curriculum design: Towards a synergic vision. *TESOL Quarterly, 47*(3), 600–614.

Piccardo, E., & Galante, A. (2018). Plurilingualism and agency in language education. The role of dramatic action-oriented tasks. In J. Choi, & S. Ollerhead (Eds.), *Plurilingualism in teaching and learning. Complexities across contexts* (pp. 147–164). Routledge.

Piccardo, E., Germain-Rutherford, A., & Lawrence, G. (2022). An introduction to plurilingualism and this handbook. In E. Piccardo, G. Lawrence, & A. Germain-Rutherford (Eds.), *Routledge handbook of plurilingual language education* (pp. 1–15). Routledge.

Rajendram, S. (2019). *Translanguaging as an agentive, collaborative and socioculturally responsive pedagogy for multilingual learners*

Tian, Z. (2020). Faculty first: Promoting translanguaging in TESOL teacher education. In S. Lau, & S. Van Viegen (Eds.), *Plurilingual pedagogies: Critical and creative endeavors for equitable language (in) education* (pp. 215–236). Springer.

Trentin, G. (2010). *Networked collaborative learning: Social interaction and active learning*. Chandos. https://doi.org/10.1533/9781780631646

Van Viegen, S. (2020). Remaking the ground on which they stand: Plurilingual approaches across the curriculum. In S. Lau, & S. Van Viegen (Eds.), *Plurilingual pedagogies: Critical and creative endeavors for equitable language (in) education* (pp. 161–183). Springer.

Vygotsky, L. S. (1991). A formação social da mente. O desenvolvimento dos processos psicológicos superiores. [Mind in society. The development of higher psychological processes]. Martins Fontes.

CONCLUSION

Telma Gharibian Steinhagen

Conclusion

Looking back to our careers as expatriate educators working in the Arabian Peninsula and realizing a necessity to transform and innovate the existing beliefs and practices on language education, we undertook the endeavor of creating this edited volume having a specific audience in mind:

- students and educators in countries where the official language is Arabic, regardless of their home/first language, who teach using the English language;
- education policy-makers who are looking for voices who live through this unique and challenging experience of growing economies in the Arabian Peninsula.

At the beginning of our journey and even before starting this volume, we reflected upon our own experience and *weltanschauung* where education is considered a means for empowerment and transformation. Soon, we discovered that there is an urgency to discuss existing practices and beliefs specific to the Arabian Peninsula in order to optimize the education and training of these emerging economies.

The principle of the Freirean concept of dialog (Freire, 1972) for discovering, learning, and transformation was a leitmotif throughout the entire process. We soon discovered that our views, knowledge, and experience should be discussed in a greater context of the region. This was crucial when we approached scholars and experts in the Arabic language from the region, moving to scholars who are researching in education and educators, and closing the argument by giving the learners and educators of the region a voice by presenting their authentic views on language education in the region. We hope that this interdisciplinary

DOI: 10.4324/9781003315971-14

multifaceted dialog in the form of the present volume was the starting point of a blueprint for a bottom-up approach while making decisions in education policies in the Arabian Peninsula, a region with immense potential for growth and transformation.

Bibliographic references

Freire, P. (1972). *Pedagogy of the oppressed.* Herder and Herder.

INDEX

Printed in the United States
by Baker & Taylor Publisher Services